Business Law in the European Union

AUSTRALIA
LBC Information Services
Sydney

CANADA and USA
The Carswell Company
Toronto

NEW ZEALAND
Brooker's
Auckland

SINGAPORE and MALAYSIA
Thomson Information (S.E. Asia)
Singapore

Business Law in the European Union

by

CHRISTOPHER BOVIS

Deputy Director, Institute of European Public Law, University of Hull
Visiting Professor, The Queen's University of Belfast

Published in 1997 by
Sweet and Maxwell Ltd of
100 Avenue Road, Swiss Cottage,
London NW3 3PF
(http://www.smlawpub.co.uk)
Computerset by Interactive Sciences Limited, Gloucester.
Printed and bound in Great Britain by
Butler & Tanner Ltd, Frome and London.

No natural forests were destroyed to
make this product: only farmed
timber was used and re-planted.

ISBN 0 421 56040 1

**A catalogue record for this book is
available from the British Library**

The Alexander Maxwell Law Scholarship Trust

Maurice W. Maxwell, whose family founded Sweet & Maxwell the law publishers, by his will established a charitable trust to be known as The Alexander Maxwell Law Scholarship Trust in memory of his great great grandfather. The Trust is committed to promoting legal research and writing at various levels by providing financial assistance to authors whether they be experienced legal practitioners, those in the early years of practice or at post-graduate level.

The author of this book received financial assistance from the Trust to enable him to complete the work.

The Trust calls for applications from time to time. Anyone interested in its work should write to The Clerk to the Trustees, The Alexander Maxwell Scholarship Trust, c/o Sweet & Maxwell, 21 Alva Street, Edinburgh EH2 4PS.

Acknowledgments

It would have been very difficult to complete this book without the instrumental and constructive support of the publishers and the generous assistance of the Alexander Maxwell Law Scholarship Trust. I am also grateful to officials from the European Commission who readily provided me with information, documents and also their opinions and views on the relevant topics under discussion in this work. Also, officials from administrations in Member States showed a very warm interest in the project and freely gave me the benefit of their experience and expertise in both legal and policy agendas. Last but not least, I record my indebtedness to Dr Christine Cnossen who kindly read the manuscript numerous times and gave me all the support and encouragement I needed for the completion of this work. As a token of appreciation, I dedicate this book to her.

C. Bovis

April 1997

Introduction

In an increasingly versatile and integrated European common market, the emerging business opportunities create an environment which can achieve the objectives of the European integration process. The uninhibited functioning of the four fundamental freedoms which are stipulated in the Treaty of Rome and its amending Maastricht Treaty on the European Union will establish genuinely competitive patterns of trade, which in turn, will result in the desirable effects of economic growth and consequently the improvement of working and living conditions throughout the common market.[1]

The European integration process, as an economic exercise with clear political spillover effects from its accomplishment, is founded upon the concept of a *customs union*[2] which will gradually move towards an economic and monetary union and finally political union. The level and degree of success of economic integration in Europe will determine the level of success in political integration, as the ultimate objective stipulated in the Treaties.

The European integration process could only succeed through the free and unobstructed mobility of factors of production (labour and capital),[3] and also the creation of a single currency and the adoption of a common economic and monetary policy.[4] Clearly, the tool for such transformation is economic integration through the approximation of Member States' economic policies and abolition of obstacles/non-tariff barriers to trade. Such responsibility lies predominately in the hands of the Member States, through harmonisation of their legislation and approximation of their administrative systems.[5]

The stages for the economic integration of the Member States, which have been implemented by European institutions and transposed to law and policy by Member States, include the abolition of all tariff and non-tariff barriers to trade amongst Member States and the establishment of an effective, workable and undistorted regime of competition within the common market.

The law plays an important role in the process of European integration as it regulates the relations of the subjects of the new legal order[6] and

---

[1] See Arts. 2, 3 and 6 of the Treaty of Rome.

[2] Art. 9(1).

[3] Arts. 48 and 67 respectively.

[4] Art. 102a.

[5] See Arts. 100, 100a, 100b, the latter two being introduced by the Single European Act.

[6] This is the term used by the European Court of Justice in the *Van Gend en Loos* case (Case 26/62, *NV Algemene Transport en Expeditie Onderneming Van Gend en Loos v. Nederlandse Administratie der belastingen*: [1963] E.C.R. 1 in order to describe the conglomerate of mutual rights and duties between the European Community and its subjects.

establishes the right patterns for the accomplishment of the objectives of the Treaties. Business law in the European Union represents a wide range of thematic areas which cover regulatory instruments of corporate behaviour within the common market.

The completion of the single market project in 1992, as a milestone for the creation of a genuine common market, as well as the third enlargement of the European Community with the accession of Sweden, Finland and Austria, has established a pan-European integrated market of 368 million consumers with ECU 5,805 billion as Gross Domestic Product. The above market is bigger in comparison with the relevant markets of the USA and Japan respectively and represents a model of openness and accessibility for international trade. The European Community has been a leading signatory to the agreements under the GATT rounds with the view to enhancing and facilitating business growth and trade patterns not only within the common market but also globally.

The application of business law in the European Union and the exposure of topics, aspects and areas of business to the regulatory regime which has been envisaged at centralised level and implemented at domestic level will also facilitate the development and evolution of European policies such as industrial policy and commercial policy. To this extent, the European Union will move towards the establishment of common policies relating to commerce and industry, a fact that could enhance the competitiveness of the European industries.

The purpose of this book is to provide for a comprehensive and often interdisciplinary analysis of seven major thematic areas within European business law. Companies, their structures and management systems in Europe, corporate law developments at European level, the regulation of corporate mobility in the European Union, the application of competition law and policy on business in Europe, the regulation of business with the public sector, the regulation of financial services and finally, social policy considerations within the framework of European business law.

The thematic areas which are discussed and investigated in this book comprise seven chapters. In Chapter 1, the forms of corporate market participation in the Member States of the European Union and the differences and similarities of company structures are exposed. The picture also shows the attempts made so far to harmonise the legal framework and operation of corporate structures in the common market. In Chapter 2, an analysis of corporate law developments at European level is provided. All the attempts of European institutions to introduce uniform *corporate animals* among the Member States are discussed. In particular, the development and evolution of laws and policies relating to the Societas Europeas, the European Economic Interest Grouping (EEIG), the European Co-operative Society, the European Mutual Society and the European Association is investigated and analysed. In Chapter 3, the regulation of corporate mobility within the common market is

The mobility of companies within the common market, the legal framework of the freedom of establishment and the freedom to provide services in other Member States are evaluated. Also, a thorough investigation on the regulation of cross-border concentrations and their impact on Europe's industrial and commercial policy is pursued. In Chapter 4, the application of competition law and policy on businesses in Europe is put into perspective. The legal control and regulation of cartels and dominance and the disposition of the law and policy towards market oligopolisation are examined. Also in this chapter, the application of anti-trust law and policy to distributive trades is analysed. In Chapter 5, the business opportunities arising from the public sector purchasing in the European Union are explored. An assessment of the impact of the European public procurement legislation and a detailed exposition of the rules in force are provided. In Chapter 6, the development and evolution of the financial services law in the European Union is analysed. The integration of the banking sector, the insurance sector, and the stock exchange and securities sectors are thoroughly investigated. Finally, in Chapter 7, the role of social policy of the European Community and its impact on businesses is assessed. Relevant legislation on equal opportunities, equal pay, equal treatment, social security, maternity/parental leave, which has been adopted at Community level and subsequently implemented at national level throughout the common market is analysed.

Contents

Table of cases xvii
Table of European legislation xxiii
Table of treaties and conventions xxix
Table of national legislation xxxi
Acknowledgments vi

INTRODUCTION vii

CHAPTER 1—COMPANIES IN THE EUROPEAN UNION

General remarks 1
Management systems of companies in the European
Union 2
    Organs of the company 2
    The general meeting and the shareholders 2
    The board of directors 4
    Supervisory boards 5
    Auditors 6
Corporate structures in European companies 7
    The distribution of powers between the organs of companies .. 7
The operation of joint ventures in Europe 11
    (i) Contractual joint ventures 12
    (ii) Partnership joint ventures 14
    (iii) Joint venture companies 14
The process of harmonisation of company laws in Europe . 17

CHAPTER 2—CORPORATE LAW DEVELOPMENTS AT EUROPEAN LEVEL

General remarks 21
The Societas Europea 22
The European Economic Interest Grouping as a vehicle of
doing business in the common market 23
    The general background 23
    The development of European Economic Interest Groupings .. 26
    The legal nature of the European Economic Interest
    Grouping 28

The objectives of the European Economic Interest Grouping .. 29
The operation of the European Economic Interest Grouping
in the context of national laws 33
   The principle of uniformity 33
   The principle of harmonisation 33
The European Co-operative Society, the European Mutual
Society and the European Association 35
   The European Co-operative Society 35
   The European Mutual Society 37
   The European Association 38
   Employees' participation in the European Co-operative
   Society, the European Mutual Society and the European
   Association 39

CHAPTER 3—THE REGULATION OF CORPORATE MOBILITY IN THE EUROPEAN UNION

General remarks 41
Industrial concentration and its control 43
   General background 43
   The principles and concepts of the merger control regulation .. 50
   The control of corporate mobility through joint ventures 52
   The legal basis of the merger control regulation 56
Corporate mobility and the control of concentrations from
an economic perspective 57
   Economic evaluation criteria for concentrations 57
   The calculation of turnover 58
   The principles of mandatory notification and automatic
   suspension 60
   The examination of the notification 63
   The conclusion of the investigations 64
   The hearing of the parties and of third parties 64
   The appraisal criteria 65
   The powers of the Commission's decision 67
   The factors for assessing dominance and compatibility 69
The exclusivity of the merger control regulation 69
   The German clause 70
   The public interest clause 72
   The Dutch clause 73
   The extra-territorial application of the merger control
   regulation 74
   The jurisdictional relationship between the merger control
   regulation and European competition law and policy 74

CHAPTER 4—THE APPLICATION OF COMPETITION LAW AND POLICY ON BUSINESS IN EUROPE

General remarks 77
The control of cartels 77
The control of market dominance 78
Anti-trust and market dominance 81
    The application of behavioural remedies (Art. 85 EEC) 81
    The application of structural remedies (Art. 86 EEC) 83
The Community's approach to collective dominance 89
    Anti-trust and distribution agreements 91
    The principle of exclusivity 91
    The principle of selectivity 92
    Territorial protection in distribution agreements 93
    Consumer redress and legal protection 95

CHAPTER 5—DOING BUSINESS WITH THE PUBLIC SECTOR

General remarks 97
The legislative framework of public procurement 97
    The public supplies regime 98
    The public works regime 103
    The public utilities regime 107
    The public services regime 113
Compliance and enforcement of public procurement
legislation 116
    The compliance directives 116
    The scope of the compliance directives 121
The operation of the public procurement directives 122
    The applicability of the directives: definitions 122
        Contracting authorities 122
        Public Contracts 122
    Specific types of contracts under the public procurement
    directives 123
        Concession contracts 123
        Subsidised works contracts 123
        Framework agreements 124
        In-house contracts and contracts to affiliated undertakings 124
        Secret public works contracts 125
        Construction projects under international agreements 125
    Size of public contracts under the public procurement
    directives 125
        Thresholds 125
        Estimation of contract value 126
The principles of the directives 127
    Mandatory advertisement and publication of public contracts . 127

Selection and qualification criteria 128
Legal requirements 128
Eligibility requirements 129
Financial and economic standing 129
Technical capacity 130
The technical knowledge and ability of a contractor 130
The technical capacity of a supplier 130
List of recognised contractors 131
The award of public contracts 131
Tendering procedures 131
Prohibition of post-tender negotiations 134
Tendering procedures for concession contracts 134
Design contests 134
Award criteria 135
The award of concession contracts 135
Additional award criteria 136
Sub contracting and public procurement 136
Local labour employment and public procurement 136
The award of public housing schemes 137
Extra-territorial effects of the public procurement regime 137
The agreement on government procurement 138

CHAPTER 6—THE FINANCIAL SERVICES SECTOR

General remarks 143
The financial services sector in Europe 143
The integration of the banking sector 146
The European banking Directives 146
The integration of the insurance sector 151
The non-life insurance Directives 151
The life assurance Directives 151
The motor vehicle insurance Directives 154
The integration of stock exchange and securities markets .. 155
The stock exchange and securities markets Directives 155

CHAPTER 7—SOCIAL POLICY WITHIN THE FRAMEWORK OF EUROPEAN BUSINESS LAW

General remarks 159
The principle of equality: The function of Article 119 of the EEC Treaty 160
The equal pay principle and its components 161
Reliance upon Article 119 at national level 163
The principle of equal treatment: The structure of the equality directives 164
Equality in pay 164

Contents

Equality in treatment 165

Equality in social security schemes 166

Equality in job evaluation schemes: equal pay for work of
equal value 168

Equality in social security 170

Reliance upon the equality directives at national level 172

The concept of indirect discrimination 173

Access to justice and the provision of legal remedies at
national level 176

CONCLUDING REMARKS 177

Index 179

Contents

Equality in Remuneration 103
Equality in social security schemes 108
Inability to compensate services, equal pay for work of
equal value 109
Principle of equal economy 170
Remedies in cases equalling discontinues at par and level ... 171
The concept of indirect discrimination 173
Access to justice and the meaning of level
playing field 177

CONCLUDING REMARKS 107

Index 170

Table of Cases

Alphabetical Table of U.K. Cases and Cases before the European Courts

A & B.C. Chewing Gum, Re; Topps Chewing Gum Inc. v. Coakley [1975]
    1 W.L.R. 579; [1975] 1 All E.R. 1017 16
Ahlstrom Osakeyhtio v. E.C. Commission, *The Times*, September 29,
    1988 82
Ahmed Saeed Flugreisen and Silver Line Reiseburo GmbH v. Zentrale zur
    Bekampfung Unlauteren Wettbewerbs E.V. [1990] 2 C.M.L.R. 102;
    The Times, April 13, 1989 .... 45, 76, 85
Aktien-Zuckerfabrik Schoppenstedt v. E.C. Council [1971] E.C.R.
    975 118
Algemene Transport en Expeditie Onderneming van Gend en Loos NV v.
    Nederlandse Administratie der belastingen [1963] E.C.R. 1; [1963]
    C.M.L.R. 105 5
Alsatel/Novasam [1986] E.C.R. 237 .... 45, 86
Arbeiterwohlfahrt der Stadt Berlin E.V. v. Botel (Monika) [1992] 3
    C.M.L.R. 423; [1992] I.R.L.R. 423 167

BRT v. SV SABAM [1974] E.C.R. 313; [1974] 2 C.M.L.R. 238 85
Bayerische HNL Vermehrungsbetriebe GmbH v. E.C. Council and Com-
    mission [1978] E.C.R. 1209; [1975] 1 C.M.L.R. D44 120
Beets-Proper v. Van Lanschot-Bankiers N.V. [1986] E.C.R. 773; [1987]
    C.M.L.R. 616 170
Bilka-Kaufhaus GmbH v. Weber von Hartz [1986] E.C.R. 1607; [1986] 2
    C.M.L.R. 701 .... 162, 167, 169
Borland's Trustee v. Steel Bros & Co. Ltd [1901] 11 Ch. 279 2
British American Tobacco Co. Ltd and R.J. Reynolds Industries Inc. v.
    E.C. Commission [1988] 4 C.M.L.R. 24 .... 46, 52, 57
Burton v. British Railways Board [1982] E.C.R. 555; [1982] C.M.L.R.
    136 170

CEI v. Bellini [1987] E.C.R. 3347 104
Carruth v. Imperial Chemical Industries [1937] A.C. 707; 2 All E.R.
    422 3
Colonial Bank v. Whinney (1886) 11 App. Cas. 426 2
Commercial Solvents Corp. v. E.C. Commission [1974] E.C.R. 223;
    [1974] 1 C.M.L.R. 309 83
Consten and Grundig v. E.C. Commission [1966] E.C.R. 299 93

Defrenne v. SA Belge de Navigation Aerienne (SABENA) [1976] E.C.R.
    473; [1976] 2 C.M.L.R. 98 .... 105, 160, 161, 162, 163
Deutsche Grammophon GmbH v. Metro-SB Grossmarkte GmbH [1971]
    E.C.R. 1; [1972] C.M.L.R. 107 .... 117, 119

E.C. Commission v. Belgium [1984] E.C.R. 1543; [1985] 3 C.M.L.R.
134 117
E.C. Commission v. Denmark [1985] E.C.R. 427; [1986] 1 C.M.L.R.
44 168
E.C. Commission v. Italian Republic [1983] E.C.R. 3273; [1984] 3
C.M.L.R. 169 .... 174, 176
E.C. Commission v. United Kingdom [1982] E.C.R. 2601; [1982] 3
C.M.L.R. 284 170
E.C. Commission v. United Kingdom [1983] E.C.R. 3441; [1984] 1
C.M.L.R. 44 175
Elopak v. Tetra-Pak [1990] 4 C.M.L.R. 47; [1990] F.S.R. 263 76
Europmballage Corp. and Continental Can Co. v. E.C. Commission
[1973] E.C.R. 215; [1972] C.M.L.R. 690 .... 44, 45, 57, 65, 66,
67, 75, 83

Foss v. Harbottle (1849) 2 Hare 461; [1957] C.L.J. 194 8
Francovich and Bonifaci v. Italian Republic [1993] E.C.R. 61 [1995]
I.R.L.R. 84 .... 118, 119
Freeman and Lockyer v. Buckhurst Park Properties (Mangal) [1964] 2
Q.B. 480; [1964] 2 W.L.R. 618 8

Garland v. British Rail Engineering Ltd [1982] E.C.R. 359; [1982] 2
C.M.L.R. 174 161
Gebroeders Beentjes B.V. v. State of Netherlands [1988] E.C.R.
4635 136
General Motors Continental N.V. v. E.C. Commission [1976] E.C.R.
1367; [1976] 1 C.M.L.R. 95 83

Habermann-Beltermann [1993] E.C.R. I–1657 175
Handels-og Kontorfunktionaerernes Forbund I Danmark v. Dansk
Arbejdsgiverforening [1990] E.C.R. I–3979; [1989] I.R.L.R. 532 ... 175
Harz v. Deutche Traddax GmbH [1984] E.C.R. 1921; [1986] 2 C.M.L.R.
430 .... 166, 176
Hely-Hutchinson v. Brayhead Ltd [1968] 1 Q.B. 549; [1967] 3 W.L.R.
1408, CA 8
Hoffmann-La Roche & Co. A.G. v. Centrafarm Vertriebsgesellschaft Phar-
mazeutischer Erzeugnisse mbH [1978] E.C.R. 1139; [1978] 3
C.M.L.R. 217 .... 83, 84
Hoffman-La Roche & Co. A.G. v. E.C. Commission [1979] E.C.R. 461;
[1979] 3 C.M.L.R. 561 .... 45, 65, 66, 83, 84, 85, 86, 87, 174
Hoffman v. Barmer Ersatzkasse [1985] I.C.R. 731; [1984] 7 E.C.R.
3047 174
Hugin Kassaregister A.B. and Hugin Cash Registers v. E.C. Commission
[1979] E.C.R. 1869; [1979] 3 C.M.L.R. 345 83
Humble v. Mitchel (1839) 11 Ad. & El. 205 2
Hurd v. Jones (Inspector of Taxes) [1986] Q.B. 892; [1986] E.C.R.
29 .... 117, 119

I.C.I. v. E.C. Commission [1972] E.C.R. 619; [1972] C.M.L.R. 557 ... 82

Jenkins v. Kingsgate Ltd [1981] E.C.R. 911; [1980] 1 C.M.L.R. 81 163,
168, 169

Johnston v. Chief Constable R.U.C. [1986] E.C.R. 1651; [1986] 2
C.M.L.R. 240 .... 175, 176

Kowalska v. Freie und Hansestadt Hamburg [1990] E.C.R. I–2591;
[1992] I.C.R. 29 167

Liefting v. Directie van het Academisch Ziekenhuis bij de Universiteit van
Amsterdam [1984] E.C.R. 3225; [1984] 3 C.M.L.R. 701 162
Lutticke (Alfons) GmbH v. E.C. Commission [1971] E.C.R. 325; [1966]
C.M.L.R. 378 118
Lutticke (Alfons) v. Hauptzollampt Saarlouis [1973] E.C.R. 57; [1973]
C.M.L.R. 309 100

Macarthys Ltd v. Smith [1978] 1 W.L.R. 1189; [1978] I.C.R. 785,
C.A. 163, 168
Marshall v. Southampton and South West Hampshire Area Health
Authority (Teaching) [1986] E.C.R. 723; [1986] 1 C.M.L.R.
688 .... 105, 170, 171, 172, 173
Metro S.B.-Grossmarkte GmbH & Co. KG v. E.C. Commission [1977]
E.C.R. 1875; [1978] 2 C.M.L.R. 1 83
Molkerei-Zentrale Westfalen/Lippe GmbH v. Haupzollampt Pederborn
[1968] E.C.R. 143; [1968] C.M.L.R. 187 100
Musique Diffusion Francaise S.A.; Pioneer High Fidelity (G.B.) v. E.C.
Commission [1983] E.C.R. 1825; [1983] 3 C.M.L.R. 221 .... 82, 91

Nederlandsche Banden-Industrie Michelin N.V. v. E.C. Commission
[1983] E.C.R. 3461; [1985] 1 C.M.L.R. 282 .... 65, 66, 68, 83, 86, 87
Newstead v. Department of Transport and H.M. Treasury [1988] 1
W.L.R. 612; [1988] C.M.L.R. 219 162
Nimz v. Freie und Hansestadt Hamburg [1991] E.C.R. I–297; [1991]
I.R.L.R. 222 167
Nungesser and Kurt Eisele v. E.C. Commission [1982] E.C.R. 2015;
[1983] 1 C.M.L.R. 278 92

Pinkett v. Wright (1842) 2 Hore 120 2
Plessey Company, The v. General Electric Company et al. [1990] E.C.C.
384 .... 16, 49
Pool v. Middleton (1861) 29 Beau 646 2
Procureur de la Republique v. Waterkeyn [1982] E.C.R. 4337; [1983] 2
C.M.L.R. 145 117
Pronuptia de Paris GmbH Frankfurt am Main v. Schillgalis [1986] 1
E.C.R. 353; [1986] 1 C.M.L.R. 414 92

R. v. Minister of Agriculture Fisheries and Food [1990] E.C.R.
I–2433 .... 117, 119
Radio Telefis Eireann v. E.C. Commission (Magill T.V. Guide) [1991] 4
C.M.L.R. 586 84
Reyners v. Belgium State [1974] E.C.R. 631; [1974] 2 C.M.L.R.
305 117
Rinner-Kuhn v. F.W.W. Special-Gebaudereiningung GmbH [1989]
E.C.R. 2743; [1989] I.R.L.R. 493 167

Roberts v. Tate and Lyle Industries Ltd [1986] I.C.R. 371; [1986] 1 C.M.L.R. 714 170
Rummler v. Dato-Druck GmbH [1987] E.C.R. 127; [1987] 3 C.M.L.R. 168

Salgoil SpA v. Italian Ministry for Foreign Trade [1968] E.C.R. 453; [1968] C.M.L.R. 181 100
Societe Italiana Vetro Spa v. E.C. Commission [1992] 5 C.M.L.R. 302 .... 84, 86
Societe Technique Minier v. Machinenbaum Ulm GmbH [1966] E.C.R. 235 .... 62, 92
Suiker Unie v. E.C. Commission [1975] E.C.R. 1942; *The Times*, December 23, 1975 .... 45, 82, 84, 87

United Brands v. E.C. Commission [1978] E.C.R. 207; [1978] 1 C.M.L.R. 429 .... 65, 66, 86

Van Binsbergen v. Bestuur van de Bedrijfsvereninging Voor de Metaalnijverheid [1974] E.C.R. 1299; [1975] 1 C.M.L.R. 298 117
Volke v. Vervaecke [1969] E.C.R. 295 85
Von Colson & Kamman v. Land Nordrhein Westfalen [1984] E.C.R. 1891; [1986] 2 C.M.L.R. 309 .... 166, 176

Walrave and Koch v. Association Union Cycliste Internationale et al [1974] E.C.R. 1405; [1975] 1 C.M.L.R. 320 105
Webb v. E.M.O. Air Cargo Ltd [1994] Q.B. 718; [1992] 2 All E.R. 43, CA 175
Worringham & Humphreys v. Lloyd's Bank Ltd [1981] I.C.R. 558; [1981] E.C.R. 767 .... 162, 163, 168
Wilhem v. Bundeskartellamt [1969] E.C.R. 1; [1969] C.M.L.R. 100 .... 117, 119

Zuchner v. Bayerische Vereinsbank A.G. [1981] E.C.R. 2031; [1982] 1 C.M.L.R. 313 85

Numerical Table of Cases before the European Courts

Case 26/62   Algemene Transport en Expeditie Onderneming Van Gend en Loos NV v. Nederlandse Administratie der belastingen vii
Joined Cases 56, 58/64   Consten and Grundig v. E.C. Commission 93
Case 56/65   Societe Technique Minier v. Machinenbaum Ulm GmbH 62, 92
Case 57/65   Luttucke, Alfonds v. Hauptzollampt Saarlouis 100
Case 28/67   Molkerei-Zentrale Westfalen/Lippe GmbH v. Haupzollampt Pederborn 100
Case 13/68   Salgoil SpA v. Italian Ministry for Foreign Trade 100
Case 14/68   Wilhem v. Bundeskartellamt 117, 119
Case 4/69   Lutticke (Alfons) GmbH v. E.C. Commission 118
Case 5/69   Volke v. Vervaecke 85
Case 48/69   I.C.I v. E.C. Commission 82

Case 78/70   Deutsche Grammophon GmbH v. Metro-SB Grossmarkte
GmbH 117, 119
Case 5/71   Aktien-Zuckerfabrik Schoppenstedt v. E.C. Council 118
Case 6/72   Europmballage Corp. and Continental Can Co. v. E.C. Com-
mission 44, 45, 57, 65, 66, 67, 75, 83
Joined Cases 40–48, 50, 54–56, 111, 113, 114/73   Suiker Unie v. E.C.
Commission 45, 82, 84, 87
Case 127/73   BRT v. SV SABAM 85
Case 2/74   Reyners v. Belgium State 117
Joined Cases 6, 7/74   Commercial Solvents Corp. v. E.C. Commis-
sion 83
Case 33/74   Van Binsbergen v. Bestuur van de Bedrijfsvereninging Voor
de Metaalnijverheid 117
Case 36/74   Walrave and Koch v. Association Union Cycliste Internatio-
nale et al 105
Case 26/75   General Motors Continental N.V. v. E.C. Commission 83
Case 43/75   Defrenne   v.   SA   Belge   de   Navigation   Aerienne
(SABENA) 105, 160, 161, 162, 163
Case 26/76   Metro S.B.-Grossmarkte GmbH & Co. KG v. E.C. Commis-
sion 83
Case 27/76   United Brands v. E.C. Commission 65, 66, 86
Joined Cases 83 & 94/76 & 4, 15, 40/77   Bayerische HNL Vermehrungs-
betriebe GmbH v. E.C. Council and Commission 120
Case 85/76   Hoffman-La Roche & Co A.G. v. E.C. Commission 45,
65, 66, 83, 84, 85, 86, 87, 174
Case 102/77   Hoffmann-La Roche & Co. A.G. v. Centrafarm Vertriebs-
gesellschaft Pharmazeutischer Erzeugnisse mbH 83, 84
Case 22/78   Hugin Kassaregister A.B. and Hugin Cash Registers v. E.C.
Commission 83
Case 258/78   Nungesser and Kurt Eisele v. E.C. Commission 92
Case 129/79   Macarthys Ltd v. Smith 163, 168
Case 69/80   Worringham & Humphreys v. Lloyd's Bank Ltd 162,
163, 168
Case 96/80   Jenkins v. Kingsgate Ltd 163, 168, 169
Case 100/80   Musique Diffusion Francaise S.A.; Pioneer High Fidelity
(G.B.) v. E.C. Commission 82, 91
Case 172/80   Zuchner v. Bayerische Vereinsbank A.G. 85
Case 12/81   Garland v. British Rail Engineering Ltd 161
Case 19/81   Burton v. British Railways Board 170
Case 61/81   E.C. Commission v. United Kingdom 170
Joined Cases 314–316/81 & 83/82   Procureur de la Republique v. Water-
keyn 117
Case 322/81   Nederlandsche Banden-Industrie Michelin N.V. v. E.C.
Commission 65, 66, 68, 83, 86, 87
Case 163/82   E.C. Commission v. Italian Republic 174, 176
Case 165/82   E.C. Commission v. United Kingdom 175
Case 14/83   Von Colson & Kamman v. Land Nordrhein Westfalen 166,
176
Case 23/83   Liefting v. Directie van het Academisch Ziekenhuis bij de
Universiteit van Amsterdam 162
Case 79/83   Harz v. Deutsche Traddax GmbH 166, 176
Case 143/83   E.C. Commission v. Denmark 168

Case 184/83   Hofmann v. Barmer Ersatzkasse 174
Case 44/84   Hurd v. Jones (Inspector of Taxes) 117, 119
Joined Cases 142, 156/84   British American Tobacco Co. Ltd and R.J.
  Reynolds Industries Inc. v. E.C. Commission 46, 52, 57
Case 151/84   Roberts v. Tate and Lyle Industries Ltd 170
Case 152/84   Marshall v. Southampton and South West Hampshire Area
  Health Authority (Teaching) 105, 170, 171, 172, 173
Case 161/84   Pronuptia de Paris GmbH Frankfurt am Main v. Schillga-
  lis 92
Case 170/84   Bilka-Kaufhaus GmbH v. Weber von Hartz 162, 167, 169
Case 222/84   Johnston v. Chief Constable R.U.C 175, 176
Case 262/84   Beets-Proper v. Van Lanschot-Bankiers N.V. 170
Case 89/85   Ahlstrom Osakeyhtio v. E.C. Commission 82
Case 192/85   Newstead v. Department of Transport and H.M. Treasury
                                                                                    162
Case 237/85   Rummler v. Dato-Druck GmbH 168
Joined Cases 27–29/86   CEI v. Bellini 104
Case 66/86   Ahmed Saeed Flugreisen and Silver Line Reiseburo GmbH
  v. Zentrale zur Bekampfung Unlauteren Wettbewerbs e.v. 45, 76, 85
Case 247/86   Alsatel/Novasam 45, 86
Case 31/87   Gebroeders Beentjes B.V. v. State of Netherlands 136
Case 171/88   Rinner-Kuhn v. F.W.W. Spezial-Gebaudereiningung
  GmbH 167
Case 179/88   Handels-og Kontorfunktionaerernes Forbund I Danmark
  v. Dansk Arbejdsgiverforening 175
Case 33/89   Kowalska v. Freie und Hansestadt Hamburg 167
Case T–68/89   Società Italiano Vetro SpA v. E.C. Commission (Hat
  Glass) 84
Case T–69/89   Radio Telefis Eireann v. E.C. Commission (Magill v. T.V.
  Guide) 84
Case 75/89   Societe Italiana Vetro v. E.C. Commission 84, 66
Case 213/89   R. v. Minister of Agriculture Fisheries and Food 117, 119
Joined Cases 6/90 & 9/90   Francovich and Bonifaci v. Italian Repu-
  blic 118, 119
Case 390/90   Arbeiterwohlfahrt der Stadt Berlin E.V. v. Botel (Monika) ..
                                                                                    167
Case 421/92   Habermann-Beltermann 175
Case IV31.043   Elopak v. Tetra-Pak 76

Table of European Legislation

DECISIONS

Dec. 80/271: [1980] O.J.
L215/1 .... 102, 138
Dec. 87/565: [1987] O.J.
L345 122
Dec. 89/22: [1989] O.J.
L78/48 .... 86, 87, 88, 89
Dec. 89/79: [1989] O.J.
L33/66 84
Dec. 93/323: [1993] O.J.
L125 141
Dec. 93/324: [1993] O.J.
L125 137

DIRECTIVES

Dir. 64/225: [1964] O.J. Spec.
Ed. 131 151
Dir. 66/683: [1966] J.O. 37 ... 99
Dir. 68/151: [1968] O.J. Spec.
Ed. 41 .... 18, 21, 24
Dir. 70/32: [1970] J.O. L13 ... 98,
99, 100
Arts. 3(1)–(3) 99
Arts. 9, 10 99
Dir. 71/304: [1971] O.J.
L185/1 .... 98, 103
Dir. 71/305: [1971] O.J. Spec.
Ed. 682 .... 98, 104, 105,
106, 107, 129
Preamble 104
Art. 1(a) 104
Art. 2 106
Art. 3(3) 105
Art. 4 106
Art. 5 106
Art. 7 105
Art. 21 .... 105, 129
Art. 29(4) 106
Art. 48 105
Art. 52 105
Art. 59 105

Dir. 71/305: [1971] O.J. Spec.
Ed. 682—cont.
Art. 119 105
Annex I 105, 106
Annex II 104
Dir. 72/166: [1972] O.J.
L103 154
Dir. 73/183: [1973] O.J.
L194 146
Dir. 73/239: [1973] O.J.
L228 .... 151, 154
Dir. 73/240: [1973] O.J.
L288 151
Dir. 75/117: [1975] O.J.
L45/9 .... 160, 164, 170
Art. 1 .... 163, 168
Arts. 3, 4 164
Art. 6 170
Dir. 76/207: [1976] O.J.
L39/40 .... 160, 165, 170,
173
Art. 1(2) 171
Art. 2(1) 165
(2) 165, 175
(3) 174
Art. 5(1) 170, 172
Art. 6 165
Dir. 77/62: [1977] O.J.
L13/1 .... 98, 100, 101,
102, 104, 107, 108,
138
Art. 1(b) 100
Art. 2 107
Art. 3 106
Art. 5(1)(a) 101
Art. 18 .... 105, 129
Arts. 20–23 129
Art. 26 106
Annex I 100, 108
Dir. 77/91: [1977] O.J. L26 ... 18,
21
Dir. 77/92: [1977] O.J. L26 ... 152

Dir. 77/780: [1977] O.J. L322 146
Dir. 78/473: [1978] O.J. L151 151
Dir. 78/660: [1978] O.J. L222 .... 18, 21, 38, 52
Dir. 78/855: [1978] O.J. L295 .... 18, 21
Dir. 79/7: [1979] O.J. L6/24 ... 160, 166, 167, 173
   Art. 7(1) 171
     (a) 171
Dir. 79/267: [1979] O.J. L63 151
Dir. 79/279: [1979] O.J. L86 155
Dir. 80/390: [1980] O.J. L100 155
Dir. 80/767: [1980] O.J. L215/1 .... 98, 101, 138
Dir. 80/987: [1980] O.J. L283 118
Dir. 82/121: [1982] O.J. L48 155
Dir. 82/891: [1982] O.J. L378 .... 18, 21
Dir. 83/189: [1983] O.J. L165/1 102
Dir. 83/349: [1983] O.J. L193 .... 18, 21, 38, 124
Dir. 84/5: [1984] O.J. L8 154
Dir. 84/253: [1984] O.J. L126 .... 18, 38
Dir. 85/611: [1985] O.J. L375 156
Dir. 86/378: [1986] O.J. L225/40 .... 160, 162, 166, 167, 173
   Art. 2(2)(c) 171
   Art. 4(a) 166
Dir. 86/613: [1986] O.J. L359/56 .... 160, 168
Dir. 86/635: [1986] O.J. L372 .... 147, 149
Dir. 87/102 149
Dir. 87/344: [1987] O.J. L185 151
Dir. 87/345: [1987] O.J. L185 155
Dir. 88/295: [1988] O.J. L127/1 .... 98, 102, 106, 107, 129

Dir. 88/295: [1988] O.J. L127/1—cont.
   Art. 1(a) 103
   Art. 3(2)(a)–(c) 103
   Art. 6(1)(c) 103
   Art. 7 103
     (2) 102
   Art. 9 103
Dir. 88/301: [1988] O.J. L131/73 109
Dir. 88/357: [1988] O.J. L172 151
Dir. 88/627: [1988] O.J. L348 155
Dir. 89/117: [1989] O.J. L44 .... 147, 149
Dir. 89/289: [1989] O.J. L124 155
Dir. 89/299: [1989] O.J. L124 146
Dir. 89/440 .... 98, 104, 106, 107, 129
   Art. 3 107
Dir. 89/592: [1989] O.J. L334 155
Dir. 89/646: [1989] O.J. L386 146
Dir. 89/647: [1989] O.J. L388 147
Dir. 89/665: [1989] O.J. L395 120
   Art. 1 121
Dir. 90/88 149
Dir. 90/211: [1990] O.J. L112 155
Dir. 90/232: [1990] O.J. L129 154
Dir. 90/531: [1990] O.J. L297 ...... 98, 109, 111, 141
   Art. 1 110
   Art. 2 110
     (4) 110
     (5)(a) 110
      (b) 111
   Art. 3 111
     (1)–(4) 111
   Art. 6(1) 112
   Art. 7(2) 112
   Art. 8 .... 110, 112
     (2) 112
   Art. 9 112
     (1)(a) 112

Dir. 90/531: [1990] O.J. L297—*cont.*
Art. 12 107
Art. 26 129
Art. 29 .... 113, 129, 141
Annex I-V 112
Dir. 90/618: [1990] O.J. L330 154
Dir. 90/619: [1990] O.J. L330 .... 151, 152
Dir. 91/31: [1991] O.J. L17 ... 147
Dir. 91/308: [1991] O.J. L168 147
Dir. 91/674: [1991] O.J. L374 152
Dir. 91/675: [1991] O.J. L374 152
Dir. 92/13: [1992] O.J. L76/7 .... 120, 122
Art. 1 121
(a) 123
Art. 3 121
Art. 7 122
Dir. 92/30: [1992] O.J. L110/52 149
Dir. 92/49: [1992] O.J. L228 . 151
Dir. 92/50: [1992] O.J. L209 ....
98, 103, 109, 111, 113, 115, 116
Art. 1(a) 123
(c), (d) 132
(g) 113
Art. 6 124
Art. 7(2)–(8) 126
Art. 11(2), (3) 132
Art. 15(1), (2) 128
Art. 16(1) 128
Art. 19(4) 133
Art. 26 129
Art. 29 129
Art. 31 129
Art. 35 131
Art. 36(1)(a),(b) 135
Dir. 92/85: [1992] O.J. L348/1 .... 160, 168
Dir. 92/96: [1992] O.J. L380 .... 151, 152
Dir. 92/121: [1992] O.J. L29 147
Dir. 92/302: [1992] O.J. L110 147

Dir. 93/6: [1993] O.J. L141 ... 156
Dir. 93/22: [1993] O.J. L141 156
Dir. 93/36: [1993] O.J. L199 .... 98, 103
Art. 1(a), (b) 122
(d), (e) 132
(f) 132
Art. 5(1)(a), (c) 126
(2)–(6) 126
Art. 6(2) 132
(3) 132
Art. 9(1)–(3) 128
Art. 12 133
Art. 17 136
Art. 20 .... 129, 136
Art. 22 .... 129, 130
Art. 24 134
Art. 25 131
Art. 26(1)(a), (b) 135
Art. 52 .... 103, 104
Art. 53 103
Art. 59 .... 103, 104
Art. 60 104
Art. 62 103
Dir. 93/37: [1993] O.J. L199 ...... 98, 103, 107, 134
Art. 1(b) 122
(d) 123
(e), (f) 132
(g) 132, 134
Art. 2(1), (2) 123
Art. 3 134
(1) 126
Art. 4(b) 125
Art. 5(a), (c) 125
Art. 6(1)–(5) 126
Art. 9 137
Art. 7(2), (3) 132
Art. 11(1), (2) 128
(3) 128, 136
(4) 128, 136
(5) 128
Art. 13 133
Art. 16 136
Art. 17 136
Art. 20 136
Art. 24 129
Art. 26 129
Art. 27 130
Art. 29 131
Art. 30(1)(a), (b) 135

Dir. 93/38: [1993] O.J.
    L199 ....
    98, 103, 109, 110, 111, 112,
                       114
   Art. 1(1), (2) 122
      (3) 124
      (4)(a)–(c) 123
      (5) 124
      (7)(a)–(c) 132
   Art. 13 124
   Art. 14(a)–(c) 126
   Art. 20(1) 132
      (2)(b) 115
        (i) 124
      (3) 132
   Art. 21 128
   Art. 22(1)(a)–(c) 128
   Art. 24 128
   Art. 26(2) 133
   Art. 31 .... 129, 130
      (b) 129
   Art. 34(1)(a),(b) 135
Dir. 94/19: [1994] O.J.
    L135 .... 146, 148

DRAFT DIRECTIVES

Directive on company structure:
   [1983] O.J. C240 .... *18,*
                      19, 22
   Art. 12 .... *23*
   Art. 21S *23*
Vredeling Directive: [1983] O.J. C217
                      18, 19

REGULATIONS

Reg. 17/62: [1959–1962] O.J.
   Spec. Ed. 87 .... 49, 74,
              75, 76, 94, 95
   Art. 3 95
Reg. 26/62: [1959–1962] O.J.
   Spec. Ed. 129 74
Reg. 27/62: [1959–1962] O.J.
   Spec. Ed. 132 74
Reg. 141/62: [1959–1962] O.J.
   Spec. Ed. 291 74
Reg. 19/65: [1965–1966] O.J.
   Spec. Ed. 35 94

Reg. 802/68: [1968] O.J. Spec.
   Ed. 165 .... 113, 137, 141
Reg. 1017/68: [1968] O.J.
   Spec. Ed. 302 70
Reg. 1983/83: [1983] O.J.
   L173 .... 93, 94
   Recitals 3–5 92
Reg. 1984/83: [1983] O.J.
   L173 .... 91, 94
Reg. 2349/84: [1984] O.J.
   L219/1 .... 53, 93
   Art. 5(2) 53
Reg. 123/85: [1985] O.J.
   L15 94
Reg. 2137/85: [1985] O.J.
   L199/1 ... 24, 26, 28, 32, 34
   Preamble 30, 32, 34
   Art. 1(2) 29, 31
      (3) 29
   Art. 2 27
      (1), (2) 27
   Art. 3 .... 29, 34
      (1) 28, **30**
      (2) 30, 32
        (c) 32
        (d) 33
        (e) 33
   Art. 4 .... 30, 31
      (1)(b) 30
      (3) 33
   Art. 5 29
   Art. 6 29
   Art. 7 .... 29, 31
   Art. 9 24
   Art. 10 29
   Art. 11 29
   Art. 12 .... 29, 31
   Art. 14 29
      (4) 33
   Art. 15 29
   Art. 16 .... 29, 31
      (1) 33
   Art. 17 .... 29, 31
      (3) 33
   Art. 18 .... 29, 31
   Art. 19 29
      (2) 33
      (3) 33
   Art. 20 29
      (2) 33
   Art. 21(1) 33, 34
      (2) 29, 31

Reg. 2137/85: [1985] O.J. L199/1—*cont.*

Art. 22 29
Art. 24(1) 34
Art. 26 29
   (2) 29, 33
Art. 27 29
   (1) 33
Art. 28 29
   (1) 33
Art. 30 29
   (1) 33
Art. 31 29
   (1) 33
Art. 32 29
   (3) 33
Art. 35 29
   (1) 34
Art. 36 .... 29, 34
Art. 38 34
Art. 40 30
Art. 42(2) 26
Reg. 4056/86: [1986] O.J. L378/4 70
Reg. 3975/87: [1987] O.J. L374/1 70
Art. 5.3(2) 84
Reg. 3976/87
Art. 7.2 84
Reg. 4064/89: [1989] O.J. L391/1 ... 48, 49, 51, 56, 90
Art. 1(2) 55, 56, 59
Art. 2 71
   (1) 58
     (a) 67, 69
     (b) 66, 67, 69
   (2) 58, 66, 67
   (3) 67, 68
Art. 3 .... 51, 70, 74
   (2) 53, 55
Art. 4 61
   (1) 61
   (4) 61
Art. 5 58
   (1) 59
   (5)(b) 60
Art. 6 .... 71, 72
   (1)(b) 71, 72
Art. 7 61
   (1) 63
   (2) 63
   (4) 63

Reg. 4064/89: [1989] O.J. L391/1—*cont.*

Art. 7(5) 62
Art. 9 .... 63, 64, 70, 71, 72
   (2) 70
   (3)(a), (b) 71, 72
   (5) 72
   (7) 69
   (10) 72
Art. 10(1) 63
   (4) 64
   (6) 63
Art. 11 64
Art. 12 64
Art. 13 64
Art. 14(1) 61
Art. 17 70
Art. 19(3), (4) 64
Art. 21(2) 69, 74
   (3) 72, 73
Art. 22(1), (2) 70
   (3) 73
   (4) 73
   (5) 73
Art. 24 74
   (3) 74
   (4) 74
Art. 36 73
Art. 85 .... 56, 57
Art. 86 .... 56, 57
Art. 87 .... 56, 57
Art. 223 73
Art. 224 73
Art. 235 .... 56, 57
Rec. 6 .... 56, 57
Rec. 10 .... 56, 57
Rec. 11 .... 56, 57
Rec. 13 .... 48, 67, 68, 69
Rec. 15 75
Rec. 24 57
Rec. 25 55
Reg. 1461/93: [1993] O.J. L146 .... 137, 141

DRAFT REGULATIONS

*1st draft merger control regulation
[1973] O.J. C92/1 ....* 46

1st draft merger control regulation [1973] O.J. C92/1 —cont.

amendment: [1982] O.J. C36/3 46

amendment: [1984] O.J. C51/8 46

amendment: [1986] O.J. C324/5 46

E.C. COMMUNICATIONS

Com. (80) 422 final (*telecommunications*) 108

Com. (84) 717 final (*public supply contracts*) 102, 108

Com. (85) 310 final (*internal markets*) 102, 108

Com. (89) 400 final (*regional and social aspects of public procurement*) 106

Com. (90) 372 final, Syn. 293 (*service concessions*) 115

Com. (91) 322 final, Syn. 293 (*service concessions*)

Com. (93) 252 final (*European Co-operative Society, European Mutual Society and European Association*) 35

Treaties and Conventions

TREATIES

1957 Paris. Treaty establishing the European Coal and Steel Community (ECSC Treaty) 43, 101
Art. 66 43

Rome. Treaty establishing the European Economic Community .... vii, 1, 43, 68, 97, 143, 176
Art. 2 vii
Art. 3 vii
Art. 3f 57, 67, 77
Art. 5 .... 117, 119, 120
Art. 6 vii
Art. 7 .... 97, 136
Art. 8(2),(4) 67
　　　(7) 98
Art. 9(1) vii
Art. 30 .... 97, 99, 100, 101, 106, 117
Art. 33(7) 99
Art. 48 vii
Art. 52 .... 97, 98, 117, 136
Art. 53 .... 97, 98
Art. 54(3)(g) 18
Arts. 59, 60 .... 97, 98
Art. 67 vii
Art. 83(3) 85
Art. 85 .... 43, 44, 46, 47, 49, 50, 51, 52, 53, 56, 57, 58, 62, 74, 75, 76, 77, 81, 84, 85
　　　(1) 26, 44, 54, 55, 77, 78, 81, 82, 84, 85, 90, 95
　　　(2) 44, 78, 95

Rome. Treaty establishing the European Economic Community—cont.
Art. 85(3) 26, 44, 48, 66, 69, 76, 85, 93, 94
Art. 86 .... 43, 44, 45, 46, 47, 49, 50, 53, 54, 56, 57, 58, 65, 66, 68, 71, 74, 75, 76, 77, 81, 83, 84, 85, 86, 87, 88, 89, 90
Art. 87 .... 46, 49, 56, 57, 76
Art. 88 76
Art. 89 .... 75, 76
Art. 90 98
Art. 92 99
Art. 100 ...... vii, 100, 101
Art. 100a .... vii, 120, 121
Art. 100b vii
Art. 102a vii
Art. 115 .... 139, 140
Art. 117 .... 159, 160, 161
Art. 118 ..... 159 160, 161
Art. 119 .... 159, 160, 161, 162, 163, 164, 166, 167, 168, 169, 170, 173
Art. 120 .... 159, 160
Art. 121 .... 159, 160
Art. 122 .... 159, 160
Art. 130a 49
Art. 130f 49, 69
Art. 169 .... 117, 173
Art. 171 117
Art. 173(2) 120
Art. 177 .... 76, 118

Rome. Treaty establishing the European Economic Community—*cont.*
Art. 186 72
Art. 189 .... 26, 100, 172, 173
Art. 215(2) 120
Art. 228(2) 138
Art. 235 .... 26, 46, 49, 56, 57, 65, 121

Rome. Treaty establishing the European Atomic Energy Community (EURATOM Treaty) 101

1987 Single European Act .... vii, 23

1991 Maastricht Treaty on European Union ... vii, 97, 176

CONVENTION

1951 International Labour Convention (ILO) No. 100 (*Equal Remuneration*)
Art. 2(1) 160

Table of National Legislation

FRANCE
Commercial Code (Code du Commerce), Loi No 66–537, on commercial societies
Art. 265 3

GERMANY
Anti-trust Act (GWB)
s. 1 53
23 53
Commercial Code (HGB)
Art. 170 5
Law of Limited Liability Companies Act (GmbHG)
Art. 15 3
(3) 3
Art. 16 3
Art. 17 3

IRELAND
1977 Employment Equality Act 163

ITALY
Commercial Legislation (Codice Civile)
Art. 2021 4

UNITED KINGDOM
1973 Fair Trading Act (c. 41) 90, 43, 51
1975 Sex Discrimination Act (c. 65) 163
1976 Restrictive Trade Practices Act (c. 34) 13
1977 Patents Act (c. 37)
s. 39(1) 13
1985 Companies Act (c. 6)
s. 182(1) 2
1986 Insolvency Act (c. 45) 15
1988 Copyright, Designs and Patents Act (c. 48)
s. 11(2) 13
s. 215(3) 13
s. 267(2) 13

Chapter 1

Companies in the European Union

GENERAL REMARKS

The examination of management systems and corporate structures in the European Union is of utmost importance and interest to business lawyers and business people as it reveals the different approaches of several European legal orders to corporate market participation. The process of European integration, as conceived by the founding fathers of the European Communities in the Treaty of Rome and reinforced by the Maastricht Treaty on European Union, is based upon the concept of a common market, where *inter alia* factors of production enjoy free and unobstructed mobility.

Movements of labour and capital and the right of establishment are relevant determinants for the integration of private markets, although recent trends have revealed the willingness and the commitment of European institutions to reform the Member States' public sectors and align them with the regime and competitive standards operating in private markets.[1]

The right of establishment and the right to provide services within the European Union are fundamental principles of the common market and inherent components for its completion and proper operation. Both principles are crucial for the development of genuine patterns of trade between Member States and are considered necessary conditions for cross-border business development.

The concept of the company and its constituents is the starting point of the following analysis on management systems and corporate structures. In all European legal systems, the company represents a collective effort of individuals to achieve a common goal. Corporate structures which allocate power within companies reveal different perceptions of corporate performance and management responsibilities among European legal orders. Decision-making and executive implementation are vested in the hands of the company's organs. The distribution and balance of power between the organs of the company, as well as the legal

---

[1] For example, the set of E.C. Directives on public supplies, works and services, opening up public procurement in the Member States. A more detailed analysis of the principles and the impact of public sector integration in the E.U. is provided in Chap. 5.

relationship between themselves and the company as a distinct personality, are the main topics of this Chapter. Attempts by European institutions to harmonise European company laws and recent corporate developments at European level will also be analysed. The examination of management systems and corporate structures in Europe reveals two distinct legal traditions, which are influenced by common law and civil law respectively.

MANAGEMENT SYSTEMS OF COMPANIES IN THE EUROPEAN UNION

Organs of the company

The company in its corporate personality is an artificial (legal) person composed of natural persons. It is distinguished from individuals who are its members, as it can own property, have rights and be subject to liabilities. The company, as a legal recognition of a nexus of contracts by a group of persons pooling their capital, delegates its management to specialist managers. The members of the company, who are individual shareholders form the *general meeting*; this appoints the *board of directors* who are the company's officers with the task to govern it. In all European Union legal orders these two organs form the core of a company. Interestingly, there are legal orders that have added more organs with a view to facilitating supervision and control of management; these organs are *supervisory boards* and *works councils*.

The general meeting and the shareholders

The general meeting includes the total number of shareholders who have a right to vote. A shareholder is a natural or legal person who has invested capital in the company and has taken shares in return. Shares constitute proof of membership or ownership for shareholders. The legal definition of the share is essential here for the understanding of the operation of the general meeting. Courts in the United Kingdom have described shares as choses in action.[2] Under British law, the share does not represent rights of property but purely contractual rights recognised by the Companies Act.[3] The fact that these contractual rights are transferable, at a time when other choses in action are not legally assignable, attaches the character of "property" to shares.[4] The Companies Act 1985, s.182(1) states that shares are personal estate and not realty. Also,

---

[2] *Humble v. Mitchel* (1839) 11 Ad. & El. 205; *Colonial Bank v. Whinney* (1886) 11 App. Cas. 426.
[3] *Borland's Trustee v. Steel Bros & Co. Ltd* [1901] 11 Ch. 279 at 288.
[4] *Pinkett v. Wright* (1842) 2 Hore 120; *Pool v. Middleton* (1861) 29 Beau 646.

---

courts described shareholders' rights as rights of property merely in order to emphasise that they may be exercised as the shareholder chooses, without regard to the welfare of the company.[5] This might be seen incompatible with the whole concept of the company as an independent personality, distinct from its members and with the right to have its own property. In fact shares do not embody property rights since shareholders are not the owners at law or in equity of the company's property.

Under French law, share appears to have a slightly different nature. The share presents the common characteristics of transferable values; it is a title of nominal value which confers to its holder a right of participation in the profits or dividends.[6] This approach seems to give precedence to the proprietary rights of the share, although the contractual element of rights and duties is not missing, as the *Code du Commerce* regulates to a great extent these rights and duties, but with respect to restrictions on transfer of shares, they are not covered as such by statutory provisions.[7] The articles of association may provide for two main restrictive clauses, namely the consent clause (*clause d'agrement*), where prior approval by the board of directors is required for transfer of shares, and the preemption clause (*clause de preemption*), where the other shareholders should be given the right of first refusal of shares offered for sale.[8]

German law follows, in principle, the same definition of the nature of shares, although distinction should be made between shares of *Geselschaft mit beschränkter Haftung* (GmbH) and *Actiengeselschaft* (AG) (limited liability and public company respectively).[9] A share of a GmbH is not embodied in a negotiable share certificate as in an AG. That means the certificates, which are seldom issued, merely serve as evidence.[10] Transfer of shares can be executed before a notary and has effect in respect to the company only after notification to it. Much care needs to be taken by the purchaser of GmbH shares, since he has no absolute guarantee that the transferor actually owns it. A list of shareholders is annually filed with the commercial register, but it is only an indication and not an evidence of ownership. In principle, shares are freely transferable, although transferability may be restricted by the memorandum or

---

[5] See *Carruth v. Imperial Chemical Industries Ltd* [1937] A.C. 707 at 765; [1937] 2 All E.R. 422 at 459.

[6] "*L'action presente les caractères communs aux valeurs mobilières; elle est un titre a valeur nominal qui confere a son titulaire un droit à la participation aux benefices ou dividendes*", see Michel de Julgart and Benjamin Ippolito in Droit Commercial (2nd ed., 1975), pp. 514 *et seq.*

[7] See *Code du Commerce* (French Commercial Code), Loi No 66–537 on commercial societies, Art. 265.

[8] *ibid.*, Art. 275.

[9] See GmbHG (Geselschaft mit beschränkter Haftung Gesetz—German Law on Limited Liability Companies), Arts. 15–17. (Law on limited liability companies of April 20, 1892 as amended).

[10] *ibid.*, Art. 15(3).

articles of association.[11] The Italian legal system regards shares as the documents representing the extent of participation of a member in a company.[12] Therefore, rights and duties of shareholders derive through the proprietary character of the share.[13] Transfer of shares may be subject to special conditions by the articles of association (pre-emption or consent clauses). The transfer has no effect with respect to the company until it is registered in the company's register of shareholders.

The above examination of company laws among European legal orders, as far as the nature of the share is concerned, unfolds a general perspective of the legal status of shareholders as the members of the company. They form the *general meeting*, the assembly of the company. While each member enjoys certain individual rights *vis-à-vis* the company, namely the receipt of dividends and the exercise of voting rights, the power to influence and control the company's policy is vested in the members collectively. Shareholders, as members of the company, through the annual general meeting or extraordinary meetings exercise their powers; these powers relate to the control of management. The general meeting appoints the board of directors which is accountable to the former. Actually, the control of management in the company is linked with voting rights of shareholders.

Divergence occurs as different European legal systems regulate voting rights in a different way. In contrast to the British system, where non-voting shares are allowed, most continental legal orders consider the right to vote as an essential function of the share. Participation in an enterprise through contribution to its share capital should also result in a proportionate degree of say, and to some extent power, within the company. On the other hand, problems may arise in respect to multiple voting. Contrary to the legal system operating in the United Kingdom, shares with a plural vote are, in principle, forbidden in many continental jurisdictions. Of course, certain exceptions both to non-voting shares and to a multiple voting system exist. In Germany for example, preference shares without voting rights may be issued provided that the amount issued does not exceed the nominal value of all the other shares and that the shares acquire the right to vote if the preference dividends are not paid. In France, when fully paid registered shares have been held for two years in the name of the same person, they may be given a double vote.

The board of directors

This organ of the company defines and executes the general policy of the company. It is appointed by the general meeting and as mentioned

---

[11] See Formmel and Thompson, *Company Law in Europe* (1975), p. 257; also R. Pennington, *Companies in the Common Market* (1970), pp. 17–18.
[12] C.C. (*Codice Civile*) (Italian Commercial Legislation) Art. 2021.
[13] Formmel and Thompson, *op. cit.*, p. 34.

above, it is accountable to the latter. The board operates collectively and acts collegiately, although it is accepted that it may delegate its powers or part of its powers to one or more of its members in a way that it authorises them to pursue the objectives of the company. In any case it is accountable *en bloc* to the general meeting.

Both the British and continental legal systems do not provide a sufficient answer as to the legal relationship between the directors and the company and it is not clear whether the former are considered agents of the latter. In the United Kingdom there is no case before the courts that has defined clearly the exact legal status of a director.[14] Distinction should be made between the fact that a director may derive his powers through the memorandum and the articles of association or through a contractual link with the company. In the former case, he acts as an officer of the company, being appointed under the provisions of its constitution, whereas in the latter case he serves the company as an employee or an agent under express or implied contract of service.

In continental legal systems two different approaches exist. French law considers the directors to be mere agents of the company whose powers are governed by the rules of "mandate" (*mandat*), a concept that is very similar to the English concept of agency.[15]

Under the French legal approach, there is a contract between the principal (the company) and the agent (the director), which includes the granting of powers to the latter to represent the former. On the other hand, German law makes a distinction between mandate, as such, and representation.[16] The power of representation is based on two systems; one is the *Prokura*, a commercial authority which is very broad and must be entered in the Commercial Register; the other is the *Handlungvollmacht* (general power of attorney), narrower than the former with no need to be registered. Consequently, in the German legal order a clear distinction is made between the power of the board of directors to manage the company and the power to represent it *vis-à-vis* third parties. This power is given to all directors jointly or two directors jointly or one director jointly with a *Prokurist*. The German example has been adopted with some modifications by the Italian legal system. It appears that legal certainty, protection of third parties dealing with the company and preservation of decency in commercial transactions are the motives behind the German model.

Supervisory boards

The board of directors exercises the policies of the company and the general meeting of shareholders controls the implementation of the decisions of the board, through the annual or extraordinary meetings. In

[14] See Pennington, *Company Law* (6th ed., 1991), p. 550.
[15] See Juglart and Ippolito, *op. cit.* at n. 6, pp. 634 *et seq.*
[16] See H.G.B. (*Handelsgesetzbuch*—German Commercial Code) Art. 170; also Formmel and Thompson, *op. cit.* at n. 11, p 241.

order to enhance control mechanisms over the board of directors, some legal orders provide for a body which lies between the board of directors and the general meeting. This corporate organ takes the form of a supervisory board and its main task is the supervision of the management. In fact, supervisory boards have another function: to provide for sufficient employees' representation to the management of the company. Indeed, workers' participation is considered by many legal systems as an essential requirement of contemporary corporate management strategies, with a view to achieving a workable and effective regime in industrial relations.

Supervisory boards as a means of employees' representation were initiated in Germany, where A.G.s (public companies) must have a two-tier management system: the board of directors and the supervisory board.[17] In France a two-tier system is optional. In Italy supervisory boards are not known. In the Netherlands a system of workers' participation in the management of the company has been introduced since 1971. This system differs from the German one to the extent that the supervisory board in an N.V. (Naanloze Vennootschap—Dutch plc) or a B.V. (besloten Vennootschap met beperkte aansprakelijheid—Dutch Ltd) may appoint the board of directors after prior consultation with the general meeting and the works' council, whereas the German system provides for appointment of the management by the supervisory board without any prior consultation. Finally, English law is not familiar with the institution of supervisory boards. Management is vested solely in the hands of the board of directors.

Auditors

Auditors are organs of the company appointed by the shareholders (general meeting) to examine the annual financial statements of the company. Their task is twofold: control and supervision of the company's finance. Their powers vary with respect to the legal order in question.

In the United Kingdom the auditor is for certain purposes an officer of the company and may be regarded as its agent.[18] He is liable to the company, if he fails to exercise reasonable care in carrying out the audit. He also may be liable to third parties for negligent misstatements on which one can reasonably expect them to rely.

The English system does not confer supervisory powers on auditors as many continental legal orders do. Furthermore, it is obligatory for auditors to be professional accountants. In France, companies (S.A.s) must have auditors, their number depending (two maximum—one minimum) on the size of the company, or on the fact that it has a Stock Exchange listing, or on whether it appeals to the public for its funds. Auditors must

---

[17] Formmel and Thompson, *op. cit.* at n. 11, p. 40.
[18] See Farrar, Company Law (3rd ed., 1991); also Pennington, *op. cit.* at n. 14.

be professional accountants and must be chosen from a list maintained by the Court of Appeal in whose jurisdiction the company is located. They have no supervisory powers.[19] In Germany a slightly different formula is followed: All A.G.s must appoint one or more auditors who must be professional accountants. On the other hand, only large GmbHs which publish their accounts annually must have them examined by independent public accountants.[20] In Belgium auditors have supervisory tasks in a way of an unlimited right to superintend and control the operations of the company. They need not be professional accountants, unless the company has made a public issue of shares or debentures or its securities are listed on a Stock Exchange; in that case one auditor must be a public accountant.[21] The Dutch system is similar to the Belgian one, but it confers more powers to the auditors of the company who can dismiss the management of the company. They are appointed by the general meeting; in fact they are members of the supervisory board.[22] The Greek system provides for the appointment of two statutory auditors (or one if he is a Certified Public Accountant) to follow corporate accounting throughout the year, review and certify the financial statements and report to the meeting of shareholders. Apart from their power to make recommendations to the general meeting, they may refer the case to the Ministry of Commerce, if they detect a violation of the law or of the charter of the company.[23] In the Italian system, auditors are organised in a board with supervisory tasks over the management. At the request of shareholders representing one-twentieth of the company's share capital, the auditors are obliged to carry out an investigation.

CORPORATE STRUCTURES IN EUROPEAN COMPANIES

The distribution of powers between the organs of companies

The most effective way in which shareholders through the general meeting can control the management is by exercising their rights to appoint and remove the directors of the company. This is one approach of management control without any provision granting rights to employees to be represented in the company. As already mentioned above, certain legal orders provide for a two-tier system where supervisory boards exercise a substantial degree of control over the management of the company. In companies where a two-tier board system is in operation,

---

[19] See Julgart and Ippolito, *op. cit.* at n. 6, p. 691.
[20] Formmel and Thompson, *op. cit.* at n. 11, pp. 256–257.
[21] *ibid.*, pp. 144–145.
[22] *ibid.*, p. 412.
[23] For a general review of Greek company law see K. Kerameus and P. Kozyris (eds.), *Introduction to Greek law*, (1988) pp. 189 *et seq.*

the supervisory board derives from the general meeting. Shareholders appoint the members of the supervisory board and then the latter selects amongst its members the members of the board of directors. The procedure differs in various European legal orders.

In the United Kingdom a company has two principal organs, the general meeting of shareholders and a board of directors. Shareholders with the right to vote appoint the board of directors and control it through the memorandum and articles of association, where provision concerning the powers conferred to directors are stipulated. Such control may be exercised by altering these provisions. The board of directors is in a strong position, as day-to-day running of the company is vested in the hands of it. It should be mentioned that British law does not regard certain powers as managerial or executive in order to be conferred exclusively upon the board. The board's powers may be as broad or as narrow as they are defined in the memorandum and articles of association. The board of directors acts collectively. That means, in principle it cannot delegate any of its powers to one or more of its members. On the other hand, following the theory of *implied powers*, it has been held by the courts[24] that a delegation of powers by the board is not *ultra vires*, since it is a part of the general power of it to manage the company's affairs. Of course, there is always the possibility for the general meeting to authorise such a delegation. The power to appoint the board of directors is a corporate one, exercisable in the manner laid down in the company's memorandum and articles of association. Although the two-tier system, in the form of employees' representation has not officially been introduced, the memorandum or articles of association may provide for the latter. It has been argued that the appointment of part-time non-executive directors serves a similar purpose. Finally, the general meeting of a British company operates in accordance with the majority rule.[25] This means that the majority of the shareholders decide framework policies to be implemented by the board of directors. A minority of the members of the general meeting who are dissatisfied with the conduct of the company's affairs by the majority or by the board of directors cannot judicially challenge decisions of the majority of shareholders or acts of the board of directors. The courts establishing the rule of judicial non-interference in the management of the company refused to substitute its organs in the decision making. The justification lies in the need to preserve the right of the majority to decide how the company's affairs shall be conducted. Furthermore, any attempt by the court to interfere would be ineffective, since its decision could be set aside by an authorisation of the general meeting.

In France, an S.A. may opt for a board of directors or for a two-tier system, the latter including a board of directors with a supervisory

---

[24] *Freeman and Lockyer v. Buckhurst Park Properties Ltd* [1964] 2 Q.B. 480; [1964] 1 All E.R. 630; *Hely-Hutchinson v. Brayhead Ltd* [1968] 1 Q.B. 549; [1968] 3 All E.R. 98.
[25] The rule in *Foss v. Harbottle*; Pennington, *op. cit.* at n. 14, pp. 649 *et seq.*

board.[26] In the first case the board of directors must have a minimum of three and a maximum of 12 members. A director cannot be appointed to more than eight boards. The board convenes shareholders' meetings; it is responsible for the book-keeping and each financial year must present to the general meeting the balance sheet, profit and loss accounts and a report on the company's activities; it appoints amongst its members the chairman of the board. The chairman of the board in his capacity as general manager has the widest powers to manage the current business of the company, always within the objectives laid down in the memorandum and articles of association. His duties and powers are twofold: first, as a chairman of the board of directors, he must observe that the latter fulfils its duties (implementation of decisions of the shareholders); secondly, as general manager, he has special powers to act on behalf of the company. The chairman of the board may bind the company *vis-à-vis* third parties even by acts performed beyond the objectives laid down in the memorandum and articles of association. Also, he may delegate his powers to certain members of the board or to employees of the company, but he retains personal responsibility for their acts.

In the second case, where a two-tier management system is opted, the supervisory board, which is appointed by the general meeting, is the only competent body to appoint the board of directors and its chairman. It should be mentioned that two members of the works' council attend meetings of the supervisory board (and of the board of directors), but without voting rights. The supervisory board permanently monitors the activities of the board of directors and for this purpose it may, at any time during the year, examine any documents and check upon its activities, although without direct interference. The board of management is limited to five members. Companies having a share capital of less than FF 250.000 may have a sole managing director. A member of the board of directors must not be a member of the supervisory board, neither may he be an auditor. The board of directors collectively and all members' terms of office expire at the same time. It enjoys wide powers to act on behalf of the company. It convenes general meetings and may receive delegated authority by the general meeting to alter the capital of the company. The company is bound by transactions entered into by its board of management, even if they fall outside its objectives.

In Germany, the shareholders' meeting is the supreme body of the GmbH. Its position is so strong that it is entitled to intervene in the day-to-day business of the company and to issue any kind of instructions to the management. It appoints the managing directors and, where it is mandatory, the supervisory board. The powers of the managing directors are distinguished between their external authority (power to represent the company) and their internal rights and obligations

---

[26] See Julgart and Ippolito, *op. cit.* at n. 6; also Formmel and Thompson, *op. cit.* at n. 11.

9

(management). The external authority of managing directors can only be limited by the provision of joint signature of a *Prokurist*. With regard to their internal rights and duties, the managing directors' authority is limited by the articles of association or by the shareholders' resolutions or by their contract of employment. As far as supervisory boards are concerned, these are mandatory in two cases: (a) if the company (GmbH) has more than 500 employees or (b) it is engaged in coal and steel manufacturing. In the first case, one third of the members of the supervisory board are employees' representatives and the other two thirds are appointed by the shareholders' general meeting. In the second case, the supervisory board must consist of at least 11 members of which five are employees' representatives and five are representatives of the shareholders. The 11th member is an independent one, to be nominated by a co-determination procedure between the general meeting and the supervisory board.

The Dutch system of corporate structure appears more complicated than the European systems previously examined. Dutch companies, whether N.V.s or B.V.s, can be divided into small and large companies. Large companies, in turn can be categorised into exempt large companies, structure companies and mitigated structure companies. The general meeting of shareholders has the power to control the company's policy. All companies must have a meeting of shareholders. The memorandum and the articles of association provide for the division of labour between the general meeting and the management. The powers of the general meeting may be weakened substantially by the so-called "oligarchic clauses". Indeed, the articles of association may include such clauses with respect to certain categories of shares (shares with multiple vote). Another way of curtailing the powers of the general meeting is the provision for a supervisory board. Furthermore, if the company employs more than 100 persons, a works' council must be instituted. There is considerable difference of management relations between on the one hand structure companies and mitigated structure ones and on the other hand small and large companies. The most striking difference is that the supervisory board of a structure or a mitigated structure company has more extensive powers than the supervisory board of any other company. In the case of a structure company the supervisory board appoints the board of directors after prior consultation with the general meeting and the works council. As for mitigated structure companies, the management is appointed by the general meeting of the shareholders, but certain decisions of the management are subject to the approval of the supervisory board, which appoints the supervisory directors by its members.

Finally, with respect to large companies, the general meeting appoints the management and the supervisory boards, where the latter advises and supervises the former without having any substantial powers. The purpose for this differentiated management structure is to limit the influence of shareholders and increase the say of the employees in a company.

THE OPERATION OF JOINT VENTURES IN EUROPE

Joint ventures, in the sense in which the term is understood in business today, are largely a development of the period since the Second World War. Their increasing importance has been attributed to two factors: (i) as a result of inflation and high production costs, large projects concerning technological innovation, research and development can frequently be undertaken only by combining the forces of two or more enterprises; (ii) in international relations it has become very noticeable that investment in a foreign country is possible only by means of participation of a local group, whether public or private.

None of the legal systems of major industrialised nations addresses itself specifically to joint ventures; statutory or other definition of a joint venture is lacking. Inevitably, general law in its different branches (company law, competition law, labour law, consumer protection, environmental law) applies to specific situations created by joint ventures.[27] A large proportion of all joint ventures transcend national boundaries, thus operating in the framework of transnational corporations. The great majority of what the business world terms joint ventures are carried on through corporations.[28]

A joint venture can be defined as an enterprise, corporation, or partnership formed by two or more companies, individuals or organisations, at least one of which is an operating entity which wishes to broaden its activities for the purpose of conducting a new profit-motivated business of permanent duration. In general, the ownership is shared by the participants with more or less equal distribution and without absolute dominance by one party.[29] Generally, joint ventures can be classified in the following different ways[30]:

(i) they may be related to a single project or they may concern setting up business on a permanent basis;

(ii) the nature of the participants and their relationship to one another outside the joint venture itself characterises a joint venture as a "horizontal" one, when the venturers are broadly in the same kind of business, or as a "vertical" one, when the venturers are engaged in different stages of the manufacturing process, or as a "conglomerate" joint venture, when the venturers intend to operate in a field unrelated to their existing activities;

(iii) joint ventures may be intended to cover the complete business cycle in the field in which they are to operate or they may be

---

[27] See E. Herzfeld, *Joint Ventures* (2nd ed., 1989), p. 13.
[28] See Crane and Bromberg, *Partnership* (1968), p. 195.
[29] See G. R. Young and S. Bradford Jr, *Joint Ventures: planning and action* (Financial Executives Research Foundation, 1977), pp. 11–15.
[30] This classification is based on the possible effects on competition, but it is also applicable in the operational level of joint ventures.

restricted to one or more facets of it, such as research and development, production, packaging, etc.

(iv) depending on the location in which it is to operate, and the residence of its participants, a distinction may be drawn between a joint venture operating at national level and a joint venture operating at international level.

Interestingly, Community law is generally not concerned with the form that a joint venture may take, or the arrangements between the parties, but rather focuses on joint ventures' substantive economic effects and their potential restrictions on competition.[31] Accordingly, when a joint venture is to be achieved by way of a new jointly-owned company, a partial merger or acquisition, a partnership or a contract is a matter of national (company) laws, which, of course, should be harmonised throughout the Community.[32]

In practice, joint ventures can be identified through three basic structural forms:

(i) Contractual joint ventures

By definition, a contractual joint venture is created by a direct contractual relationship between the venturers through one or several contracts and is governed entirely by the law of contract, as it is a contract between the parties concerned and it does not include the establishment of an independent legal entity or a "vehicle" capable of owning its own property, or contracting in its own right with third parties, undertaking an independent business activity as a profit centre.[33] A contractual joint venture is well suited to specific commercial collaborations, where its activity is strictly ancillary to the activities of its members. Typical examples include collaboration in specific stages of manufacture and production, joint production or processing of essential components or raw materials, collaboration in packaging and distribution.[34] The above-mentioned structure is identified with the so-called "horizontal" arrangements, although it is used sometimes to pursue other commercial relationships such as distribution, licensing and sub-contracting agreements.[35] In principle, there is no obligation to register details of the contract with an independent body such as the Registrar of Companies.

---

[31] See *GEC-Weir Sodium Circulators* [1977] O.J. L327/26.
[32] See Kapteyn and Verloren Van Themaat, *Introduction to the Law of the European Communities* (2nd ed., 1989), pp. 448 *et seq.*
[33] See Bentham, "Joint Ventures in Europe: a comment" in *Commercial Operations in Europe* (1978) Vol. 1, pp. 335 *et seq.*; also Herzfeld, *op. cit.*, p. 36.
[34] See Bulton, *Business Consortia* (1961), p. 59.
[35] See Kling and Ellison, *Joint Ventures in Europe* (1991), p. 221.

However, domestic competition law might require the registration of the agreement.[36]

In addition to a statement on their objectives and the means to be taken to achieve them, the parties must define precisely the extent of their rights and obligations. In spite of the absence of a separate legal entity, the joint venturers have certain obligations, which if not complied with pursuant to the joint venture contracts, will entail general penalties under the applicable contractual law and possibly specific penalties which may be stipulated in such contracts, enforceable through court proceedings or, more often, arbitration proceedings.[37] The joint venture contracts usually contain, *inter alia*, provisions on the duration, the sharing of obligations, the sharing of the results of the venture, management structure, industrial property rights and dispute settlement procedure.

As far as management is concerned, the manner and extent of supervision and monitoring of the performance of the collaboration is to be agreed between the parties and specified contractually. Two kinds of structure are met, often in combination[38]: the collective structure and the executive structure. The former consists of committees known as coordinating committees or steering committees. These committees constitute an internal organ of the joint venture. The latter structure comprises the leader, who represents the other(s) in dealings with third parties. Problems may arise with intellectual property rights generated by seconded personnel; in the absence of agreement to the contrary, these rights will belong to their employers, as they procure their availability.[39]

Each member of a contractual joint venture is liable for its own acts and omissions ("several" liability). However, the absence of a predetermined legal category and structure involves certain difficulties, particularly in relations with third parties, in that the venturers may be deemed to have created a *de facto* partnership or an apparent partnership, thus rendering their liability unlimited and joint.[40]

A contractual joint venture normally enjoys tax transparency; income expenses and tax benefits (including investment, tax credits, and deductions from depreciation) are posed directly to each joint venturer. If the joint venture is characterised as a *de facto* partnership pursuing commercial activities, then its profits are taxed in accordance with the corporate taxation system.

[36] Under the Restrictive Trade Practices Act 1976, which is the principal mechanism by which U.K. law seeks to control the anti-competitive effects of commercial agreements, the parties of a commercial agreement covered by the Act shall notify it to the Office of Fair Trading, which will assess the possible anti-competitive effects of the agreement.

[37] See Dubisson, *Les groupements des enterprises pour les marchés internationaux* (1979) pp. 24 et seq.

[38] See Krassilchik, "L'investissement connexe a une operation d'exportation" (1981) *Droit et Pratique du Commerce International*, pp. 603 *et seq.*

[39] Under the Copyright Designs and Patents Act 1988, ss.11(2), 215(3) and 267(2) and Patents Act 1977, s.39(1).

[40] See Julgart and Ippolito, *Droit Commercial* (2nd ed., 1975), pp. 241–242.

(ii) Partnership joint ventures

In contrast to the contractual joint venture structure, the establishment of a partnership gives rise to a vehicle that can be used for the creation and operation of a jointly owned business.[41] Partnerships are characterised by the unlimited liability of the partners and the fact that in most cases they do not form a separate legal entity.[42]

A partnership offers a joint venture a kind of independent *persona* or identity. However this "independence" of the partnership from its members is not, strictly speaking, recognised in English law.[43] Although the partnership may operate under a name that differs from those of its partners, may open a separate bank account, and may sue or be sued in its own name, it is not, as a matter of law, regarded as being an entity independent of, or having separate interests from, its member-partners. English law looks not to the identity of the firm, but to the identity of the individual partners. The partnership cannot contract in its own name; instead, each partner is entitled to contract on behalf of the firm and his act, on the condition that it falls within his authority, will bind all the other partners.[44] The members of a partnership operate in a "double capacity", that of an agent and that of a principal. The partners have personal and unlimited liability against third parties, irrespective of the quantum of their respective capital contributions.[45]

A partnership joint venture offers tax transparency. Thus, its profits only bear tax by reference to the position of its partners and not by reference to the partnership as a joint venture vehicle itself.[46] Corporate partners can directly offset losses accruing from the operation of the joint venture, whereas individual partners are also able to offset their share of losses against other income. There are no filing requirements in respect of the constitution, management, capitalisation or audited results of a partnership, although, when a partnership consists solely of corporate partners, its contribution to each corporate partner's results will be ascertainable from their individual returns to the Registrar of Companies.

(iii) Joint venture companies

The most common form of joint venture structure for collaboration between corporate undertakings is through a joint venture company, where the parties' objectives contemplate the creation and operation of a jointly owned business in the form of an independent entity with

---

[41] See Crane and Bromberg, *op. cit.* at n. 28, p. 208.
[42] See Ripert, *Traite Elementaire de Droit Commercial* (8th ed., 1974), pp. 417–430.
[43] A partnership is treated as a person in Scotland; for more details on the subject see Lindley, *Law of Partnership* (14th ed., 1985), pp. 70 *et seq.*
[44] See Farrar, *Company Law* (3rd ed., 1991), p. 5.
[45] See Pennington, *Company Law* (6th ed., 1991) p. 14.
[46] See Kling and Ellison, *op. cit.*, at n. 35, p. 232.

distinct and separate interests from those of its members.[47] The resulting relationship that subsists between the parties is that of shareholders in a commonly owned and controlled company. Normally, the vehicle for the formation and operation of a joint venture company is a (private) limited company, but in exceptional cases a public limited company may be used, particularly if some of its financial needs are to be raised directly from the public. In most cases, the joint venture company will not be a subsidiary of any of its parent companies, as the latter share control of it; it will be dealt with by its parents as an associated company.[48]

Although their constitution (memorandum and articles of association), their operation and the rights and obligations of shareholders therein are regulated by company law, it is customary for joint venture companies to provide expressly for the manner in which they will be funded and the nature of the venturers' rights as shareholders in a principal document, namely the shareholders' agreement. The memorandum and the articles of association of the company, the issue and the allocation of its share capital, the appointment of its officers and its audited accounts must be filed with the Registrar of Companies and they will be open to public inspection. The contents of the shareholders' agreements, which will contain the true commercial terms of collaboration between the parties, will not be open to public inspection.

Funding takes one of two basic forms (frequently applied in combination): either by joint venturers' contributions, or via recourse to a third party external funder.[49] In practical terms, the provision of funding through an external funder, by means of a loan, affords the venturers more flexibility in the event that the collaboration is not successful and the parties wish to withdraw. This means that if the parties have funded the venture by means of equity, they will only be able to obtain the return of their investment by following the relatively time-consuming and costly procedure for a corporate winding-up.[50] The procurement of external funding, to cover normal overdraft facilities, will almost certainly rely upon the creation by the joint venture of a floating charge over its assets.[51] On the other hand, an attempt to procure external finance for a start-up joint venture, may remove the availability of "limited liability" for the parents, unless the joint venture has, from the outset, material assets; otherwise, the venturers should provide adequate security for a start-up loan and they will be under an obligation to guarantee repayment of it, in the event of the venture's default.[52]

---

[47] See Broden and Scanlan, "The legal status of Joint Venture corporations", (1982) 95 *Harvard Law Review* 831; also Bentham, *Joint Ventures in Europe, op. cit.*, p. 483.

[48] See Herzfeld, *op. cit.* at n. 27, pp. 42 *et seq.*

[49] See Bentham, *op. cit.*, p. 297; also Kling and Ellison, *op. cit.* at n. 35, p. 247.

[50] Winding-up proceedings are contained in the Insolvency Act 1986.

[51] A floating charge is a form of security that, in contrast to a fixed charge, is not attached to specific items of the company's assets. It should be noted that a partnership is not able to grant a floating charge and must rely upon fixed charges over identified assets or personal guarantees from the partners.

[52] See Herzfeld, *op. cit.* at n. 27, p. 55; also Kling and Ellison, *op. cit.* at n. 35, p. 249.

It should be mentioned that, under normal circumstances, the max-imum liability of the shareholders-venturers, in respect of the liabilities of the joint venture, is the amount paid-up on their shares, or in the case of partly paid-up shares, the amount owing in respect of their shares. However, from an economic point of view, the availability of "limited liability" for the parents is curtailed, when in the case of venturers whose shares are listed, the value and price of their shares are likely to be seriously and negatively impacted by a potential failure of the joint venture. Also, as mentioned above, banks and lender contractors may require shareholders' guarantees and bonds as extra security for financ-ing the joint venture.

Corporate joint ventures, in their shareholders' agreement, regulate, *inter alia*, issues concerning the issue and allotment of share capital, minority protection, dispute settlement procedures, transferability of shares and termination of the joint ownership of the venture.[53] Although it is possible to entrench such rights in the articles of association, it is generally preferred to keep the commercial details in terms of control at the level of the board and the shareholders' agreement, since this docu-ment, unlike the articles of association, is not subject to filing with the Registrar of Companies and public inspection.[54] It is customary to allocate a different class of share to each party-venturer, depending upon the relevant number of participants. Minority protection can be achieved at the level of the board of directors, by using decision-making clauses requiring unanimity or a board resolution in respect of which all the directors shall have voted in favour; at the level of the general meeting of the company (joint venture), minority protection is generally achieved by stipulating either that changes to the joint venture memorandum and articles of association will require the consent of the majority holders of each class, or that in respect of such matters, each class of shares will have only one vote, namely the decision of the majority of its holders.[55] As far as the transferability[56] of shares in conjunction with the termina-tion of the joint ownership of the venture is concerned, two methods are commonly used: either providing for buy and sell share options, or utilising "pre-emption" rights that would typically be contained in the articles of association.

When drafting the articles of association, attention should be paid to the following issues: (a) the protection of minority shareholders, (b) the possible creation of a holding company through which the venturers may control the joint venture, (c) the selection of a two-tier system and (d) the application of the so-called procedure of special advantages, which

[53] See Brown, "International Joint Venture Contracts in English Law", (1979) 5 *Droit et Pratique du Commerce International*, 193 *et seq.*
[54] See Kling and Ellison, *op. cit.* at n. 35, p. 250.
[55] See Herzfeld, *op. cit.* at n. 27, p. 47; also the case *A & BC Chewing Gum Ltd, Re; Topps Chewing Gum Inc. v. Coakley* [1975] 1 W.L.R. 579.
[56] Note the recent court proceedings in *Plessey PLC v. General Electric Company et al.* [1990] E.C.C. 384.

involves the appointment by the court of a special auditor who will be required to submit a report to the shareholders.

The best method to provide protection for joint venturers who are minority shareholders appears to be the allocation of shares by class. In France for example, the establishment of a holding company to look after the interests of the venturers depends on whether a foreign partner participates in, and on whether third parties will be investing in the holding company's capital. As far as the management system is concerned, the two-tier system with a supervisory board to monitor the board of directors, appears at first sight cumbersome, but it has the advantage of offering more independence to the latter, which freely assumes the day-to-day management of the corporation, subject only to the supervision of the former. Finally, the procedure of special advantages (the appointment by the court of a special auditor) is mandatory when special advantages, such as the allocation of classes of shares with special rights, are given to a shareholder, but it can be avoided when the special advantages are granted equally to all shareholders at the time the joint venture is created or when such advantages are not the result of personal preference but can be justified as recognition of an investor's contribution to the joint venture.

THE PROCESS OF HARMONISATION OF COMPANY LAWS IN EUROPE

One of the most important goals of European institutions is the achievement of sustainable economic growth and the enhancement of competitiveness among European industries. This goal has been pursued through the application of the competition policy by the Commission of the European Communities as well as through the provision of a legal environment for European enterprises,[57] which has been developed along two lines: (i) the provision of uniform legislation on the protection of the various interests associated with the activities of enterprises, such as the interests of shareholders, investors, employees, creditors and third parties; (ii) the provision of a new framework, appropriate for exercising cross-border collaborative economic activities and for the control of industrial concentration and rationalisation of mergers regulation, both at national and Community levels.

With reference to the provision of uniform legislation which aims to harmonise and approximate existing company laws at domestic level, it should be mentioned that only limited progress has been made. A number of instruments have been successfully enacted by Member States, such as the First and Second company law Directives on the protection of shareholders and third parties, the Fourth Directive on

---

[57] See Kapteyn and Verloren van Themaat, *Introduction to the Law of The European Communities* (2nd. ed., 1989), Chap. II.

company accounts and the Seventh Directive on consolidated accounts.[58] The First Directive introduced the co-ordination requirement which is stipulated in Article 54(3)(g) and provided for publicity of certain documents concerning the annual report and accounts of companies and the capacity of directors. The Second Directive provided for minimum requirements regarding the formation of companies and the maintenance, or alteration of capital. It provided, *inter alia*, for a new classification among private and public companies and introduces compulsory valuation of non-cash consideration provided to a public company for return of shares. The Fourth Directive dealt with disclosure of financial information and the contents of a company's annual accounts. It complements the First Directive and is supplemented by the Seventh Directive which deals with group accounts. The Eighth Directive[59] deals with the qualifications and independence of auditors of both public and private companies. The Eleventh Directive the Commission has adopted is a proposal for a directive dealing with disclosure requirements in respect of branches opened in a Member State by certain types of companies governed by the law of another state. The Twelfth Directive allows the operation of one-member private companies. This is permitted already in a number of jurisdictions.

With respect to the provision of a new framework for exercising cross-border collaborative economic activities, only the Third company law Directive (on mergers at national level) and the Sixth company law Directive (on division of public companies) have been enacted.[60] The Third Directive provided for co-ordination of procedures applying to internal mergers within a Member State. The directive only applies to public companies and does not cover take-overs by acquisition of shares. The Sixth Directive deals with scissions or divisions. "Scission" means the transaction whereby a public company transfers to a number of public companies within the same Member State which are already incorporated or yet to be formed, all its assets and liabilities in exchange for the issue of shares to the shareholders of the original company.

Other proposals are still pending, and have been met with strong opposition, in particular those regarding employees' rights of information and participation in management.[61] The Draft Fifth Directive deals with corporate structure and worker participation and as mentioned above, has been the subject of much controversy. The most recent draft refers to a distinction between the directors of a public limited company who will be responsible for its management and those responsible for

---

[58] See Council Directives, respectively: 68/151: [1968] O.J. Spec. Ed. 41; 77/91: [1977] O.J. L26; 78/660: [1978] O.J. L222; 83/349: [1983] O.J. L193.

[59] Council Directive 84/253, [1984] O.J. L126.

[60] See Council Directives, respectively: 78/855: [1978] O.J. L295; 82/891: [1982] O.J. L378.

[61] This is one of the reasons for the standstill of the amended proposal for a Fifth Directive on company structure ([1983] O.J. C240) and the so-called "Vredeling Directive" ([1983] O.J. C217).

their supervision. Provision is made in order that the above distinction between managing and supervisory directors can be achieved either through a two-tier board or a one-tier board. In the latter case, the distinction would be achieved by a division between executive directors who would manage, and non-executive directors who would supervise. One of the most difficult topics in the Fifth Directive is that of employee participation in corporate decision-making. The directive provides for three ways of employee participation. The first way initiates employees' representation at supervisory boards, whereas the second introduces employee participation through the operation of works' councils. Finally, a third way of employee participation could be achieved through collective agreements.

In addition, the directive includes provisions concerning the duties and liability of directors, the powers of the general meeting, the rights of shareholders and in particular minority shareholders, approval of annual accounts and the functions and liability of auditors. It should be mentioned here that there is also a draft directive on procedures for informing and consulting employees which overlaps with the Fifth Directive. This instrument is known as the "Vredeling Directive". It does not form part of the company law harmonisation programme as it applies to other employers as well as companies. It would require head offices of large companies to inform and consult employees of subsidiaries or separate establishments through local management.

The draft Ninth Directive deals with certain aspects of groups of companies and the relationship between the participating corporations. The directive has been mainly influenced by the relevant German law on groups. The directive seeks to provide an organised legal structure for the unified management of a public company which is controlled by any other undertaking (whether a company or not) and of that other undertaking. The directive also stipulates for a conduct of groups which are not subject to unified management, although in the latter case the code of conduct could only apply to the parent or dominant undertaking and those members of the group which are public companies. The directive provides for two methods for establishing a group; through a control contract or a unilateral declaration of control. It should be mentioned that the directive appears flexible to the extent that it would leave Member States free to introduce other methods in order to achieve similar results. A proposal for a Tenth Directive is designed to facilitate on a Community-wide basis the type of merger between public companies dealt with in the Third Directive. Finally, a proposal for a Thirteenth Directive deals with takeovers and is influenced to a large extent by the City of London takeover code.

Chapter 2

Corporate law developments at European level

GENERAL REMARKS

An important goal of European institutions is the growth and enhanced competitiveness of European enterprises. This goal has been pursued through a careful application of the competition policy by the Commission of the European Communities and through the provision of a better legal environment for these enterprises.[1] The two main lines along which this project has been developed are:

   (i) the provision of a uniform legislation on the protection of the various interests touched by the activity of the enterprises, such as shareholders and investors, employees, creditors and, more generally, third parties;

   (ii) the provision of more suitable forms for the exercise of an economic activity and for industrial concentration, and a rationalisation of existing ones, in particular mergers—both at national and international level—and groups of companies.

It should be mentioned that only some of the provisions belonging to the first category have so far been successfully enacted, like the First and Second company law Directives, whose aim is the protection of shareholders and third parties; the Fourth Directive on company accounts and the Seventh Directive on consolidated accounts.[2]

Other proposals are still pending, and have been met with strong opposition, in particular those regarding employees' rights of information and participation in management. In respect of the second category, only the Third company law Directive (on mergers at national level) and the Sixth (on division of public companies) have been enacted,[3] whereas there are several proposals or draft proposals whose approval is not

---

[1] See Kapteyn and Verloren van Themaat, *Introduction to the Law of The European Communities*, (2nd ed., 1989), Chap. II.

[2] See Council Directives, respectively: 68/151: [1968] O.J. Spec. Ed. 41); 77/91: [1977] O.J. L26; 78/660: [1978] O.J. L222; 83/349: [1983] O.J. L193.

[3] See Council Directives, respectively: 78/855; [1978] O.J. L295; 82/891; [1982] O.J. L378.

---

easy to foresee: they range from the Fifth Directive on company structure to the draft of the Ninth Directive on groups of companies, the draft
regulation on the statute of the European company and the proposal for
a Tenth company law Directive on cross-border mergers.

THE SOCIETAS EUROPEA

In an attempt to achieve a Community-wide corporate structure and a
general framework for the so-called European company law, European
institutions have introduced a common denominator by harmonising
and approximating national laws. All started in 1966,[4] when the Commission took up proposals of the professional and other bodies to pre-
pare draft legislation for a European-type company, the *Societas Europea*,
a genuine transnational corporation which would provide a suitable
vehicle for cross frontier mergers within the Common Market.

With regard to management, the draft legislation organised the structure of a *Societas Europea* along the same lines as German law does.
Initially, the Commission proposed that a *Societas Europea* should follow
the two-tier system, with a supervisory board consisting of one-third by
members appointed by the employees and two-thirds by members
appointed by the general meeting of the shareholders. However, in 1974,
after advice given by the European Parliament, the Commission subsequently modified the abovementioned proposal, so that one-third of the
members of the supervisory board would be appointed by the employees
of the company, one third by the general meeting and one-third would be
co-opted by these two groups. This reveals a combination of the German
and the Dutch system.

Alongside the proposed legislation for a European-type company, the
Fifth Directive of the Commission[5] deals with important topics of company structure and workers participation. Its current version, as
amended in 1989, provides for an option between the two-tier system
and the conventional one-tier board known in the United Kingdom. The
difference is that in the former situation management should be accountable to the supervisory board, which is to be composed in accordance
with the German or the Dutch system; in the latter situation, the conventional one-tier board provides for non-executives, who are to supervise
the management. Non-executives are members of the management
appointed by the meeting of shareholders by a maximum of two-thirds
and by employees of the company by a maximum of one-third. In both
systems employee participation seems to be guaranteed, not only
through their representation to the management but also through the

---

[4] See Formmel and Thompson, *Company Law in Europe* (1975), pp. 407 *et seq.*
[5] See Pennington, *Companies in the Common Market*, (1970) p. 121.

institution of works councils. In both systems the structure of the company, in respect to the division of powers between its organs appears the same. The fact that by virtue of Article 12 of the Fifth Directive, when a company opts for a two-tier system, the authorisation of the supervisory board must be obtained for certain decisions of the board of directors, whereas on the other hand, by virtue of Article 21S, when a company opts for a conventional one-tier system, the management cannot delegate its powers for the decisions mentioned in Article 12.

This may cause some problems of interpretation as to the role of management in the one-tier system. In the writer's view, and based on the difference in language between Articles 12 and 21S of the Fifth Directive, prior authorisation by the supervisory board, in case of the two-tier board, weakens the position of the management; on the other hand, the management as such, in the one-tier system company, being comprised of executives and non-executives is in a stronger position, since it retains the power to decide on the same aspects where in the two-tier system authorisation by the supervisory board is required. The European Commission, taking into account the new dimension created by the introduction of the Single European Act and the new dynamics of the project of the internal market, has revitalised the idea for the *Societas Europea* in conjunction with the involvement of employees in it. Indeed, in 1989 it proposed a regulation[6] on the statute for a European Company and at the same time a directive[7] on the participation of employees in the company. The initial draft legislation concerning the *Societas Europea* and the Fifth Directive were the substantive legal bases for the proposed regulation and directive. Unfortunately, these proposals remain as controversial as their predecessors were in the early seventies. It is argued that the bone of contention is taxation of the *Societas Europea* in different European legal orders.

THE EUROPEAN ECONOMIC INTEREST GROUPING AS A VEHICLE OF DOING BUSINESS IN THE COMMON MARKET

The general background

The attempts of European institutions to provide European enterprises with an appropriate framework for their mobility through cross-border integration can be traced throughout the 1970s. The European Commission indicated intermediate forms between co-operation and integration of enterprises, in order to develop an effective industrial policy within the common market.[8] Intermediary forms were seen as a first step

---

[6] [1972] O.J. C240.
[7] See [1989] O.J. C263.
[8] Memorandum from the Commission to the Council: "The Industrial Policy of the Community, Part II, Improvement of the environment of enterprises in the Community", Brussels, March 19, 1970.

towards integration and to a large extent had been influenced by the operation of the French *groupement d'interet economique* (GIE).

Bearing in mind the obstacles that the proposals aimed at corporate integration had encountered, the idea of an extension at Community level of an institution similar to the French GIE appeared as a viable substitute for inter-firm co-operation. Indeed, the loose structure of a grouping and the fact that it preserves the autonomy of the participants, came as the solution to the reluctance of European firms to embark on mergers or other forms of integration, particularly after the failures which occurred in the 1970s.[9] The European Commission considered a priority objective the need for European enterprises to collaborate more closely in order to be able to compete with US and Japanese rivals.

The instrument chosen for such corporate collaborative activities is the European Economic Interest Grouping (EEIG), which is closely modelled on the French GIE. Its regulation at Community level reduces to a minimum the interference of national laws and it might be considered as the first successful attempt to create a *forum* of European company law. The EEIG regulation[10] allows a great deal of contractual freedom for the participants, with the exception of the rules on publicity and disclosure, which aim to protect third parties contracting with an EEIG and present striking similarities to the provisions of the First company law Directive.[11]

The progressive consolidation of an enlarged and European-wide common market led to a noticeable movement towards industrial concentration, in line with the Community's industrial policy. Although an industrial policy as such is not included among the objectives of the Treaty of Rome, the need for it appeared already in the late 1960s[12] and the first formulations by the EEC Commission were published in the same period and more fully developed in the early 1970s.[13] The main objective of such a policy was, and still is, the controlled encouragement of concentration and collaboration among private enterprises from different Member States; its main features are the competition policy provided for in the Treaty, and the desire to strike a balance between large enterprises and small and medium-sized firms.

This has resulted mainly in a wave of mergers at national level, whereas cross-border mergers and other forms of collaboration have

---

[9] See Bayer in [1985] *Horizontal Groups and Joint Ventures in Europe: Concepts of Reality* (Hopt ed., 1982).

[10] Council Reg. 2137/85: [1985] O.J. L199.

[11] Art. 9 of Reg. 2137/85.

[12] It should be recalled that this was precisely the time when, after the successful implementation of the provisions of the EEC Treaty at the end of the transitional period, the dominance of US-based multinationals loomed increasingly over the European industry, which had just emerged from the post-war recovery. See Servan-Schreiber, *The American Challenge*, (1968).

[13] See the Commission's Communication, published in the Official Journal, July 29, 1968; also the Commission's Memorandum on the Community industrial policy; *op. cit.* at n. 10.

been hampered by several factors, not least those linked with considerations of national pride.[14] The other side of the coin is the political perception of the need for an integrated European industry, especially in high technology sectors, to maintain an acceptable level of indigenous technological advancement, even though such a perception clashes with considerations of strategic self-sufficiency at national level.[15] Thus, a real need has emerged for forms of collaboration, capable of preserving the separate identity of the co-operating enterprises.

The same scenario applies to smaller firms, but in less politically sensitive industrial sectors, where the need for collaboration is based more on economic reasons (economies of scale, more efficient allocation of resources, in particular in relation to non-production activities such as marketing, advertising, research and development). More specifically, in this case serious drawbacks may be implied in a merger: even if differences in national laws would not prevent such firms from merging, such mergers would not necessarily be desirable in view of the characteristics of many of the firms potentially involved. Firms of small or medium size, firmly rooted in their national—or perhaps local—business environment, generally lack the flexibility to adapt suddenly to a broader horizon, especially as far as management resources are concerned. Such firms also lack the knowledge needed for a merger, as regards information about potential partners and ability to evaluate the potential of the resulting entity.[16]

These kinds of problems which arise in respect of mergers at a purely national level, can often be overcome; at international level, on the other hand, they are exacerbated by greater diversity and difficulty of communication. Therefore, it is apparent that a chance for initially limited co-operation, capable of being gradually increased, is needed as a sort of a pre-merger trial.[17] This could take the form of a *joint venture* or a *consortium* and at European Community level since 1989, of a *European Economic Interest Grouping*. The European Economic Interest Grouping is a new corporate instrument which aims to facilitate cross-frontier co-operation for businesses within the common market engaging in certain activities such as, for example, research and development, purchasing, production and selling, operation of specialised services, quality control of substances, computerised data processing and the formation of multidisciplinary consortia in the construction industry to tender for public or private contracts.[18] It was created as a result of the adoption,

[14] An interesting account of the failure of some of these attempts at international mergers among European enterprises is given by Bayer, *op. cit.*

[15] See the conference organised by the *Financial Times* and the Institute for Research and Information on Multinationals, (Munich, April 1985), reported in the *Financial Times* of April 25 and 26, 1985.

[16] In this respect, in order to help them, The E.C. Commission instituted an Office for Co-operation among Enterprises, [1973] 4 E.C. Bull.

[17] See Herzfeld, *Joint Ventures* (1983), Part 1.

[18] See [1987] 3 E.C. Bull. Supp. 2.

on July 25, 1985, by the Council of Ministers of the European Community of Regulation 2137/85.[19] The regulation came into force in August 1985. However, it was not possible to form the first EEIG before 1 July 1989,[20] in order to give Member States time to make their legislation compatible with the requirements of the Regulation.[21]

The development of European Economic Interest Groupings

The initial distrust of the European Commission towards the French GIE was based on the GIEs' nature of agreement between enterprises, an agreement which could potentially or actually restrict competition within the meaning of Article 85(1) of the EEC Treaty. The operation of GIEs appeared somehow controversial, because such (potentially) anti-competitive agreements enjoyed the legal protection of national laws of Member States. That perspective, however, was soon changed, as the Commission developed its policy towards industrial concentration[22] and recognised the need for corporate collaborative activities which in the long run may have pro-competitive effects. This shift in policy led not only to a more permissive attitude towards GIEs, but also to the proposal, in 1973, of a regulation on a "European Co-operation Grouping",[23] based on Article 235.

In the context of the Commission's policy, such a grouping was meant to have a specific objective: the necessity for closer co-operation among European industries with a view to enhancing competitiveness and productivity.[24] At the same time, the Commission was aware of the importance of further corporate integration and the efficiency gains obtainable through such an exercise, so it proceeded with the creation of a legal environment for the regulation of cross-border groups and mergers.

It should be mentioned that collaborative business activities had to be cleared of any potential or actual anti-competitive effect on intra-Community trade. The only instrument provided for such purpose by the Treaty is the provision in Article 85(3), which enables the Commission to exempt some agreements and some categories of agreements from the

---

[19] [1985] O.J. L199.

[20] Art. 42(2) of Reg. 2137/85.

[21] This is peculiar, since implementation periods are given only with respect to E.C. Directives, which are the optimum instrument for harmonization of laws, and not to regs. which provide for uniformity of laws; see also Art. 189.

[22] See the Commission's Communication, published in the *Official Journal* of July 29, 1968, relating to the co-operation among firms—especially small and medium-sized ones—as a means of improving the industrial structure of the Community and thus within the provision of Art. 85(3). Such an approach was later developed in the Commission's Memorandum on the Community Industrial Policy (Brussels, 1970) and subsequently refined and carried on as a fundamental component of both competition and industrial policies.

[23] [1974] E.C. Bull. Supp.

[24] Commission's Communication *op. cit.* at n. 22 *supra*.

prohibition contained in paragraph 1, when some permanent advantages may be obtained through them,[25] even though they may restrict competition within the Community.

The proposed "European Co-operation Grouping" (ECG)[26] was meant to fill the *lacuna*,[27] and to provide firms with the required framework in order to achieve the advantages of co-operation, without losing their independence and their identity.[28] The draft lay dormant for a few years, until the Commission submitted to the Council, in 1978, an amended proposal.[29] The substantial provisions remained virtually unchanged, apart from some minor amendments; but other provisions regarding protection of employees' interests and their participation in the decision-making process were inserted. Such a move was part of the more general trend, at Community level, towards employees' participation, as shown also by several other proposals in those years. It might well be that this has been the reason why the amended ECG proposal shared the same destiny as these others and stayed dormant for more years. In 1983 the Commission showed a renewed interest for the grouping proposal and in the meantime renamed it "European Economic Interest Grouping". The change of name was attributed to the fear that the word "co-operation" might lead to confusion with co-operative societies and associations operating in various ways under the laws of Member States.

A major difference between the EEIG and the French GIE lies in its very objective and purpose. Article 1 of the Ordinance No. 67–821 states that a GIE is formed with a view to providing the proper ways in order to facilitate or to develop the economic activities of its members and to improve or to increase the results of such activities. Article 2 of the Regulation 2137/85 states likewise, but it adds that the objective of a grouping shall be defined in the contract forming the grouping and must conform to the requirements of paragraph 2 of the same Article, which lays down that the activities of a grouping shall be limited to the provisions of services exclusively to its members and to the processing of goods or the packaging of finished products, exclusively for the purposes of its members.

Article 2 of the Ordinance states the grouping is not created for the making of profits, whereas Article 2(1) of the Regulation 2137/85 stipulates that groupings shall not seek to make profits for themselves, thus laying emphasis on the difference between the pursuit of profit in an ordinary venture between enterprises and the wider economic purpose of the grouping, in respect of which increased profits are a longer-term

[25] See Bellamy and Child, *Common Market Law on Competition* (3rd ed., 1987).
[26] See [1974] 1 E.C. Bull. Supp.
[27] See Drury, "The European Co-operation Grouping", in [1976] 13 C.M.L. Rev. 7 at 9.
[28] This issue of identity, and especially of national identity, has always been a major obstacle on the road of transnational concentrations; Commission's Communication 1968, *op. cit.* at n. 22.
[29] See [1978] O.J. C103.

objective of the participants. The latter provision apparently reflects the initial mistrust of the Commission towards GIEs as a possible instrument of unlawful cartels.[30]

The legal nature of the European Economic Interest Grouping

In terms of its legal classification, the nature of the EEIG appears unclear. This is attributable to the fact that the EEIG represents a substantial transposition of the French GIE at Community level. The French GIE has been mainly influenced by the law of contract and has been a novelty in French law due to its deviation from the traditional classification of companies as profit-seeking legal persons.[31]

It is worth pointing out the contrast between on the one hand, the emphasis put on the grouping by Regulation 2137/85 as a contractual arrangement and on the freedom that the grouping's participants enjoy in defining its structure according to their requirements by means of the "formation contract", and on the other hand some mandatory features of its organisation, which reflect corporate dimensions in the sense of business associations.[32]

The EEIG represents a vehicle for collaborative business activities based upon a contractual framework, rather an economic entity in its own right, even though it has a separate legal *persona*.[33] The contractual nature of the grouping can be justified by reference to provisions of Regulation 2137/85, particularly the provisions determining its aims and objectives. The members of an EEIG are not supposed to seek gain in itself.[34] Their individual interests, therefore, cannot be absorbed by the common interests for which they join the grouping. The grouping is being set up with a view to pursuing some common—although limited—goals, without setting aside the participants' individual aims,

---

[30] See Guyenot, "Groupements d'Interet Economic—An Institution in French Law at the European Level", in [1972] 6 J.W.T.L. 327.

[31] *ibid.* at p. 328, where he states that when viewed against the background of traditional company law, there is no denying the element of novelty in creating, alongside commercial companies, an institution whose essential objective is no longer only making profits; the novelty of the GIEs must not be sought in their structure, which has been adopted from company and partnership law.

[32] The expression "business association" is meant here to have the most general meaning, inclusive of both companies and partnerships, as well as other legal forms for carrying on a business. However, the word "company" could equally well be used, as it has no strictly legal meaning, thus implying an association of a number of people for some common object(s), normally associated with economic purposes; see Gower, *Principles of Company Law*, (4th ed., 1979), p. 3.

[33] See Drury, "The European Co-operation Grouping", *op. cit.*, at n. 27, where he states that the draftsmen of the reg. did not see it (the grouping) as an economic entity distinct from its members, even though it is a separate legal entity.

[34] Art. 3(1) of Reg. 2137/85.

which may well diverge. In addition, there is the absence of any provision, explicit or implicit, for a common fund made up by members' contributions.[35]

On the other hand, there appear to be several elements which reflect the corporate dimension of a grouping. There is no doubt that an EEIG is a legally separate entity from its participants/members, as Article 1(2) of the Regulation 2137/85 gives them full legal capacity, and Article 1(3) allows Member States to give them also legal personality. One could possibly argue that legal independence should be underlined by common economic objectives, although profits as such for the grouping are not allowed. Furthermore, there are several provisions of Regulation 2137/85 which resemble the relevant provisions for traditional corporate entities. Briefly, they include rules relating to:

(a) identification of the grouping (Articles 5 and 12);

(b) publicity, documentary evidence and its effects against third parties (Articles 6, 7, 10, 11, 14);

(c) organs of the grouping, *i.e.* the manager(s) and the members' body and their distribution of powers between them (Articles 16–20);

(d) changes in membership (Articles 26, 27, 28, 30);

(e) winding up, liquidation and nullity (Articles 31, 32, 35, 36 and 15).

Among the most interesting of the above provisions are Article 20, on the exclusive power of the manager(s) to represent and bind the grouping in dealing with third parties; and Article 26, paragraph 2, on the liability of a new member for debts arising out of the grouping's activities before his admission.

The objectives of the European Economic Interest Grouping

Although the European Economic Interest Grouping represents a new legal form for an economic activity, its limited scope classifies it as being different from other corporate structures. The difference is expressed in principle by the definition of the objectives of an EEIG in Article 3 of the Regulation 2137/85 and relates to the economic function that groupings are meant to perform: that is, co-operation among independent and autonomous enterprises Article 3(1) defines the objective of a grouping with a view to (a) safeguarding the autonomy of participating enterprises; and (b) complementing the business of such enterprises (and not replacing it). The Article reads as follows:

[35] Arts. 21(2) and 22 of Reg. 2137/85.

"The purpose of a grouping shall be to facilitate or to develop the economic activities of its members and to improve or to increase the results of those activities; its purpose is not to make profits for itself. Its activity shall be related to the economic activities of its members and must not be more than ancillary to those activities".

The EEIG lays down rules, applicable to all members, on the structure and method of operation, thus providing companies, particularly small and medium-sized ones, with a framework which is more capable of responding to their needs and their potential. The EEIG will enable them to group part of their economic activity, while still retaining their economic and legal independence within a structure enjoying full legal capacity.[36]

The aim of the EEIG is to facilitate or develop the economic activities of its members and to improve or increase the results of those activities; its purpose is not to make profits for itself.[37] Its activity shall be related to the economic activities of its members and must not be more than ancillary to those activities.[38] On the basis of its very broad definition, therefore, no sector of activity is automatically excluded, the only condition being that the grouping's activity must relate to the economic activity of its members and cannot replace it.[39] The grouping also enjoys neutrality in respect of its profits, both for commercial and for tax purposes, in so far as its profits or losses are taxable only in the hands of its members.[40]

The possibility of forming an EEIG is wide open to natural persons, companies or firms and other legal bodies from Community Member States.[41] These bodies (that is to say, entities, which, in legal terms, are independent of their members without necessarily being companies or legal persons) may include, for example, certain public bodies or public or semi-public scientific organisations.[42] Natural persons who are members of the EEIG must carry on an industrial, commercial, craft or agricultural activity or provide other services in the Community.[43] The last category includes professional people.[44]

---

[36] See the Commission's Communication 1968, *op. cit.* at n. 22.

[37] See preamble of Reg. 2137/85, 9th consideration.

[38] See Art. 3(1) of Reg. 2137/85.

[39] *ibid.*, Art. 3(1), (2).

[40] *ibid.*, Art. 40.

[41] Art. 4 of Reg. 2137/85. A legal entity (firm or company) operating outside the European Community can be a member of an EEIG if it has legal and economic presence in the EEC by means of a subsidiary operating in one Member State; this is not the same as when a firm or company gains representation in the EEC by establishing a branch. The reason, in the writer's view, could be that a branch is not a taxable entity in the legal regime in which it operates, therefore not being eligible to establish a legal entity (EEIG) which enjoys tax transparency.

[42] See [1987] 3 E.C. Bull. Supp. 4.

[43] Art. 4(1)(b) of Reg. 2137/85.

[44] For example professional groups such as lawyers, who have begun to use the form as a vehicle for European-wide co-operation; see Kling and Ellison, *op. cit.* at n. 33, Chap. 1.

The official address of the EEIG must be situated in the Community.[45] The regulation gives the members a fairly wide scope in respect of criteria for fixing the official address. It enables the official address to be transferred from one Member State to another, and even to be transferred within the same state, without affecting the legal capacity of the grouping.[46] The formalities involved in the formation of a grouping are very simple. A contract is concluded and filed at the appropriate registry of the Member State in which the grouping has its official address.[47] Registration confers full legal capacity on the EEIG throughout the Community and even outside it.[48]

The regulation gives the members of the EEIG a large amount of freedom in organising their internal relations and in the choice of the grouping's methods of operation. It leaves such matters chiefly to the free choice of the parties. While it does lay down some mandatory and suppletive measures, this is to protect third parties and, to a certain extent, the members themselves. The latter must assess beforehand the extent of their personal commitment. Nevertheless, the prevailing principle is that of freedom, and there are none of the restrictions imposed on some types of companies.

The EEIG must have at least two organs: the members acting collectively and the manager(s).[49] The members of a grouping, acting as a body, may take any decision for the purpose of achieving the objects of the EEIG. The grouping is managed by one or more managers who have extensive powers for representing the grouping in dealings with third parties. The latter are protected by means of widespread publicity at the time of the grouping's formation, during its existence, and when it is wound up, and also by the unlimited joint and several liability of the members for debts of every kind incurred by the grouping.[50] This personal commitment of the members is the counterpart to contractual freedom, which is the basis of the EEIG, and to the fact that members are not required to provide a mandatory capital representing a minimum guarantee offered to creditors. Indeed, one of the features of the EEIG is that it does not necessarily have to be formed with capital. Members are free to choose ways of financing the grouping. All types of contributions are possible: in cash, in kind, or in skill (know-how, commercial or professional knowledge, etc.).[51] Members can also decide not to contribute in this way if they consider that the EEIG can operate through the payment of regular contributions or by making funds available on current account.[52] This flexibility in financial matters is important for companies, particularly small and medium-sized businesses, which will

---

[45] Art. 12 of Reg. 2137/85.
[46] *ibid.*, Art. 4.
[47] *ibid.*, Art. 7.
[48] *ibid.*, Art. 1(2).
[49] *ibid.*, Art. 16.
[50] *ibid.*, Arts. 17 and 18.
[51] See the preamble of the draft regulation, [1974] 1 E.C. Bull. Supp.
[52] Art. 21(2) of Reg. 2137/85.

thus be able to increase co-operation depending on the opportunities or the results of joint action. Consequently, the EEIG is a completely flexible instrument of co-operation in business activities.

Analysis of the objectives of the EEIG as stipulated by various provisions of Regulation 2137/85 reveals the following considerations.

A grouping does not represent a fusion or amalgamation of its members

Regulation 2137/85 aims to exclude from the sphere of a grouping's operation the possibility of using it as a legal means for integration among participating enterprises. A grouping differs from a traditional company principally in its purpose.[53] The activity of a grouping aims to facilitate or to develop the business of the participants. By definition, the grouping's activity cannot absorb the activities of its members, and the latter cannot be reduced to the role of sub-contractors. The grouping's activity must be ancillary to the activities of its members/participants. However, the term ancillary should not be interpreted in a strict manner, as if it meant accessory.[54] The link between the activity of the grouping and those of its members may well be a functional one, as in the case of complex operations requiring skills, know-how and other capacities involving engagements in any sector of economic activity.

A grouping does not represent a holding company

Article 3(2) of the Regulation 2137/85 sets out some specific restrictions which define the relationship between the grouping and its participants/members. In particular, a grouping may not "(a) exercise, directly or indirectly, a power of management or supervision over its members' own activities or over the activities of another undertaking, in particular in the fields of personnel, finance and investment; (b) directly or indirectly, on any basis whatsoever, hold shares of any kind in a member undertaking; the holding of shares in another undertaking shall be possible only in so far as it is necessary for the achievement of the grouping's objectives and if it is pursued on its members' behalf".

Rules on workers' participation do not apply to groupings

There is a limit of 500 employees in an EEIG, a figure which seems to have been set to prevent the application of the German law on employees' participation in management. (Article 3(2)(c)).

A grouping may not evade national company laws

There are certain limits on loans and transfers of property which aim to prevent companies from making use of groupings to circumvent relevant

---

[53] See preamble to Reg. 2137/85, 5th consideration.
[54] See Israel, "Une avancee du droit communautaire: le groupement europeen d'interet economique (GEIE)", [1985] 28 R.M.C. 645.

rules in national company law (Article 3(2)(d)). The prohibition of an EEIG being a member of another EEIG aims to avoid the creation of a chain of liabilities, which might dilute the liability of the participants/members in the domestic legal orders (Article 3(2)(e)).

The operation of the European Economic Interest Grouping in the context of national laws

The underlying concept of the EEIG was the provision of a new legal instrument at Community level, which would replace the various national frameworks under which cross-border co-operation could take place. The regulation establishing the EEIG has been based on two principles: *uniformity* of rules concerning the establishment of groupings throughout the common market and *harmonisation* of existing legal regimes concerning their operation at domestic level.

The principle of uniformity

The applicability and effectiveness of rules concerning the establishment and structure of groupings within the common market is direct. This means that these rules take precedence over national law without the need of implementation by the Member States. The rules are mandatory and relate mainly to the legal structure of the EEIG and to the protection of third parties and members, the establishment of groupings by means of contract, the organs of the grouping, the powers of the manager(s), publicity and registration requirements and their effects as against third parties and finally, grounds for winding up.

The principle of harmonisation

The regulation leaves a great deal of freedom to the members, especially as regards the functioning of the grouping's structure, through the formation contract or through a subsequent decision of the members acting collectively.[55] When it was impossible to agree on uniform rules, a considerable margin of appreciation has been left to national laws. The regulation introduces a language similar to that employed in Directives and allows Member States to implement some of its provisions in accordance with national company laws.[56] In other cases, the regulation simply refers to the application of national law. This is the case for

---

[55] See for instance, Arts. 16(1), 17(3), 19(3), 20(2), 21(1), 26(2), 27(1), 30(1) and 31(1) of Reg. 2137/85.
[56] See for example, Arts. 4(3), 14(4), 19(2), 28(1) and 32(3) of Reg. 2137/85.

insolvency and cessation of payments (Article 36) and for liquidation (Article 35(1)),[57] and also for the consequences of members' unlimited, joint and several liability (Article 24(1)).

The regulation does not make express provision for the exercise of the groupings' activities. All relevant aspects have been left to the domestic company laws, where the establishment of a grouping is or its activity takes place. The preamble to the regulation states that in matters which are not covered by this regulation, the laws of the Member States and Community law, such as social and labour law, competition law, and intellectual property law[58] are applicable. These examples do not represent an exhaustive list as Member States are free to apply or to adopt any laws, regulations or administrative measures which do not conflict with the scope or objectives of this regulation.[59] The preamble itself gives some other instances: whereas Article 21(1) says only that the profits resulting from a grouping's activities shall be deemed to be the profits of the members and shall be apportioned among them, the fourteenth consideration says that otherwise national tax laws apply, particularly as regards the apportionment of profits, tax procedures and any obligations imposed by national tax law. Whereas the relationship between the activity of a grouping and those of its members is determined at length in Article 3, Article 38 states that when a grouping carries on any activity in a Member State in contravention of that state's public interest, a competent authority of that state may prohibit that activity and, more generally, the sixteenth consideration of the preamble says that activities of groupings are subject to the provisions of Member States' laws on the pursuit and supervision of activities; in the event of abuse or circumvention, that Member State may impose appropriate sanctions.

Regulation 2137/85 has introduced a very original example of harmonisation of company laws. The regulation required a complex implementation and adaptation in order to achieve a more harmonious amalgamation of EEIGs with national company laws and seemed to be the only way of removing existing barriers for cross-border co-operation. Other possibilities of inter-company co-operation (establishment of joint subsidiaries, inter-company co-operation contracts, joint ventures etc.) rely predominantly on a specific national legal system and involve certain constraints[60] and territorial limitations which may act as a deterrent[61] for corporate mobility within the common market.

---

[57] The problem that may arise here is that the regulation does not specify which national law applies; but it appears logical to suppose that it refers to the law of the court where insolvency proceedings are brought, or the liquidation is carried on, including the conflict of laws rules of such a system, since the reference is not made solely to the "internal" law, as it is, instead, in other cases.

[58] See preamble to Reg. 2137/85, fifteenth consideration.

[59] See preamble to Reg. 2137/85, seventeenth consideration.

[60] See Kling and Ellison, *Joint Ventures in Europe*, (1991), pp. 2–11.

[61] See Caves, *Multinational Enterprises and Economic Analysis* (1982), pp. 48 *et seq.*

THE EUROPEAN CO-OPERATIVE SOCIETY, THE EUROPEAN MUTUAL SOCIETY AND THE EUROPEAN ASSOCIATION

European institutions have been keen in establishing corporate bodies which will facilitate cross-border business, not only in economic relations within the European Union, but also in external economic relations with the rest of the world. In pursuance of the above objective, the European Union has achieved considerable progress in the adoption of three legal instruments in the form of Council regulations for a *European Cooperative Society*,[62] for a *European Mutual Society*,[63] and finally for a *European Association*.[64] The establishment of these corporate bodies will be accomplished in a uniform manner throughout the European Union, as their legal bases will be regulations, whose direct applicability and direct effectiveness leaves no implementing discretion in the hands of Member States.

The European Co-operative Society

In order to facilitate European co-operatives to engage in cross-border business, by creating legislative provisions which take into account their specific features and also provide for the involvement of employees, European institutions established a transnational corporate structure in the form of a European Co-operative Society. The proposal has been influenced by previous company law developments in the European Union during the 1970s and 1980s and includes a Council regulation on the statute for the European Co-operative Society, as well as a Council directive supplementing the statute with regard to the involvement of employees in its management.

The European Co-operative Society is to be a private-law body with legal personality and a capital not less than ECU 100,000 or the equivalent in national currency. Its registered office, which is to be specified in its rules, must be within the European Union and must be in the same place as its central administration. It may be set up by any two or more legal entities formed under the law of a Member State, provided at least two of them have their registered offices and central administrations in different Member States.

The European Co-operative Society must provide for a general meeting and for either a management board, with a supervisory board monitoring its activities (the two-tier system), or for an administrative board (the one-tier system).

A general meeting must be held at least once a year, not later than six months after the end of the financial year. Meetings are to be convened by the management board or administrative board on its own initiative or at the request of at least 25 per cent of the members.

[62] Com. (93) 252 final; [1993] O.J. C263.
[63] *ibid.*
[64] *ibid.*

In the two-tier system a management board is to manage the European Co-operative Society. The members of the management board have power to represent it in dealings with third parties and in legal proceedings. They are to be appointed and removed by the supervisory board. The same person may not serve on both boards at the same time. The supervisory board may nominate one of its members to occupy a vacancy on the management board. The member concerned then ceases to exercise his functions on the supervisory board.

In the one-tier system a single administrative board is to manage the European Co-operative Society. Powers to represent it in dealings with third parties and in legal proceedings are vested in the member or members of the administrative board. The administrative board may delegate powers of management, but not other powers, to one or more of its members. Certain operations require the authorisation of the supervisory board or the deliberation of the administrative board.[65]

The European Co-operative Society may offer "investor" shares, carrying no voting rights, for subscription by interested parties. To offset these disadvantages such shares may be given preferential entitlements. Where rules authorise persons who do not expect to use its services to subscribe for voting shares, they must make special provision for the benefit of such non-user members with regard to the distribution of surpluses.

With reference to the drawing-up, auditing and disclosure of its annual accounts, and its consolidated accounts if any, the European Co-operative Society is to be subject to the law of the State in which it has its registered office giving effect to the Community legislation in force. It may be wound up either by a decision of the general meeting, in particular where the period fixed in the rules has expired or where the subscribed capital has been reduced below the minimum capital laid down in the rules, or by the courts, in particular where the registered office has been transferred outside the Community. As regards liquidation, insolvency and suspension of payments, the European Co-operative Society is to be subject to the laws of the State in which it has its registered office.

---

[65] These are:
- any investment project costing more than the subscribed capital;
- the setting-up, acquisition, disposal or closing down of undertakings, establishments or parts of establishments, where the purchase price or the proceeds of disposal account for more than the subscribed capital;
- the raising or granting of loans, the issue of debt securities and the assumption of liabilities of a third party where the total money value in each case is more than the subscribed capital;
- the conclusion of supply and performance contracts where the total turnover provided for is more than the percentage of turnover for the previous financial year.

The percentage concerning the following transactions is to be determined by the rules of the *European Co-operative Society*, but it may not be less than 5 per cent nor more than 25 per cent.

The European Mutual Society

A European Mutual Society comprises of a grouping of natural or legal persons, or both, which guarantees its members, in return for a subscription, full settlement of contractual undertakings entered into in the course of the activities authorised by its rules (whether concerned with providence, insurance, health assistance, credit, or otherwise). The European Mutual Society has legal personality from the day it is registered in the state in which it has its registered office and a formation fund of no less than ECU 100,000 or the equivalent in national currency. The regulation does not affect obligatory social security schemes which in certain Member States are managed by provident mutual societies, nor the freedom of Member States to decide whether and in what circumstances to entrust the management of such schemes to European Mutual Societies.

The Mutual Society's registered office, which is to be specified in its rules, must be within the Community and must be in the same place as its central administration. The European Mutual Society must provide for a general meeting of the members and either a management board, with a supervisory board monitoring its activities (the two-tier system), or an administrative board (the one-tier system).

A general meeting is to be held at least once a year, not more than six months after the end of the financial year. Meetings may be convened by the management board or administrative board on its own initiative or at the request of at least 25 per cent of the members. In the two-tier system a management board is to manage the European Mutual Society. The member or members of the management board have the power to represent it in dealings with third parties and in legal proceedings. They are to be appointed and removed by the supervisory board. The supervisory board may appoint one of its members to occupy a vacancy on the management board. The member concerned will then cease to perform his functions on the supervisory board.

In the one-tier system a single administrative board is to manage the Mutual Society. The member or members of the administrative board have power to represent it in dealings with third parties and in legal proceedings. The administrative board may delegate powers of management, but not other powers, to one or more of its members. Certain operations require the authorisation of the supervisory board or the deliberation of the administrative board.[66]

---

[66] These are:
- closing or transferring a large establishment or a substantial part of such an establishment;
- substantially reducing, extending or altering the activities of the Mutual Society;
- making substantial organisational changes within the Mutual Society;
- establishing co-operation with other legal persons which is both long-term and of importance to the activities of the Mutual Society, or terminating such co-operation;
- raising loans in respect of operations in excess of the ceiling laid down in the rules, issuing securities and assuming or guaranteeing liabilities of a third party.

As regards the drawing-up, auditing and disclosure of its annual accounts, and its consolidated accounts if any, the European Mutual Society is to be subject to the law of the State in which it has its registered office giving effect to the fourth Council Directive (78/660) on annual accounts, the seventh Council Directive (83/349) on consolidated accounts, the eighth Council Directive (84/253) on the approval of persons responsible for carrying out the statutory audits of accounting documents. A European Mutual Society may be wound up either by a decision of the general meeting, in particular where the period fixed in the rules has expired or where the formation fund has dropped below the minimum laid down in the rules, or by the courts, in particular where the registered office has been transferred outside the Community. As regards liquidation, insolvency and suspension of payments, the European Mutual Society is to be subject to the laws of the State in which it has its registered office.

The European Association

A European Association is to be a body whose members pool their knowledge or their activities either for a purpose in the general interest or in order directly or indirectly to promote the interests of particular professions or groups. It has legal personality from the day of its registration in the Member State in which it has its registered office and may be set up directly either by any two or more legal entities formed under the law of a Member State, provided at least two of them have their registered offices and central administrations in different Member States, or by at least 21 natural persons, being nationals of and resident in at least two Member States.

An association which has been formed in accordance with the law of a Member State may set up a European Association by converting into the required European Association's form if it has an establishment in a Member State other than that of its registered office. It must be able to show that it is carrying on a genuine cross-border activity. The European Association's registered office, which is to be specified in its rules, must be within the Community, and must be in the same place as its central administration. The rules must also provide for a general meeting and for an executive committee. A general meeting is to be held at least once a year, not more than six months after the end of the financial year. Meetings may be convened at any time either by the executive committee on its own initiative or at the request of at least 25 per cent of the members; the rules may set a lower proportion. Every member is entitled to one vote. Decisions are to be taken by a majority of the votes of the members present or represented. The general meeting has sole power to amend the rules of the European Association; any such resolution is to be passed by a majority of two-thirds of the votes of the members present or represented.

The member or members of the executive committee have the power to represent the European Association in dealings with third parties and in legal proceedings. They are to be appointed and removed by the general meeting.

Members of the executive committee are to be appointed for a period which may not exceed six years. They may be reappointed at the end of the six-year period. The European Association is to draw up a budget for the forthcoming financial year. It may be wound up either by a decision of the general meeting, in particular where the period fixed in the rules has expired or where no accounts have been disclosed as required in the European Association's last three financial years, or by the courts, in particular where the registered office has been transferred outside the European Union. As far as liquidation, insolvency and suspension of payments are concerned, the European Association is to be subject to the laws of the state in which it has its registered office.

Employees' participation in the European Co-operative Society, the European Mutual Society and the European Association

The Council directives on employees' participation, complementing the regulations for a European Co-operative Society, the European Mutual Society and the European Association refer to the domestic rules governing the participation of employees in the supervisory or administrative boards of domestic companies and societies in general. If the Member State in which the European Co-operative Society, the European Mutual Society and the European Association have their registered office has no rules on the participation of employees, or does not wish to apply such rules, it must nevertheless comply with some minimum requirements concerning informing and consulting of employees. Where most of the employees are members of the European Co-operative Society the requirements of information and consultation do not apply, as they *de facto* participate in the management in their capacity as members. Information and consultation procedures must be adopted in European Co-operative Societies, European Mutual Societies and European Associations with at least 50 employees. The management boards or administrative boards of European Co-operatives and Mutual Societies and the executive committee of a European Association must inform and consult the employees in good time, particularly with reference to issues which affect the interests of the employees and any question concerning conditions of employment.

The regulation of corporate mobility in the European Union

GENERAL REMARKS

The European integration process relies on the unobstructed mobility of goods and factors of production (labour and capital) and of persons (natural or legal) seeking establishment and the right to provide services within the common market. The migration of companies follows patterns which are shaped by competitive forces and the need for profit maximisation. By dismantling all internal barriers to trade, the European Community has prepared the legal and socio-economic background for the necessary transfer of resources to the most optimal location within the common market. Corporate migration depicts *inter alia* the market response to the allocation of resources and to performance optimisation *vis-à-vis* European and international competition.

The mobility of companies in the common market follows two distinctive trends. The first one includes the traditional market penetration through the establishment of a subsidiary or a branch in another Member State and reveals the need for harmonisation of existing company and corporate tax laws among Member States, in order to provide the appropriate framework for company mobility. The static effect of this trend is indicated by the utilisation of existing domestic corporate structures which are available to companies wishing to penetrate a geographical market, where domestic company and contract laws regulate such trade patterns.

The second trend involves cross-border corporate mobility based on co-operation or collaboration agendas or on take over and merger activities and reveals the positive and dynamic involvement of European institutions and Member States in establishing new ways for cross-border corporate mobility by means of regulating industrial concentration.

Industrial concentration may take place in different economic forms. Vertical integration usually refers to expansion of a firm's activities through integration of successive forward steps in the production, financing or distribution of goods and services. Diversification normally refers to the growth of a firm either by internal expansion or by merger through production and distribution of various products or ranges of products. The multi-product or the multi-range enterprise is also labelled as a conglomerate but sometimes the latter term is used in reference to products or activities that are neither technologically nor otherwise functionally related and with a disparaging implication that it may be irrational and undesirable. Growth through mergers involving acquisition by one corporation is classified as horizontal integration. It should be noted that market or activities expansion relates to reaching into new geographic markets while product expansion refers to the acquisition of new but related product lines. The possible impact on the market by concentrations can take the form of either operational concentration between individual enterprises or of structural concentration where structural, durable changes take place between two or more enterprises. Operational concentration has a conservative character, as in most cases it takes place for the sake of a weak, inefficient partner. Under such form of corporate mobility, it is difficult to see effective competition arising from such protective bounds. On the other hand, structural concentration can be seen as part of the dynamic development of an economy and in most cases is the result of industrial restructuring due to competition.

If concentrations deem to threaten the viability of the common market and to prevent the maintenance of an effective and undistorted competition regime, it is of vital importance to determine the measurement of economic concentration. The most common method of measuring concentration is the so-called aggregate concentration including measurement of assets, sales, number of employees, size of payroll, value added by the manufacturer or new capital expenditure. Competent anti-trust authorities should decide against the concentration *ex post* (the American system) or legislate *ex ante* preventing threatening mergers within the common market (the European system). A public policy approach to the concept of industrial concentrations is decisive in an attempt to place concentrations within the regulatory framework of competition law and policy. Not only political and economic philosophy but also more objective circumstances prevailing in a country prescribe a policy to regulate industrial concentration.

This chapter focuses on the dynamic trend of corporate migration within the common market and analyses its legal framework. The thematics which will be investigated are *industrial concentrations* and *mergers and their control*. Corporate mobility based on these patterns has been considered as a priority issue for the completion of the common market and its effective operation and European institutions have decided to provide a regulatory framework in an attempt to control corporate mobility at centralised level based on a cautious application of competition law and policy.

Industrial Concentration and its Control

General background

After the devastation of the Second World War, Europe had to build up its economy and restructure its industry with a view to increasing competitiveness not only within the common market but also in world markets. Concentrations were deemed to have temporarily *pro-competitive* effects. During the 1960s Europe witnessed a merger wave and many realised the potential impact of uncontrolled concentrations on competition and on national economies. In Germany, a great deal of discussions before the parliament led to the introduction of a merger control in 1973.[1] It should be mentioned that even before its accession to the European Communities, the United Kingdom was applying a merger control since 1965[2] to concentrations.

In Germany and in the United Kingdom, where the necessity for the control of industrial concentration was recognised, measures regulating mergers were contained in statutes and national legislative provisions which were quite distinct from provisions concerning anti-competitive cartels and exploitatively abusive behaviour.

Unlike the EEC Treaty, its predecessor, the Treaty of Paris establishing the European Coal and Steel Community (ECSC) includes detailed provisions for the control of concentrations. Indeed, under Article 66 ECSC, concentrations are subject to the thorough scrutiny of the high authority (now the Commission). The EEC Treaty did not provide any provision for regulating industrial concentration and controlling mergers at Community level. Apart from the two legal pillars of competition law and policy of the European Community (prohibition of unlawful cartels and of abuse of dominance) which have been based upon two primary Treaty provisions, Articles 85 and 86 and a variety of secondary legislation (mainly regulations) with a view to complementing them, the control of industrial concentration seemed not to be a priority objective of the Treaty of Rome.

The public discussion on the control of industrial concentration started in 1966, when the Commission published the so-called concentration memorandum[3] on concentrations in the common market. The Commission, in the absence of relevant primary or secondary Community legislation to control the merger wave which occurred in the 1960s, addressed the issue of regulating concentrations by having recourse to the provisions of the EEC Treaty. A panel of experts consulting the Commission[4] suggested that Articles 85 and 86 EEC Treaty (EEC)

---

[1] See Gezetz gegen Wettbewerbsbeschränkungen, para. 22, as amended by Bundesgesetzblatt, BGB1 I 761 1980.

[2] See Fair Trading Act 1973 (c. 41), *Halsbury's Law of England*.

[3] See "The problem of Industrial Concentration in the Common market" in Competition Series, Study no. 3 (Brussels 1966).

[4] *ibid.*

could apply to mergers. However, the Commission was of the opinion that Article 85 was inapplicable to concentrations due to the following reasons:

— the limited in time exemption criteria under Article 85(3) are inappropriate to concentrations since the latter perform on a permanent basis, thus requiring an indefinite exemption;

— the sanction of nullity under Article 85(2) is inappropriate to concentrations since a merger includes not only agreements but basically transactions;

— Article 85(1) cannot apply to concentrations which may affect intra-Community trade since there are conceptual difficulties in defining an "agreement", "decision" or "concerted practice" between undertakings with a view to restricting competition;

— Article 85(1) is inapplicable to undertakings which merge without an agreement (*e.g.* hostile takeover);

— finally, application of Article 85 to mergers would result in a massive amount of notifications and the Commission could not cope with them in the relatively short time-limits which an efficient system of merger control requires.

The above inherent shortcomings of Article 85 relating to its inapplicability to concentrations led to the opinion that the only Article of the Treaty of Rome capable of regulating corporate mobility based in merger patterns was Article 86. The doctrine that Article 86 could apply to concentrations was judicially established in the *Continental Can* case,[5] where in the absence of specific provisions on mergers at Community level and based on the need for consistency in the existing policy with regard to restrictions on competition resulting from industrial concentration, the Court of Justice held that even potential exploitative monopolisation of the market by a merger had to be condemned as it could breach the letter and the spirit of Article 86 EEC.

The applicability of Article 86 to mergers leaves a great deal of concentrations unaffected, as there are two conceptual obstacles that have to be cleared before a concentration is stricken down. The first relates to the element of pre-existing dominance, which must be well defined for all parties involved in the concentration. The second obstacle

---

[5] See Case 6/72 *Europmballage Corp. and Continental Can v. E.C. Commission*: [1973] E.C.R. 215. In this case the Court held that Art. 86 prohibited a concentration between undertakings where one of the participants held a dominant position prior to the concentration and the concentration eliminated any residual competition in the relevant market.

concerns the definition of abusive exploitation of the collective dominance prior to the merger within the common market or in a substantial part of it. As a result of the above considerations, European institutions felt that only secondary Community legislation, particularly, a regulation with directly applicable and directly effective provisions in Member States could efficiently control concentrations.

In 1972 the European Council (Heads of States) following an EEC summit conference in Paris issued a statement confirming *inter alia* that

> " . . . it is necessary to seek to establish a single industrial basis for the Community as a whole. This involves the formation of measures which ensure that mergers affecting firms established in the Community are in harmony with the economic and social aims of the Community and the maintenance of fair competition as much within the Common Market as in external markets, in conformity with the rules laid down by the Treaty."

One could realise that a legal framework to control concentrations was envisaged not only in order to implement the Community's competition policy but also to form the basic framework for the Community's industrial policy. The *Continental Can* case paved the way for the first draft of the merger control regulation. Indeed, the Commission put forward its first proposal to the Council of Ministers in 1973.[6] It should be mentioned that the European Council (Heads of States) were satisfied with the solution given by the Court in the *Continental Can* case. They considered that Article 86 represents a sufficient framework to control concentrations. The only shortcoming which they recognised was the absence of proceedings covering prior notification and clearance.

On the contrary, the Commission held that the *Continental Can* doctrine—the application of Article 86 to concentrations—was inefficient to control all types of corporate mobility based on merger activities. Two arguments supported that position: first, the argument that the Commission could act *ultra vires* by applying Article 86 to undertakings which do not have a dominant position before the merger is supported by the fact that the Court of Justice had not ruled so far on the issue of joint or collective dominance[7]; secondly, the provisions of Article 86 could not require companies to notify concentration activities in advance and a merger could be controlled only after its accomplishment.

---

[6] See [1973] O.J. C92/1.
[7] Although the Court has never spelled out a positive definition of joint market dominance, it has at least spotlighted the situations where joint market dominance does not exist. See Case 85/76, *Hoffman-La Roche*: [1979] E.C.R. 520 No. 39; Joined Cases 40–48, 50, 54–56, 111 & 113–114/73 *Suicker Unie*: [1975] E.C.R. 1942; Case 247/86, *Alsatel/Novasam*: [1986] E.C.R. 237; Case 66/86, *Ahmed Saeed*: [1990] 4 C.M.L.R. 102.

However, it should be mentioned that in practice an informal system of prior notification was developed before the introduction of any centralised industrial concentration control system.[8] Undertakings involved in merger activities deemed wise to conduct *ex ante* the Commission. The fact that this procedure was informal seemed to have diminished its validity. The informality on the one hand and the absence of legal certainty and of clearly defined time-limits for the assessment of mergers led to the formation of a coalition between the international business society and the Commission. The plan was the introduction of a centralised, "one stop shop" system of merger control, less stringent than those in force in the Member States (Germany, France and the United Kingdom) that had introduced relevant legislation.

The first draft merger control regulation[9] was based on the combination of Articles 87 and 235 EEC. The latter provision was deemed necessary in order to cover the situation of hostile takeovers or concentration of undertakings not holding a dominant position before the merger. The former provision was invoked as the merger control had been seen as part of the legislation concerning competition policy. The fate of the first Commission proposal was a reaction by Member States which varied between indifference and hostility, underlying the political and economic sensibilities at stake.

Three subsequent amendments to the initial proposal of the Commission followed, respectively in 1982,[10] 1984,[11] 1986.[12] With each amendment the thresholds at which a merger could be classified as Community dimensional and subsequently be caught by a Community legal system were raised and compromises were made to suit national sensibilities. In 1987 the Commission decided to put the Council before an alternative: either the Council would agree to a political commitment for the idea of merger control or the Commission would exercise its rights under Articles 85 and 86 EEC in order to control concentration within the common market. This ultimatum from the Commission was backed by the Court's ruling on the applicability of Article 85 to partial mergers and acquisitions in the *Philip Morris* case.[13]

---

[8] See Commission Decisions: Michelin/Actor, AVEBE/KSH and Peugeot Citroen/Chrysler in 8th Rep. on Competition Policy; Kaiser/Estel, Coats Patons Ltd/Gutermann Co. and Fichel & Sachs/Huret in 9th Rep. on Comp.; Pilkington/BSN Gevrais-Danone, Michelin/Kleber-Colombes and Baxter Travenol Labs/Smith Kline RIT in 10th Rep. on Comp.; Amicon Corp./Fortia A.B. in 11th Rep. on Comp.; Eagle Star/Allanz Versicherung and British Sugar/Berisford in 12th Rep. on Comp.; Berisford/Napier Brown in 13th Rep. on Comp.; Philip Morris/Rembrant/Rothmans and Ahsland Oil Inc./Cabot Co. and Pont-a-Mousson/Stanton & Stavenly in 14th Rep. on Comp.; Carnaud/Sofreb in 17th Rep. on Comp.; Irish Distillers and British Airways/British Caledonian in 18th Rep. on Comp.; see also I.P. (89) for cases: Consolidated Gold Fields/Minorco and GEC-Siemens/Plessey.
[9] See [1973] O.J. C92/1.
[10] See [1982] O.J. C36/3.
[11] See [1984] O.J. C51/8.
[12] See [1986] O.J. C324/5.
[13] See Joined Cases 142 & 156/84, *British American Tobacco Co. Ltd and R. J. Reynolds Industries Inc. v. E.C. Commission*: [1988] 4 C.M.L.R. 24.

The fact that concentrations differ substantially from restrictive agreements and abuse of dominance, and the above mentioned shortcomings in the applicability of Articles 85 and 86 to concentrations led the Council to a political commitment in favour of the proposed merger control regulation. On December 21, 1988, the Council of Ministers, after further concessions to national sensibilities by the Commission announced that they had reached agreement in principle for the Commission to draw up a merger control regulation. The bargaining between the Commission and the Member States and among the Member States themselves was hard and complex. The most difficult issues were:

- the relationship between the E.C. merger control regulation and national competition law, or in different words how low or how high the thresholds should be; the relevant thresholds, as quantitative criteria, classify concentrations as Community dimensional, falling within the jurisdiction of the European Commission and as sub-dimensional, falling within the jurisdiction of Member States and their competent authorities were determined to secure their jurisdiction on mergers. Great surprise followed the initial proposal by the German Federal Cartel Office (*Bundeskartellamt*) which was holding out for a threshold of ECU 10 billion, below which a merger would not be subject to the European Commission's scrutiny; the Commission's initial proposal was ECU 1 billion.

- the concept of distinct national markets where a Member State should be entitled to intervene despite the concentration falling within the Commission's competence; the thresholds which determine the jurisdictional exclusivity of the regulation are quite high. The regulation itself has been based on the division of labour between the Commission and the competent anti-trust authorities of Member States. This division enables the Commission to deal with 40 to 50 Community dimension concentrations every year, which is a quite small number in comparison with cases dealt with by the *Mergers and Monopolies Commission*[14] and the *Bundeskartellamt*. Member States which had in force merger control legislation were reluctant to see any jurisdiction and competence transfer from their authority to the Commission. It should be recalled that the United Kingdom and (West) Germany have had their own domestic merger control acts since 1965 and 1973 respectively. France introduced its national merger control in 1977. The reluctance to accept low thresholds, proposed by the Commission, can be justified by reference to the conceptual approach of these legal orders to concentrations. The German approach was based on the legal aspects of competition

---

[14] The mergers regulation, M 77/89 of December 22, 1989. Also the *Financial Times* January 4, 1990. In the 17th Report on Competition the Commission stated that there had been 67 mergers whose aggregate turnover exceeded ECU 5 bn.

law and it appeared to be pragmatically based. On the other hand, the British approach represents a political choice on anti-trust as it was primarily based on public interest elements such as the protection of the environment, public security and concern the manipulation of mass media. The insistence of the Federal Republic of Germany on the inclusion of a provision concerning distinct national markets resulted in the insertion of Article 9 of the regulation, the so-called *German clause*, which has the potential for giving the authority to Member States to interfere in the process of controlling a concentration, even if, subject to review by the Court of Justice, the Commission ultimately retains the power of decision. It should be mentioned here that in the draft regulation of April 1988 there was no provision concerning jurisdiction of a Member State over a Community-dimensional concentration and in the draft proposed by the Commission in January 1989,[15] only in Article 8(2) was there a possibility for the Commission to refer a merger under its jurisdiction to the competent authorities of the Member State affected by that concentration. The insistence of the *Bundeskartellamt* on the opportunity to deal with Community dimension mergers which affect only a distinct national market was mitigated by the insertion of a provision demanded by the Dutch government—the so-called *Dutch clause*, Article 22(3) of the regulation—under which the Commission can control mergers that are incompatible with the Common Market, even if they do not have a Community dimension.

• finally, the question of whether the regulation was to serve competition law and policy aspects or whether it should also take into account industrial and other related policies was a point of controversy between Member States. France shared the view that a merger control system must take into account not only competition policy but regional policy, economic and social cohesion and technical innovation. The above approach and the insistence of the French government led to the inclusion of a recital which suggests that factors other than competition law may, to some extent, be taken into consideration in assessing concentrations. Indeed, Recital 13 of the regulation refers to factors other than competition, but the weight to be given to those factors is limited by the requirements, similar to those in Article 85(3), that consumer benefits and competition would not be impeded. Article 2(1)(b) of the regulation stipulates the development of technical and economic progress provided that is to the consumers' advantage and does not form an obstacle to competition. In both cases, (Recital 13 and Article 2(1)(b) of the regulation), there is no reference to primary Community law concerning industrial

---

[15] See [1989] O.J. C22/14; this proposal is the same as the one dated November 30, 1988.

policy (Article 130(f). On the contrary, in Recital 13 there is reference to Articles 2 and 130(A). Although Article 2 refers to the fundamental objectives of the Treaty, Article 130(a) aims at the strengthening of economic and social cohesion in the Community in order to promote a harmonious overall development and goes further than a competition law and policy provision. There is no specific reference to Article 130(f) as the legal basis for taking into account industrial policy aspects when assessing a merger. The reason for this could be attributed to the different approach of the concept of concentrations by Member States. As mentioned above, Germany went along the opinion which, in the framework of a centralised domestic competition law system, considers concentrations as possible restrictions on competition similar to restrictive agreements and the abuse of dominance. This approach places a merger only within a competition law framework. Other Member States, although not opposed to the inclusion of industrial policy considerations in the process of assessing a concentration, seemed unwilling to transfer any authority in this regard to the Commission by referring specifically to Article 130(f). On the other hand, the reference to Article 130(a) is rather inoffensive, as it is a general, neutral and vague enough provision to expand effectively the Commission's powers in fields other than competition policy.

After two subsequent amendments in 1988,[16] the regulation was finally approved by the Council of Ministers unanimously on December 21, 1989 and based on Articles 87 and 235.[17]

The reasons for the adoption of the regulation can be categorised as legal, economic and political. It could be maintained that the legal reasons were the inefficiency of Articles 85 and 86 to cover concentrations, the absence of a mandatory *ex ante* notification procedure which forced the Commission to intervene only *ex post facto* as in the recent case of *British Airways* and *British Caledonian*,[18] and finally the inadequacy of Regulation 17[19] to provide for an indefinite exemption as a merger requires. In addition, under Regulation 17 an exemption need not have a necessarily retroactive effect, thus leaving the merger open to challenges before national courts. The *Guerelain* case[20] and the *Plessey/GEC/Siemens*[21] litigation illustrated this problem.

---

[16] See Commission's proposals of April 1988, [1988] O.J. C130/4 and of November 1988, [1989] O.J. C22/14.

[17] Reg. 4064/89: [1989] O.J. L395/1. Had it not been for the fact that the Commission was increasingly utilising Articles 85 and 86 EEC on a case-by-case basis in order to control concentrations, such as its intervention in the British Airways takeover of British Caledonian, the IDG bid for Irish Distillers, GEC and Siemens and their bid for Plessey, it is perhaps doubtful that the regulation would ever have been passed.

[18] See [1988] 4 C.M.L.R. 258.

[19] See [1962] O.J. 13/204.

[20] See [1980] E.C.R. 2327.

[21] Unreported judgment of December 20, 1988.

The economic reasons for the adoption of the regulation echoed the concerns that the industry would be at the mercy of different national rules with regard to cross-frontier takeovers, and secondly, the regulation was seen as an instrument of increasing European industrial competitiveness *vis-à-vis* American and Japanese conglomerates.

Finally, the political reason for the adoption of the regulation was the fulfilment of the objectives of the single market programme. An effective merger control at community level was deemed to constitute an essential element of the European integration process. The completion of the internal market relies, to a large extent, on an industry structure which consists of mergers, acquisitions and other lasting forms of co-operation.

The principles and concepts of the merger control regulation

The Commission's intention was to achieve a "one stop shop" control in order to ensure a centralised system of regulating concentrations throughout the Community. On the other hand, it had to take into account not only national sensibilities but existing domestic merger controls in three Member States as well, namely the United Kingdom, Germany and France. The merger control regulation, as a result of political compromise and of tough bargaining, has the following underlying principles:

— The first principle is that it applies only to Community dimension concentrations (above certain thresholds);

— The second principle is the principle of mandatory *ex ante* notification and of automatic suspension[22];

— The third principle concerns the assessment of Community scale mergers. Concentrations that create or strengthen a dominant position which then impedes effective competition will not be allowed.

Although the regulation could be regarded as one step further than Article 86, it remains silent about the concept of abuse of dominance. Behind this principle, there is the need to prevent the establishment of monopolies and oligopolies that can exploit the common market. Due to the existing national merger controls operating in some Member States,

---

[22] As mentioned above, the Commission had developed an informal system of prior notification in the pre-regulation period. That considerable administrative practice was built up initially under Art. 86 and more recently under Art. 85. Apparently, the informality of the system diminished to a great extent its worth. As for the period between December 21, 1989 and September 21, 1990, the Commission made clear that it would apply the substantive criteria of the regulation.

references to national competent authorities as a deviation from the principle of "one stop shop" should be dealt with rapidly and in close co-operation with the Commission.

The title of the regulation refers to "the control of concentrations between undertakings". The term "undertakings" covers all kind of operators carrying out economic or commercial activities, supplying services or goods. The concept is the same as that which is considered an "undertaking" under general Community anti-trust law (Article 85).

The definition of what is to be understood as concentrations is found in Article 3 of the regulation. According to this provision, a concentration arises through a real merger between two or more previously independent undertakings or through acquisition of control by one undertaking over another. In the former case, the key issue is the abandonment of independence by the firms that merge and the creation of a new, separate economic entity. Independence indicates that the firms were actual or potential competitors in a market. In the latter case, where a concentration takes place through acquisition of control, it has to be defined what is direct or indirect control over an undertaking. The regulation itself seeks to clear up this matter, laying down in Article 3(2) and (3) that control means the possibility of exercising decisive influence by rights, contracts or other means, over a firm. Things become more complicated when trying to determine the exercise of influence and when the latter is decisive. The regulation makes no distinction between influence and decisive influence but only sets out that decisive influence takes place by ownership or the right to use all or part of the assets of an undertaking, and on the other hand, by rights or contracts which confer decisive influence on the composition, voting or decisions of the organs of an undertaking (Article 3(2)(b)). At first sight, the use of the term "decisive influence on the composition . . . " in order to define the decisive influence[23] as the element of control over an undertaking appears rather confusing, but the drafters of the regulation should have had in mind a situation similar to the holding of the majority of the voting shares in a company. It is not clear whether the provisions of Article 3 of the regulation constitute an exhaustive list or are illustrative examples of acquiring control by exercising decisive influence on an undertaking.

The fifth paragraph of Article 3 sets out three exceptions where a concentration shall not be deemed to arise. The first one concerns credit or financial institutions or insurance companies which under certain conditions hold, on a temporary basis, securities that have been acquired in an undertaking, with a view to reselling them. The conditions are the following:

---

[23] The term "decisive influence" seems to be a higher level of influence than that implied by the concept of "material influence" under the Fair Trading Act 1973, under which control is held to exist where a shareholding level exceeds 20 per cent.

(a) The acquisition of securities must result from normal activities of the credit institution or the insurance company.

(b) Normal activities are commercial or economic activities that do not go beyond the scope and the purpose of the company concerned.

(c) If the acquisition of securities consists of the exercise of voting rights, such an exercise should not determine the competitive behaviour of the undertaking concerned, but it is only allowed with a view to preparing the sale of that undertaking, or of its assets, or of the securities already acquired, within one year from the date of the acquisition.

The second exception refers to control acquired by an office holder in regard to procedures related to liquidation, insolvency, winding-up or relevant proceedings.

The third one regards activities within the terms of paragraph 1(b), (c) of Article 3 by financial holding companies referred to in Article 5(3) of the fourth company law directive.[24] According to this directive, financial holding companies are those with the sole objective of acquiring holdings in order to turn them into profit without involving themselves directly or indirectly in the management of those undertakings. The above is without prejudice to their rights, with a view to maintaining the value of their investments.

The principles concerning control enunciated in the regulation are narrower than those set out by the Court in the famous *Philip Morris* judgment,[25] where it referred to "influence" on the commercial conduct of a company in an anti-competitive way by minority share acquisitions. The concept of control under the regulation seems to be one step further than the mere influence of conduct of an undertaking. The *Philip Morris* case survives the enactment of the regulation and will continue to haunt companies whose acquisition of shares falls short of "control" as defined in Article 3 of the regulation. Here it is questionable why minority share acquisitions should be subject to the vigorous grip of Article 85 whilst full takeovers enjoy the relatively less severe treatment provided by the provisions of the regulation.

The control of corporate mobility through joint ventures

The merger control regulation covers friendly and hostile takeovers as concentrations but explicitly excludes joint ventures, except in the case of a partial merger having only the form of a joint venture but acting on

---

[24] See Council Directive 78/660, [1978] O.J. L222/11 (as amended).
[25] See n. 13.

a lasting basis as an autonomous entity without co-ordination of competitive behaviour between the parties involved. This is to cover situations similar to the *SHV/Chevron* link-up,[26] provided they meet the relevant thresholds.

Although joint ventures in the framework of anti-trust law deserve a separate analysis, it is useful now to examine the partial merger/permanent joint venture phenomenon which is caught by the regulation.

A joint venture can be characterised as a co-operation framework between two or more separate undertakings under which each party is obliged to make a substantial contribution to the implementation of a common project, usually in the field of research and development of new products or methods of production. The joint venture exists as a separate legal entity but it is jointly owned and controlled by the parent undertakings. It is worth to be noted that under EEC anti-trust law the term "joint venture" does not exist as a defined legal concept. It appears in Article 5(2) of the block exemption for patent licence agreements.[27]

The merger control regulation distinguishes between co-ordinative and concentrative joint ventures,[28] whereas the former category falls into the provisions of general Community anti-trust law (Articles 85 and 86) and the latter within the framework of the regulation.

It is well known that Community competition law has been greatly influenced by German cartel law. Regarding anti-trust treatment of joint ventures, German law distinguishes concentrated from co-operative joint ventures. Indeed, this distinction is of great importance since it defines the scope of the merger control provision of Section 23 of the German Anti-trust Act in relation to cartel prohibition of Section 1 of that Act.[29] In fact, the German Anti-trust Act explicitly provides for merger control of joint ventures if they meet certain quantitative criteria. This gave rise to the question of whether the merger control regulation provisions are exclusive and exhaustive or whether joint ventures are also subject to general cartel provisions.

If one adopts the view that merger control provisions are exclusive for joint ventures, one has to face the unacceptable result that operations not meeting certain quantitative criteria completely escape anti-trust control even if they involve serious restraints of competition. On the other hand, if joint ventures are also subject to general cartel prohibitions, there are two alternatives: either a double control system could be established under which all kinds of joint ventures should be subject to investigation under both the merger control provisions and the cartel prohibitions; or a distinction has to be developed in respect to certain kinds of joint ventures requiring a merger control and others falling under general cartel prohibitions.

---

[26] See [1974] O.J. L38/14.
[27] See Reg. 2349/84, [1984] O.J. L219/1.
[28] Art. 3(2) of Reg. 4064/89.
[29] See above n. 1 (Gezetz gegen Wettbewerbsbeschränkungen).

The German anti-trust theory and practice opted, as mentioned above, for a distinction between merger control and cartel prohibitions for assessing joint ventures, since the double control approach results in inconsistency as the standards of appraisal of merger control differ in substance and effect from those of cartel control. While a merger control is mainly based on quantitative criteria constituting dominance, cartel control relies on the appraisal of appreciable effect on competition regardless of the market power of the undertakings concerned. Moreover, there is no time limit for the invocation of cartel prohibition by a competitor even though the *Bundeskartellamt* has cleared an operation on the basis of merger control provisions.

The distinction between "concentrative" and "co-operative" joint ventures adopted in the guidelines of the Federal Cartel Office (*Bundeskartellamt*) was upheld by the German Federal Supreme Court in a decision in 1985.[30]

Thus, the concept of a partial merger enjoying the so-called merger privilege (exclusion of cartel provisions) was established. The merger privilege is limited to the formation of joint ventures and extends to ancillary or necessary competitive restraints. It should be mentioned how the German Federal Supreme Court defined the notion of a concentrative joint venture:

" . . . the essential feature of a concentrative joint venture is to be seen in the fact that it represents an independent business entity planning, determining and implementing its activities on its own responsibility, whereas the parent companies are basically confined to exercising their voting rights deriving from their shareholdings."

In the light of and in accordance with the above mentioned development in Germany, the European Commission has followed the same approach in various instances with the most striking example the *SHV/Chevron* case.[31] Before the introduction of the merger control regulation, the Commission's policy of considering concentrative joint ventures as partial mergers resulted in their escape from the framework of Article 85(1). In the absence of a separate Community merger control system, the partial merger theory was unsatisfactory since the question was whether joint ventures fall under the provision of Article 85(1) or escape anti-trust control altogether. Of course, as *ultium refugium* there is Article 86, but it requires pre-existing dominance and abuse of it as applicability criteria.

The Commission's criteria[32] in order for a joint venture to be characterised as a "concentration" are the following:

---

[30] See Court of Appeals of Frankfurt, 1989 WuW/E OLG 4323, following the decision of the German Federal Supreme Court, 96 BGHZ at 85.
[31] See above, n. 26.
[32] See Commission's Guidelines [1990] O.J. C203/10.

— first, the partners have to transfer a complete business to joint venture status and not merely a particular function such as research and development;

— secondly, the parents have to abandon business permanently and irreversibly in the field of joint venture;

— thirdly, the joint venture should be under a single management while the parents are becoming pure holding companies, and

— finally, there must be elimination of the so-called spill over effect of joint venture, namely the possibility of affecting competition between its parents in other areas.

The second paragraph of Article 3(2) of the merger control regulation illustrates the above mentioned principles and requires all "concentrative" joint ventures to be notified to the Commission pursuant to the provisions of the regulation. These joint ventures will be exclusively dealt with under the EEC merger control system, even with the existence of ancillary restraints (Recital 25 of the regulation). All other co-operative joint ventures fall into the framework of Article 85(1).

A grey area arises as to whether a simple share or asset acquisition establishing a joint venture is to be considered as a pure concentration or a co-ordination between undertakings.

The most important concept of the regulation, as regards corporate mobility based on concentration patterns, is that of mergers of "Community dimension". Once it has been clear what is meant by concentrations and what kind of concentrations require control under the framework of the regulation, it has to be established which of the above concentrations are capable of falling under the Commission's jurisdiction.

The regulation applies only to Community-scale concentrations. It seeks to achieve a clear cut division between large mergers of a European dimension where the Commission will have responsibility, and smaller mergers where competent national authorities will apply national provisions.

Article 1(2) of the regulation defines the term "Community dimension" quantitatively. It lays down three cumulative criteria:

(i) the extremely high world-wide turnover threshold of ECU 5 billion;

(ii) a *deminimis* limitation to this aggregate world-wide turnover figure, a Community-wide turnover of more than ECU 250 million; and

(iii) two thirds of the aggregate E.C. turnover must not be achieved within the same Member State.

The calculation of turnover, a quite complicated and complex process, will be given detailed analysis below.

It is evident from the text of the regulation that the only criterion for the definition of Community dimension is the turnover of the undertakings concerned. They are not required to have a legal presence in the Common Market. A question arises when reading Recitals 10 and 11 of the regulation—a reference to a geographical nexus is made. Thus, in addition to the quantitative criteria, Community dimension exists

> "where at least two of the undertakings concerned have their sole or main fields of activities in different Member States or where, although the undertakings in question act mainly in one and the same Member State, at least one of them has substantial operations in at least another Member State; whereas that is also the case the concentrations are effected by undertakings which do not have their principle fields of activities in the Community but which have substantial operations there."

This geographical test had appeared in the draft regulation submitted to the Council in April 1988 (Article 1(2)), but in the final text appears only in Recitals 10 and 11. Of course, it has some legal significance but only the future will show whether the Commission intends to enforce this additional test. In its nineteenth Report on Competition Policy, the Commission states that, in co-operation with the Council, it will take into account other factors in addition to turnover when the thresholds are revised.

The legal basis of the merger control regulation

As a legal instrument of secondary Community legislation, the regulation is based on Articles 87 and 235. It has been enacted by the Council unanimously, thus in accordance with the decision-making procedure of Article 235. The reason for the regulation being based on both Articles 87 and 235 is the following: Article 87 provides for measures implementing Articles 85 and 86. It is an instrument for the application of general Community anti-trust law. Article 87 requires a qualified majority as the decision-making procedure, thus being proved a flexible tool in the hands of Community institutions as far as proper application of competition law and policy are concerned. Article 235, the "catch all" provision, provides for measures that can fill gaps, that is, where the Treaty has not provided the necessary powers, the Council can unanimously adopt the appropriate measures for the attainment of the objectives of the Treaty. Whilst a Community act under Article 87 implements primary Community law (Articles 85 and 86), a measure under Article 235 creates new substantive rules.

It can be maintained that the regulation partly implements Articles 85 and 86. Although at first sight the regulation's test of compatibility with the Common Market, which is neither that of Article 85 nor Article 86, and its legislative history support the view that it cannot really be regarded as an implementing measure, a careful reading of Recital 6 reveals a link between general Community anti-trust law and the merger control regulation. Recital 6 reads: "whereas Articles 85 and 86, while applicable according to the case law of the Court of Justice to certain concentrations, are not, however, sufficient to cover all concentrations which may prove to be incompatible with the system of undistorted competition envisaged in the Treaty". Thus, Articles 85 and 86 apply, in principle, to concentrations, although they are inefficient to cover all kinds of concentrations which may be incompatible with the common market.

Whereas reference to Article 87 as a legal basis of the regulation seeks to capture *Continental Can* type mergers and concentrations of the kind that would be covered by Recital 24, reference to Article 235 is envisaged to cover all concentrations that Articles 85 and 86 cannot reach. Indeed, Article 235 is the necessary additional legal basis for merger control since both the application of the *Continental Can* doctrine and the *Philip Morris* doctrine results in a great deal of concentrations escaping from the Community's regulatory framework of competition law and policy. The regulation should be viewed as creating novel rules which derive from the principles of Article 3(f) but differ from those laid down in Articles 85 and 86, as implemented by the Commission and the Court of Justice.

CORPORATE MOBILITY AND THE CONTROL OF CONCENTRATIONS FROM AN ECONOMIC PERSPECTIVE

The merger control regulation has been introduced within a background of increasing industrial concentration in the European Community, as industries attempt to maximise the benefits of the creation and operation of the single market. The key economic issue behind the regulation is the introduction of clear, simple, predictable criteria for dividing competence between the Commission and national anti-trust authorities over concentrations. The regulation as a Community act seeks to take jurisdiction on mergers out of the hands of national authorities. Two reasons justify this economic rationale: the first is the avoidance of regulatory duplication; the "one stop shop" approach, at Community level, prevents delays and cost incurred in obtaining multiple clearance and creates an environment of certainty for business. Furthermore, it is necessary to make European industry more competitive *vis-à-vis* American and Japanese conglomerates. A unified approach is more preferable to the situation of several separate inquiries by different Member State authorities. The other reason is the need to meet the socioeconomic parameters of the Single European Market.

Economic evaluation criteria for concentrations

The regulation gives the Commission a relatively narrow ambit, focusing on competition policy issues but broad enough on the whole to give the discretion to carry out a thorough rule of reason analysis of the effects of a merger on market structure. In assessing the compatibility of a merger with the Common Market, Article 2(1) of the regulation lays down that the Commission should take into account:

"(a) the need to preserve and develop effective competition within the Common Market in view of, among other things, the structure of all the markets concerned and the actual or potential competition from undertakings located either within or without the Community;
    (b) the market position of the undertakings concerned and their economic and financial power, the opportunities available to suppliers and users, their access to supplies or markets, any legal or other barriers to entry, supply and demand trends for the relevant goods and services, the interest of the intermediate or ultimate consumers and the development of technical and economic progress provided that is to consumers' advantage and does not form an obstacle to competition."

Although the above mentioned evaluation criteria are wide enough and are not confined solely to a legal approach, it could be maintained that the regulation seeks a narrow focus on pure concentration issues neglecting social and industrial policy. This could reflect the influence of the German legal approach to merger control system in contrast with the British public interest approach. The regulation goes on to state in Article 2(2):

"A concentration which does not create or strengthen a dominant position as a result of which effective competition would be significantly impeded in the Common Market or in a substantial part of it, shall be declared incompatible with the Common Market."

The key issue in this analysis is the concept of dominance and the possible deviation from what is deemed dominance under Article 86.

On a case-by-case basis, dominance under Article 86 has been defined according to an overly rigid market share test at around 40 per cent. The regulation itself poses a *de minimis* rule, namely a market share of less than 25 per cent is unlikely to impede intra-Community trade. Article 2(1) of the regulation pleads for a wider definition than the rule of reason under Article 86 approach, when assessing mergers.

The evaluation criteria prominently consist of economic analysis which goes further from the essentially rule-based approach of the Commission decisions under Articles 85 and 86. The extremely thorough list of requests in the merger notification form confirms the above mentioned remark.

The calculation of turnover

One of the most complicated and complex issues of the regulation is the calculation of the turnover of the undertakings involved in a merger. Article 5 of the regulation sets out the relevant provisions.

For normal commercial enterprises their turnover will be calculated on the basis of their total revenue from the sales of products and services resulting from the company's ordinary activities in the preceding financial year, after deduction of sales rebates and of value added tax and other taxes directly related to turnover.

For banks and insurance companies, turnover will be calculated on the basis of 10 per cent of their total assets, since their actual turnover is considered to be an inappropriate method of evaluating whether a merger has Community dimension.

In the first case, normal commercial enterprises must meet the three cumulative conditions laid down in Article 1(2) of the regulation for being characterised Community dimensional, that is the aggregate world-wide turnover of all undertakings concerned must exceed ECU 5 billion. This will include both the turnover of the bidding and the target undertakings, undertakings which control the undertakings concerned (parents), undertakings which the parents control (sister companies), jointly-controlled undertakings, as well as those undertakings over which they exercise control directly or indirectly by means of :

— owing more than half of the capital or business assets, or

— having the power to exercise more than half of the voting rights, or

— having the power to appoint more than half of the members of the supervisory board, the administrative board or bodies legally representing the undertakings, or

— having the right to manage the undertaking's affairs.

In addition, each of at least two of them should achieve a Community-wide turnover of more than ECU 250 million and finally, each of the undertakings concerned must not achieve more than two thirds of its Community-wide turnover within one and the same state.

Under the above assessment, horizontal inter-group sales between the enterprises involved in a merger are disregarded, when calculating the worldwide turnover of a concentration. By virtue of Article 5(1), evaluating turnover either in the Community as a whole or in any particular Member State a geographical and commercial limitation is posed. The second indent of Article 5(1) reads: "turnover . . . shall comprise products sold and services provided to undertakings or consumers in the Community or in that Member State as the case may be". It seems that products and services exported beyond the Community are excluded in calculating the ECU 250 million Community turnover or the two thirds rule of Article 1(2) of the regulation.

Where credit and financial institutions are involved in a concentration, their Community dimension is considered by artificially calculated figures. In order to meet the first test of Article 1(2) of the regulation, the value of one tenth of total assets of banks or credit and other financial institutions is required to exceed the amount of ECU 5 billion.

The assessment of the ECU 250 million—the Community-wide aggregate turnover—demands a complex calculation: one tenth of the total assets multiplied by the ratio between loans and advances to credit institutions and customers in transactions with Community residents and the total sum of those loans and advances.

The same method is used in determining the two-thirds rule: one tenth of the total assets multiplied by the ratio between loans and advances to credit institutions and customers in transactions with residents of the Member State and the total sum of those loans and advances.

In the case of insurance undertakings, the assessment of their Community dimension is made by replacing the turnover by the value of gross premiums written. This figure comprises all amounts received and receivable in respect of insurance contracts issued by or on behalf of the insurance undertakings and also includes outgoing reinsurance premiums, but not taxes and parafiscal contributions or levies charged by reference to the amounts of individual premiums or the total value of premiums.

In evaluating a partial merger-concentrative joint venture, problems arise as to whether the turnover of the parent undertakings is included in the calculation. The regulation does not give an answer to this question but it appears that the Commission should opt for an interpretation conferring the greater jurisdiction, that is, the turnover of the parent companies should be taken into account.

Furthermore, things become more complicated when the parent undertakings, operating a concentrative joint venture, decide to merge. In that case, the turnover of the joint venture will exclude all the transactions with its parents, and the remaining turnover (with third parties) will be apportioned equally between the parent undertakings irrespective of their shareholdings in the venture (Article 5(5)(b) of the regulation).

Finally, the calculation of turnover for the purpose of evaluating whether a concentration is to be characterised as Community dimensional or not requires detailed accountancy work. If it is unclear whether the thresholds have been exceeded, the undertakings involved in the concentration must notify the Commission, which is obliged to examine the figures and issue a decision on whether the concentration has or does not have a Community dimension.

The principles of mandatory notification and automatic suspension

Once a concentration falls within the scope of the regulation the Commission must be notified within one week of the conclusion of the agreement or the announcement of the bid or the acquisition of the controlling interest (whichever comes first).[33] Where the merger is consensual or a joint acquisition, the notification must be made jointly by all the parties. In case of hostile acquisition, the notification must be made by the acquired party. Supply of incorrect or misleading information, intentionally or negligently, renders the undertakings liable to fines up to ECU 50,000 (Article 14(1)).

The result of the notification is a three week automatic suspension of the concentration.[34] In total, the merger will remain inactive for approximately four weeks, since the Commission is not notified until one week, at the most, after the initial agreement, announcement or acquisition.

It could be argued that one drawback of the notification is that it would be more appropriate as a second-stage information request, once a prima facie investigation of the concentration concerned has been conducted. The Commission should have the power to waive the need for parties to provide a full response to a notification form, if the detailed market analysis is not relevant to the examination of the case. This may occur, for example, when the Commission takes into account primarily industrial policy issues or social and economic cohesion aspects and at a later stage the market analysis assesses a concentration.

Interestingly, the regulation is silent as far as unnotified concentrations are concerned. If the undertakings involved in a merger fail to notify the Commission, they should face indefinite suspension. Indeed, in the absence of a clear provision the above solution is de lege ferenda.

The suspension of any activity of the concentration, a principle introduced by the regulation as substantive procedural provision, aims at giving the Commission the time to thoroughly examine the case and decide whether the merger is compatible or not with the Common Market.

The Commission, following a preliminary examination of the notification, may, on its own initiative, decide to suspend the merger for more than three weeks, wholly or partly until it takes a final decision, or it may take other interim measures. The unspecific meaning of "its own initiative" could be interpreted as an incentive to block legal proceedings by third parties aiming to extend the suspension period.

In order to mitigate the possible impact of the above, the suspension of the concentration shall not impede the implementation of a public bid which has been notified to the Commission, in accordance with Article 4(1), by the date of its announcement, provided that the acquirer does not exercise the voting rights attached to the securities in question or does so only to maintain the full value of those investments and on the basis of a derogation granted by the Commission pursuant to paragraph 4 of the same Article. Thus, shares in a public bid may continue to be purchased but the voting rights may not be exercised without permission from the Commission.

---

[33] Art. 4 of Reg. 4064/89.
[34] ibid., Art. 7.

The Commission may also, on request, grant a derogation from the obligation to suspend in order to prevent serious damages to one or more undertakings concerned with a concentration or to a third party. That derogation would be subject to conditions. The latter possibility opens the door for legal proceedings to be instituted by the parties concerned or by third parties, according to the Commission's decision, positive or negative in this regard. The maximum period for which the Commission may suspend a concentration is up to five months.

The legal relationship between the private parties concerned and transactions that they may have made is addressed in Article 7(5), where a distinction between, on the one hand, transactions in securities, including those convertible into other securities, admitted to trading on a market which is regulated and supervised by authorities recognised by public bodies, which operates regularly and is accessible directly or indirectly to the public, and on the other hand, all other transactions.

The former category (stock exchange transactions) will be unaffected by the suspension of the concentration, unless the buyer and the seller knew or ought to have known that the transaction was carried out in contradiction of such a suspension.

All the other transactions performed during the suspension period of a concentration will be examined *ex post facto*, that is, their validity will be determined in accordance with the final decision of the Commission. So, if the concentration is incompatible with the Common Market all the transactions made during its suspension, when it was being examined by the Commission, are invalid and vice versa.

It remains to be examined whether the pronouncement of the invalidity of those transactions is total or partial. In other words, would it be possible to apply the rule deriving from the judgment of the Court of Justice in *Société Technique Minier* case[35] where, under Article 85 national courts are allowed to assess valid parts of an agreement infringing the first paragraph of that Article. It could be said that the *Technique Minier* rule illustrates an inherent flexibility in Article 85 and represents a principle of selectivity, that is, the chance to save parts of an agreement where these parts do not constitute an essential element of the rest of the infringing agreement.

The regulation appears to having been drafted so as to deliberately pre-empt any possibility of saving valid parts of an agreement. Perhaps it is the principle of legal certainty, or of legitimate expectation which is sought to be preserved, or on the other hand the recognition that a merger is such a complex phenomenon that it should not be allowed to split up.

Finally, the fines provided by the regulation for failure to notify or suspend a concentration are quite severe. The failure to notify as such

---

[35] See Case 56/65, *Société Technique Minier v. Machinenbaum Ulm* (preliminary ruling): [1966] E.C.R. 235.

results in fines between ECU 1,000 and 50,000. The wrongful implementation of a Commission decision pursuant to Article 7(4) (derogation from suspension) may result in fines up to 10 per cent of the aggregate turnover of the undertakings concerned; the same fine may be imposed when a concentration has been put into effect in breach of Article 7(1) and 7(2) of the regulation. In addition, periodic penalty payments of up to ECU 100,000 per day may be levied in the event that there is a breach of an obligation imposed by the Commission: either in allowing a concentration to proceed despite the application of the suspensory period, or the granting of permission to exercise voting rights attached to securities acquired as a result of the implementation of a public bid.

The examination of the notification

The Commission is obliged to examine the notification as soon as it receives it and has a period of one month commencing on the day after receipt of the notification (or, where incomplete information is supplied with the notification, beginning on the day following the eventual receipt of the complete notification) to decide whether the concentration is compatible or not with the Common Market.[36] The period of one month may be increased to six weeks if the Commission is advised by a Member State that the merger particularly affects its domestic market.

The Commission, within the above mentioned period, must end the first procedural step in assessing a merger by issuing a formal decision, declaring that: either the notified transaction is not a concentration within the meaning of the regulation, or, if it is, it does not have a Community dimension therefore falling outside the scope of the regulation; either the notified concentration has a Community dimension but it does not raise serious doubts about its compatibility with the Common Market; or the notified concentration having a Community dimension raises serious doubts as to its compatibility with the Common Market and therefore requires further examination.

In the latter case, the Commission should notify without delay the parties concerned and the competent authorities of the Member States that it is going to proceed with its investigation. It has four months to conclude its investigation and to announce the results by means of a formal decision. If the Commission fails to meet the time limit of four months, the concentration shall be deemed compatible with the Common Market without prejudice to Article 9 of the regulation (referral to the competent authorities of the Member States). Here again, the Commission should issue a formal decision. Although the relevant article (10(6)) of the merger control regulation does not provide for a decision, it is logical and *de lege ferenda* for the Commission to cover the declaration of a concentration's compatibility with the Common Market under

---

[36] Art. 10(1) of Reg. 4064/89.

the cloak of a formal decision, as the latter is subject to an appeal before the Court of First Instance. Thus, the third parties concerned can contest the compatibility of a concentration with the Common Market, when it has been deemed compatible.

Finally, it will normally take a maximum of five months before the Commission assesses the compatibility of a concentration. Only very exceptionally (Article 10(4) of the regulation) will it be allowed to take longer. Of course, there will be a possible delay due to Member States appealing the Commission's decision under Article 9 of the regulation, or obtaining interim measures in order to apply their domestic provisions to a merger. The five month period within which a concentration will be cleared is not excessively long compared to the deadlines in the United States and German merger control systems. In U.S. a merger will be cleared in 50 days at the most, and in Germany there is a four month suspensory period following notification (which under certain circumstances may be extended), although approval may come sooner. It should be remembered that the basic difference between the two systems is that the American has opted for an *ex post* investigation whilst the German (and the European) for an *ex ante* investigation.

The conclusion of the investigations

The Commission, in carrying out its investigation, has a wide range of powers. Under Article 11 of the regulation it can request further information from the parties, and as has been seen the provision of misleading information gives rise to fines. By virtue of Article 12, it can request the co-operation of the competent authorities of the Member States to carry out investigations and it may assist them in carrying out these duties.

Under Article 13, the Commission is empowered to examine the books and other business records of the undertakings concerned, to take or demand copies or extracts from the books and business records, to ask for oral explanation on the spot or to enter any premises, land and means of transportation of the undertakings.

The competent authorities of the Member States must be in constant liaison with the Commission and express their views upon those procedures. Provision is made under Article 19(3) and (4) that an Advisory Committee on Concentrations comprising of representatives of each of the Member State is established in order to consult the Commission when assessing concentrations.

The hearing of the parties and of third parties

Before taking any decision, the Commission shall hear the parties affected and allow representation to be made at every stage of the procedure. Any Commission decision to extend the period of suspension, attach conditions to a concentration, order divestiture or declare a concentration incompatible with the Common Market will be based only on objections which the parties have been able to submit in their observations. All the files on the case shall be open to the parties directly concerned, subject to the protection of business secrets.

Third parties, natural or legal persons, may be heard insofar as the Commission and the competent national authorities of the Member States deem it necessary. If they have a legitimate interest, they should be entitled, upon application to be heard. The regulation poses no limitations on the number of natural or legal persons, but it shows a preference for administrative or management organs of the undertakings concerned or recognised workers' representatives. What is to be held as "legitimate interest" and when this condition is fulfilled remains to be seen. The requirement that both the Commission and the competent authorities should regard the hearing of third parties as necessary may create some problems.

The appraisal criteria

The regulation, as a new legal instrument based primarily on Article 235, establishes substantive rules that create a complex situation. On the other hand, it is designed to deal with the lasting structural changes effected by mergers, acquisitions and other concentrations which are different from the behavioural changes raised by an abuse of dominant position under Article 86; thus, the aim of the regulation is not the control of *behavioural* change but rather of *structural* change, which is a new concept for the EEC Treaty only introduced by the regulation.

On the other hand, in order to assess the compatibility of a concentration with the Common Market, the regulation employs terms like "dominant position" which is questionable if it is the same as under Article 86, having developed and acquired a definition through the jurisprudence of the Court of Justice.

The complexity which the regulation creates derives from the question of whether the concept of "dominance" under Article 86 is the same as that used under the regulation, and further, what is the relationship between the two criterion. Since Article 86 has already been applied to mergers (*Continental Can* case) the situation becomes more complicated as far as the appraisal criteria of a concentration are concerned.

The concept of dominance under Article 86 and under the administrative practice built up by the Commission prior to the adoption of the regulation, was based on the equation of dominance with an absence of effective competition, without the concept being quantitatively or qualitatively related to market share.

Indeed, the Court in the *Hoffman-La Roche*,[37] *United Brands*[38] and *Michelin*[39] cases established a definition of dominance as the ability of a

---

[37] See Case 85/76, *Hoffman-La Roche v. E.C. Commission*: [1979] E.C.R. 520.
[38] See Case 27/76, *United Brands v. E.C. Commission*: [1978] E.C.R. 207.
[39] See Case 322/81, *NV Nederlandsche—Banden Industrie Michelin v. E.C. Commission*: [1983] E.C.R. 3461.

company to hinder the maintenance of effective competition by acting independently of competitors, customers and consumers, having the power to exercise an appreciable influence on conditions under which competition will develop, even where lively competition exists. That approach was followed in the *Continental Can* case.

In fact there are three elements: the independent behaviour, the hindering of effective competition which constitutes the core of the abuse, and finally, the exploitative use of this dominance. The Commission, in the *Akzo* case,[40] sought to deviate from the above mentioned definition with a view to de-emphasising the element of independence of a dominant firm in respect of pricing and other competitive decisions. In particular, it stated that the power to exclude effective competition is not coterminous with independence from competitive factors, but may also involve the ability to eliminate or weaken existing competitors or to prevent potential competitors from entering the market. It could be argued that the Commission sought to broaden the concept of dominance, giving it the form of a market power whose very existence results in the ignoring of competitors.

The regulation uses this concept of dominance and in Article 2(2) and (3) describes those effects which, if present, will trigger a declaration of incompatibility. Interestingly, it does not use the language of the Court's definitions endorsed in the *United Brands, Hoffman-La Roche, Michelin* and *Continental Can* cases, omitting respectively the reference to independent action and to the absence of any serious possibility of competition. This approach represents a deviation from the principles of Article 86 and reflects the regulation's structural, as opposed to behavioural, concerns. But this deviation does not mean that "dominance" is to be defined differently than under Article 86. In fact it indicates that dominance and its effects are to be examined from an objective perspective of competitive structure, rather than from a perspective of an undertaking's ability to pursue a course of conduct insulated from competitive pressures.

The different approach that the regulation has in assessing dominance in the context of concentrations, employs criteria previously relied on by the Court and the Commission in assessing dominance. As is made clear by Article 2(1)(b) of the regulation, these criteria are market share, financial and economic power, opportunities available to suppliers and users, access to supplies and markets, barriers to entry, and trends in supply and demand. There is also additional criteria which relate to the development of technical and economic progress, provided that it is to consumers' advantage and to the preservation of competition, which implies an efficiency defence mechanism such as it might be found under Article 85(3).

---

[40] See ECS/A, [1985] O.J. L374/1.

The inclusion of the provision referring to technical and economic progress and Recital 13 indicate that, although the appraisal of compatibility involves a one-step analysis which will lead to one of the two alternative determinations set out in Article 2(2) and (3) of the regulation, this analysis is not limited to a mere determination as to whether a dominant position has been created or strengthened; it includes an evaluation of the effects of the concentration and also takes into account other limited considerations, although the latter may be overridden where dominance becomes an obstacle to all competition and is thus incompatible with Article 3(f).

The powers of the Commission's decision

If the Commission finds a concentration incompatible with the Common Market, it has the power to attach and accept at a later date modifications by the undertakings concerned, so the concentration will become compatible with the Common Market (Article 8(2)). In case the Commission declares a concentration incompatible with the Common Market by way of a formal decision, it may order divestiture of the assets or order a cessation of joint control or any other action that may be appropriate in order to restore conditions of effective competition (Article 8(4)).

Under Article 2(2), (3), the Commission is obliged to declare incompatible all concentrations that create or strengthen a dominant position, as a result of which effective competition would be significantly impeded in all or in a substantial part of the Common Market.

There are two options for this analysis. The first is to define the creation or strengthening of dominance and to condemn it as such. The second is to add a qualification clause to the concept of dominance under the terms " . . . as a result of which effective competition would be significantly impeded".

Under the former analysis, where the creation or the strengthening of dominance will result in a *per se* prohibition of a concentration, there is no room for a flexible evaluation, except for the definition of the relevant product and geographical markets and the assessment of the factors defined in Articles 2(1)(a) and (b) of the regulation, which are only to determine whether dominance exists or if it has been strengthened.

Under the latter analysis, two elements deserve attention: (i) the creation or the strengthening of dominance (ii) of such a magnitude that can impede effective competition. As the Court did in the *Continental Can* case, it could be argued that the regulation focuses on the effects of the creation or the strengthening of dominance, *e.g.* the abuse of it and not on the dominant position as such; and abuse derives from excess dominance. A dominant position as such is not prohibited. One may ask whether a dominant position is conceivable without the effect of impeding competition. In most cases it is not. But when assessing a merger, one has to take into account the dynamic factor of time and various desirable restrictions on competition which will finally result in an increase of competitiveness.

Here, the analysis concerning the lifetime of a product market, future barriers to entry and the comparison of the post-merger situation to the previous one is decisive. It is interesting to note that the American merger control system focuses only on the concept of dominance as such, and even hypothetical abuse of dominance may be prohibited.

The concept of economic and social cohesion (Recital 13) should be understood under the perspective of the dynamic development of a market and with consideration to the short, medium and long term impacts of a concentration. However, the effort to encourage economic development in poorer regions of the Community should not be used as a cohesion defence to dominant positions.

The abandonment of the reference to "independence" as an element of dominance, and the need for a flexible analysis in the absence of a prohibition, as such, of the existence of dominance in the EEC Treaty, may lead to the conclusion that the regulation does not intend such an approach *vis-à-vis* dominant concentrations.

Thus, the significant impediment of competition referred to in Article 2(3) may not be synonymous with dominance in every case, but may be intended to signify the unacceptable consequences resulting from a degree of dominance that has either been created or strengthened by the concentration. The above interpretation is to some extent supported by the Commission's prior administrative practice under Article 86 when dealing with mergers; for instance in *Michelin/Kleber-Colombes*, in *Michelin/Actor*, in *British Airways/British Caledonian*, in *British Sugar/Bensford*,[41] the Commission either has not opposed concentrations that created or strengthened dominant positions or adopted the view that although pre-existing dominance may have been strengthened to some extent, its intervention was not required since effective competition continued to exist.

It is admitted that the drive to market integration will result in major corporate reorganisation and the effects of the resulting structural changes may lead the Commission to adopt a flexible approach to concentrations. Such a flexibility may be desirable as dominant positions exist in different sizes and shapes, in different degrees and for different reasons, and concentrations involving smaller and low profile dominant positions will be harder to stop; as a result more and more oligopolies will emerge. Under this situation and bearing in mind that the Court has left open the issue of joint dominance leading to abuse, the Commission may have to introduce the theory of collective dominance in respect to concentrations.

---

[41] See above, n. 8.

The factors for assessing dominance and compatibility

Article 2(1)(b) of the regulation lays down the criteria for assessing the existence of market power. Although it does not refer to a definition of the relevant product market, it seems logical that the Commission will apply a product market analysis taking into account demand and supply structure, demand and supply substitution and cross elasticities of both.

It is not clear whether the Commission will seek a geographical market analysis. The reference to the distinct market in Article 9(7) appears to emphasise local peculiarities, thus deviating from the case law of the Court in regard to the geographic element of the relevant market at a Community level. A geographical test for determining the relevant market should have more economic than political aspects. In addition, the requirement set out in Article 2(1)(b) that the Commission shall take into account the access of suppliers and users to supplies or markets, indicates the need to avoid vertical integration.

One of the most difficult criteria in appraising a concentration and assessing its dominance is the actual or potential competition outside the Community. Article 2(1)(a) reads: " . . . actual or potential competition from undertakings located either within or without the Community". There are two elements here: first the Commission shall take into account competition from outside the Community when its effects emerge within the Community. Problems arise as to the second element, namely whether the Commission, when evaluating the effects of a concentration in the Community, should consider the need of European undertakings to increase their competitiveness in order to meet international competition outside the Community. The wording and scope of the regulation concerns competition within the Community and from the beginning the Commission rejected the argument that a competitive world market may justify dominance at Community level.

On the other hand, there is a connection between indents (a) and (b) of Article 2(1) of the regulation. It has been stated that European competitiveness is lagging in respect to American and Japanese multinationals. Competition from outside the Community should promote technical and economic progress; international competition should serve as a vehicle to industrial policy, although in Article 2(1)(b) the development of technical and economic progress is subject to a defence mechanism similar to that under Article 85(3) and there is no specific reference to Article 130(f).

THE EXCLUSIVITY OF THE MERGER CONTROL REGULATION

Under the regulation the Commission has exclusive jurisdiction for mergers above the thresholds. Article 21(2) reads: "no Member State shall apply its national legislation on competition to any concentration that has Community dimension". Furthermore, by virtue of Article 22(1), (2) there is exclusive applicability of the regulation to concentrations as defined in Article 3 and the repeal of Regulation 17 and its analogues[42] with reference to concentrations.

The purpose is clear: the achievement of a "one stop shop" to ensure a centralised system of concentration control and a uniform policy towards Community concentrations. The regulation based on the principle of exclusivity divides the task of merger control between the Commission and the Member States.

There are three exceptions to the "one stop shop" rule. Member States may invoke two exceptions to the Commission's exclusive jurisdiction and there is one exception to their exclusive jurisdiction.

The German clause

Under Article 9 a concentration, although falling under the definition of the regulation, meeting the thresholds and having a Community dimension, may be subject to control by competent authorities of the Member State. Article 9 works as follows: a Member State may seek jurisdiction to control a notified concentration that threatens to give rise to a dominant position within its territory. The Commission may do one out of three things. It may send the case to the competent authorities of the Member State to apply national merger provisions, or deal with the case itself. It may also disagree with the Member State's application, disputing the relevance in competition law terms of the market identified by the Member State, namely the concept of a distinct market, or if the market is properly defined the Commission may dispute the alleged dominance. Finally, if the Commission finds that the Member State's application is not founded, it will reject it by decision.

Uncertainties arise in respect to what kind of domestic competition law has a Member State to apply to a Community dimension concentration, in case the Commission refers the merger to it. As mentioned above, only three Member States, namely the United Kingdom, Germany and France have effective merger control systems to apply to European scale concentrations. Other Member States do not possess relevant legislation and it could be inconsistent to apply general national cartel law to a merger, since merger control rules are *lex specialis* in respect to general competition law. Article 9 appears to have limited application only to the three larger Member States. It could be argued that the German clause is an unofficial invitation for Member States to introduce their own merger control systems.

Things become more complicated when one reads in Article 9(2) that a distinct market can be a substantial part of the Common Market or not. If the national distinct market is a substantial part of the Common

---

[42] See Regs. 1017/68, [1968] O.J. Spec. Ed. 302; 4056/86, [1986] O.J. L378/4; and 3975/87, [1987] O.J. L374/1.

Market the Commission may apply Article 86 to restore effective competition. This is quite an unclear situation which creates significant problems. It has been argued that since the Commission has the discretion to refer a merger to national authorities and as it has stated that it will not use Article 86 at Community level in respect to concentrations, no important difficulties arise. But if one transfers the matter to an academic sphere, it would seem wise to delete the wording "substantial part of the Common Market" from the regulation, thus eliminating the theoretical possibility of using Article 86 at Community level and creating a clearer situation.

In addition to the above considerations, the concept of "distinct market" requires further elaboration. A strict application of Article 9 of the regulation pleads for limitation to local markets of a Member State and not the whole territory of the Member State concerned, because in the latter case it will normally be a substantial part of the Common Market. Only exceptionally could the provision apply to a national market as a whole, which is to some extent isolated from the rest of the Community. The wording of Article 9 (whether the distinct market is a substantial part of the Common Market or not) seems to opt for a solution where the whole national market can be characterised as a distinct market.

With regard to the definition of a distinct market, there are some more problems concerning the mutual exclusivity of the regulation. The relationship between Article 9 and Article 6 of the regulation appears to be a complex matter leading to uncertainty. Indeed, under Article 6(1) the Commission shall declare in the form of a decision that a concentration either (i) does not fall within the scope of the regulation, (ii) does fall but does not create serious doubts as to its compatibility, or (iii) requires further investigation since it raises serious doubts as to its compatibility.

When a Member State seeks jurisdiction under Article 9 of the regulation, where the Commission can choose between Article 6(1)(b) solution, namely that the Community dimensional concentration in question does not raise serious doubts, or a solution under 9(3)(a) and (b), it can either deal with the concentration itself or refer it to the competent national authorities with a view to the application of that state's national provisions.

If the distinct market is a substantial part of the Common Market, Articles 6(1)(b) and 9(3)(a) and (b) are mutually exclusive. However, where the distinct market is not a substantial part of the Common Market the mutual exclusivity is demolished, since a concentration perfectly compatible with the Common Market and eligible without any qualification for an Article 6(1)(b) decision, could be prohibited pursuant to an Article 9(3)(a) decision. This result also undermines the logic behind Article 2 of the regulation and the standard of legality, which only deals with the whole Common Market or a substantial part of it.

The Commission should be aware of this situation, and in order to reduce to a great extent the uncertainty, it may limit the use of Article

9(3)(a) to cases where the distinct market constitutes a substantial part of the Common Market, whilst the alternative of Article 9(3)(b) could be used in cases where the distinct market is not a substantial part of the Common Market.

Of course, the discretion of the Commission in the third paragraph of Article 9 may mitigate the impact of the German clause, if for example the Commission uses in most of the cases the 9(3)(a) option; but on the other hand, the ninth paragraph of Article 9 provides for a safeguard against this possibility. Member States are entitled not only to appeal a Commission's decision but they can request the application of Article 186 EEC (interim measures). It cannot be denied that in a case under Article 9 of the regulation, the Commission will be under enormous pressure.

Another problem concerning the relationship between Articles 6 and 9 of the regulation is the omission to provide a time-limit under Article 9, in respect of a 6(1)(b) Commission decision whereby a Community dimensional concentration does not raise serious problems as to its compatibility with the Common Market. On the contrary, Article 9(5) lays down that if the Commission fails to take a decision on referral within three weeks at the most from notification, it shall be deemed to have referred the case to the Member State concerned. Most probably, Article 9(5) will apply by analogy to cover a 6(1)(b) situation. Article 9 is to be reviewed within four years of the adoption of the regulation,[43] but the decision making procedure for such a review is not clear.

The public interest clause

The other exception to the "one stop shop" rule is the so-called public interest clause. Article 21(3) of the regulation provides for the possibility for Member States to invoke legitimate interests other than those protected by the regulation, in order to take appropriate measures whenever a concentration threatens them. These interests include public security, plurality of media and prudential rules and are far removed from competition policy.

One can recall the distinction between "newspaper" mergers and other mergers under the U.K. merger control legislation. Article 21(3) is the fully-fledged "double barrier" so feared by the international business community. Indeed, even when a merger has been cleared by the Commission at Community level, it can be condemned at national level on grounds that have nothing to do with competition law. The range of legitimate interests to be taken into account is open-ended. Apart from the three explicitly mentioned there are various others, subject to their being recognised as such by the Commission before a Member State invokes them, and after an assessment of their compatibility with general principles and other provisions of Community law. Interestingly, there is

---

[43] See Art. 9(10) of Reg. 4064/89.

no provision for time-limits within which these additional national procedures should be terminated. Under these national proceedings a Member State may take the appropriate measures to protect its interest by prohibiting a concentration or making its approval subject to additional conditions or requirements. In no case may a Member State authorise a concentration which has been prohibited by the Commission.

The legitimate interest of public security is to be defined in accordance with Article 36 following a strict interpretation, and Article 224 and covers matters outside the scope of the general derogation contained in Article 223. Plurality of media recognises the legitimate concern to maintain diversified sources of information for the sake of plurality of opinion and multiplicity of views. Prudential rules relate to the financial services sector authorities and concern the good repute of individuals, the integrity of transactions and solvency rules.

Since the Commission and the Council stated that the public interest clause creates no new rights for Member States, one could expect a development of the principles of proportionality and non-arbitrary discrimination or disguised restrictions. A rule of reason approach will create legal certainty and legitimate expectation with respect to the vagueness referred to in Article 21(3).

Finally, there is no guarantee to exclude the possibility that Member States will use Article 21(3) in a projectionist manner in order to cope with international competition, particularly when a multinational merger cannot otherwise be faced. To everybody's surprise there is no provision for review of Article 21(3) of the regulation.

The Dutch clause

As has already been mentioned, below the thresholds the Member States have exclusive jurisdiction on mergers with only one exception, the so-called Dutch clause. Article 22(3) of the regulation works in the following manner: if a Member State believes that a merger could create a dominant position within its territory, it may ask the Commission to intervene, even if the concentration is sub-dimensional, that is, falling below the thresholds. The Commission's intervention will aim at preventing the merger if it poses a real threat to competition within a Member State and will be limited to what is needed to restore effective competition.

It could be argued that the Dutch clause seeks to undermine the high thresholds and counterbalance the impacts of the German clause. Article 22(3) to (5) is to be reviewed with the revision of the thresholds. However, the real purpose is to avoid discrimination, or to use a more moderate word, unequal treatment, between Community dimension and sub-dimensional concentrations. The original text of the Dutch clause even provided for a request by the parties concerned for a Commission intervention. But this would have resulted in an enormous wave of complaints, since the "one stop shop" control at Community level is much more preferable than extremely complex and stringent national provisions.

The extra-territorial application of the merger control regulation

Article 24 of the regulation deals with relations with non-member countries. Initially it had been proposed that these relations should be covered under the principle of reciprocity where the latter refers to mutual recognition of rights between Community Member States and third countries. The final text of the regulation uses the notion of (national) treatment but the criterion is whether a third country grants Community undertakings the same treatment that enterprises from that country enjoy within the Community. This proviso was inserted as a result of the insistence of the French government which wished to see reciprocity provisions incorporated into the regulation.

The consequences of a finding of failing reciprocity are quite reasonable.[44] Interestingly, no automatic sanctions are provided; only a Commission proposal to the Council for the appropriate mandate for negotiations, with a view to obtaining comparable treatment for Community undertakings.

Multilateral or unilateral treaties are to be respected; this is added in paragraph 4 of Article 24 and refers particularly to the GATT. The regulation provides for an equal treatment of third-country enterprises. Discrimination towards certain undertakings would require a unanimous amendment of the regulation, since there is a great deal of Member States' interest at stake.

The jurisdictional relationship between the merger control regulation and European competition law and policy

A final point on jurisdiction is the relationship between the regulation and Articles 85 and 86. The regulation does not exclude the application of Articles 85 and 86 to concentrations. It merely sets out the framework within which, subject to exceptions, the Commission will have competence to take decisions on mergers with Community dimension in respect of which Member States shall not apply their national legislation on competition (Article 21(2)). This is because general Community anti-trust law is not sufficient to cover all concentrations (Recital 6 of the regulation).

By virtue of Article 22(2), the applicability of Regulation 17 and its sister regulations[45] in other fields to concentrations as defined in Article 3

---

[44] See Art. 24(3) of Reg. 4064/89.
[45] Reg. 26/62, [1959–1962] O.J. Spec. Ed. 129; Reg. 27/62, [1959–1962] O.J. Spec. Ed. 132; Reg. 141/62, [1959–1962] O.J. Spec. Ed. 291.

of the merger control regulation has been repealed. As Regulation 17 is the procedural legislation implementing Articles 85 and 86, it is impossible for the Commission to apply these articles to concentrations as defined in the regulation. Irrespective of them having or not having a Community dimension, a concentration is not subject to Articles 85 and 86.

On the other hand, the regulation does not prohibit the application of Article 89, so there is a possibility for the Commission to apply general Community cartel law to concentrations. Article 89, which does not provide for investigatory powers, periodic penalties or fines, empowers the Commission to adopt a reasoned decision recording the existence of an infringement and to authorise Member States to take the necessary measures, as determined by the Commission, to remedy the situation. The effectiveness of this provision as an enforcement mechanism is doubtful.

It remains to see whether the possibility for the Commission of applying Articles 85 and 86 through Article 89 to concentrations is plausible. Recital 15 of the regulation indicates that where the market share of the participants of a concentration does not exceed 25 per cent either in the Common Market or in a substantial part of it, the concentration may be presumed compatible with the Common Market. Furthermore, the Commission has stated that concentrations with a worldwide turnover of less than ECU 2 billion and Community-wide turnover less than ECU 100 million would not normally affect intra-Community trade. Under the above consideration three kinds of concentration appear: (i) the Community dimension ones, (ii) the sub-dimensional ones and (iii) the *de minimis* concentrations. All the controversy will focus on the first two categories. Here it should be mentioned that under Article 86 there is no *de minimis* defence mechanism, although the Treaty requires that the abuse occur in a substantial part of the Common Market and the Court has said that where there is no effect on intra-Community trade Article 86 does not apply. It is possible that the Commission will consider compatible with the Common Market concentrations falling under revised thresholds, in cases where trade between Member States is not affected.

At Community level, the *Continental Can* doctrine (application of Article 86 to mergers) has been abandoned by the repeal of Regulation 17. In contrast however, the application of Article 85 is possible. The *Philip Morris* doctrine survived the enactment of the regulation and will continue to catch mergers which are not characterised as concentrations within the scope of the regulation.

The Commission has indicated in its nineteenth Report on Competition that it is not willing to apply Article 86 to concentrations at Community level, although it has reserved its rights under Article 89. Indeed, this would be a legal paradox as the regulation seeks to cover situations that Article 86 does not. There are some doubts concerning the application of Article 86 to a merger after it has been cleared in accordance with the regulation, having in mind the *Tetra-Pak* case,[46] where the Court said that it is possible for a merger to be prohibited even though it has firstly been granted an exemption under Article 85(3).

The joint application of Articles 85(3) and 86 gives rise to arguments trying to make a comparison between the regulation and exemptions under Article 85(3). In the *Tetra-Pak* case, an abuse of dominance was the inevitable consequence of the takeover. It could be argued though that a comparison between the regulation and Article 85(3) having on the other side Article 86 is not possible, since the regulation is a kind of legal continuation of Article 86 and not something similar to an exemption under Article 85(3).

At national level things are more complicated. Article 85 is no longer enforceable before national courts in merger cases; in contrast Article 86 is directly applicable and it can be invoked by individuals before national courts. In the absence of Regulation 17, the Commission cannot apply Article 85(3) and in this situation individuals cannot invoke Article 85 before national courts. Article 86 is directly applicable in national courts as the Court has ruled recently.[47] In this situation, it is not clear what the national courts will do. They will most probably request a reference from European Court of Justice for a preliminary ruling pursuant to Article 177. A more confusing situation may arise where multiple actions in various national courts under Articles 86 and 89, if the effects of a concentration were felt in more than one Member State, could give rise to conflicting or inadequate results. The same problems of an unco-ordinated approach would arise if Member States were to act under Article 88, applying Article 86 to concentrations.

---

[46] See *Elopak v. Tetra-Pak (Tetra-Pak I)* and the recent judgment of the Court of First Instance 51/89.

[47] See Case 66/86, *Firma Ahmed Saeed Flugreisen v. Central zur Bekampfung des unlauteren Wettbewerbs* [1989] O.J. C122/4. In this case the Court established the direct applicability of Art. 86 in national courts even in the absense of implementing legislation under Art. 87.

The application of competition law and policy on business in Europe

GENERAL REMARKS

The main purpose of the competition law and policy of the European Community is to achieve the four freedoms through a system which prevents exploitative market abuse and manipulation. Article 3(f) which provides for the above mentioned requirement, is implemented by primary Community legislation, namely Articles 85 and 86, and secondary legislation (regulations) in accordance with the requirements laid down in the above Articles.

Competition is distorted when there is collusive conduct between independent undertakings (Article 85), or when abuse of dominance by one or more undertakings takes place in the relevant market (Article 86). Article 86 complements Article 85 in that it strikes at the abuse of the economic power, whereas Article 85 prohibits agreements, decisions or concerted practices between undertakings which have collusive effect with a view to restricting competition in the relevant market. Article 86 is the logical continuation of Article 85, to the extent that it seeks to capture advanced methods of distortion of competition. The spirit of Article 86, reveals the effort to prevent the development of monopolies, which threaten the market by achieving supra-competitive profits. The control of monopolies under E.C. competition law is a structural one, based on the test of performance (abuse) of undertakings having a dominant position in the market.

THE CONTROL OF CARTELS

Cartels under E.C. anti-trust law are prone to restrict or distort competition when involved in a range of collusive activities. When cartels engage in collusive behaviour in order to limit price competition or to segment geographical or product markets, the applicability of Article 85(1) renders their agreements, decisions or concerted practices incompatible with the common market. Such incompatibility denotes the automatic invalidity of the elements of the above collusive behaviour by virtue of paragraph 2 of Article 85. However, when cartels contribute to the improvement of production or distribution of goods, or to the promotion of technical and economic progress and the benefit of consumers, they are deemed to have pro-competitive effects and the inapplicability of Article 85(1) may be declared by the European Commission on a case-by-case basis or based on a bundle of regulations which provide for exemption from paragraph 1 of Article 85. Such pro-competitive agreements which benefit from block exemptions cover a wide range of distributive trades as well as commercial activities based on industrial property rights.

THE CONTROL OF MARKET DOMINANCE

A monopoly acts without consideration of the demand and supply structures in the market,[1] has absolute dominance in the market and can achieve supra-competitive profits, either by price-fixing methods or by output control. However, in the long run, a monopoly will face competition, since its supra-competitive profits constitute an incentive for other firms to enter the market. Theoretically speaking, the monopoly will gradually become a duopoly, a monopolistic competitive market, an oligopoly, an imperfectly competitive market and finally, a perfectly competitive market.[2]

In practice, perfect competition is unattainable. What modern antitrust legislation seeks to achieve is the model of imperfect competition in a market. Imperfect competition is a situation where workable and effective competitive forces are developed and operate in a market, which is not dominated by monopolies or oligopolies.[3] There are two ways of achieving this: the first is to leave market forces to remedy the situation without intervention. This, however, may take time, as factors ensuring monopolization, such as patent licences, know-how and other barriers to entry will hinder the restoration of the market by "invisible" forces. The second way is to intervene and strike down monopolies and oligopolies.

If the latter method is to be followed, workable and effective competition will be achieved by the exercise of behavioural and structural control over the undertakings participating in a market. Behavioural control comprises remedies seeking the prohibition of anti-competitive action between undertakings; structural control focuses on the mere existence

---

[1] See Scherer, *Industrial Market and Economic Performance* (2nd ed., 1979), pp. 384–403.
[2] See Fisher and Pegg, *Introduction to Economics*, (3rd ed., 1990), pp. 141–143.
[3] Scherer, *op.cit.*, p. 415.

of monopolies (and oligopolies) and attacks concentration of market power.[4]

Modern anti-trust laws are against the development and operation of monopolies. In fact, what they wish to avoid is the making of supra-competitive profits by a monopoly, since there is no competition in the market. Although it is recognised that a monopoly is not evil in itself[5] —it may boost technological innovation, improve product efficiency and develop new product markets[6]—competition policy focuses on the control of monopolies through structural remedies, though its inability to make satisfactory contact with oligopolies is evident.[7]

On the other hand, an oligopolistic market is one which is characterised by the presence of a few suppliers, none of which is individually in a position to dominate the market, but each of which is relatively large.[8] Oligopolistic markets vary to a great extent from one to another. Concentration ratios[9] reveal symmetrical oligopolies, where the firms in question have the same market share and asymmetrical ones, where different market shares of the oligopolists pose formidable problems in deciding at what point oligopoly ceases and dominance by the largest firm begins. However, the term oligopoly does convey the essence of the idea: the control of the market by a few large firms.

The main argument against oligopolies is that the structural conditions of the market in which oligopolists operate are such that they will not compete with one another on price and will have little incentive to compete in other ways (e.g. technological innovation). This is the theory of oligopolistic interdependence,[10] which asserts that oligopolists will be able to earn supra-competitive (quasi-monopoly) profits without entering into any type of collusive agreement proscribed by competition law.

In the absence of deliberate collusive agreement to restrict competition, an oligopoly could be controlled by reference to its performance in the relevant market.[11] Performance tests concentrate on the alleged abuse of dominant position. Since none of the oligopolists has a dominant position, their aggregate dominance should be taken into account when investigating an alleged abuse.

---

[4] See Whish, Competition Law, (2nd ed.,1989), pp. 481 *et seq.*

[5] See Bellamy and Child, *Common Market Law of Competition* (3rd ed.), p. 389.

[6] See Joliet, *Monopolisation and Abuse of Dominant Position* (1970), pp. 226 *et seq.*

[7] *ibid.*, p. 237.

[8] Scherer, *op.cit.*, p. 394.

[9] Concentration in a market is often measured by the so-called aggregate concentration method, which includes measurement of assets, sales, number of employees, size of payroll, value added by the manufacturer or new capital expenditures; see Scherer, *op.cit.*, pp. 214–218. In U.S. anti-trust enforcement, the so-called Hirfindahl Index of market concentration is widely used, especially when the oligopolists concerned do not have dominant position individually.

[10] On the theory of oligopolistic interdependence see Scherer, *op.cit.*, at n. 1 above; Hall and Hitch, *Price Theory and Business Behaviour* (1939), pp. 12–45; Sweezy, *Demand under Conditions of Oligopoly* (1937), pp. 568–575.

[11] Whish, *op.cit.*, p. 585.

If workable and effective competition is to be preserved through anti-trust legislation, three possible approaches towards oligopolies exist: the structural, the conduct and the performance approaches.[12]

The structural approach concentrates on the structure of an industry as a barrier to effective competition. In this case it would be necessary to prevent oligopolistic structures in the first place by having strong merger controls and by preventing the elimination of competitors from the market. Also, logic would suggest that further powers would be needed to deconcentrate industries that had become oligopolistic.[13] There are two main drawbacks to the structural approach: First, economies of scale may be distorted or prevented. Indeed, oligopolies, in many cases, are the result of superior efficiency associated with economies of scale. In this case, it is necessary to consider at what point the advantages arising from economies of scale offset the adverse effects of a loss of price competition deriving from an oligopoly. Secondly, compulsory deconcentration may have a disruptive impact on the market in question and on economic life in general.

The conduct approach focuses on the pricing behaviour of the oligopoly and seeks to control price-fixing in oligopolistic industries by direct public regulation.[14] Prices would be fixed at what might be considered to be a "competitive" or at any rate a "reasonable" level. The disadvantage here is that this ad hoc governmental intervention and the litigation which may follow, represents a waste of resources. On the other hand, a precedent established on a case-by case basis can be used as a disincentive to anti-competitive conduct on the part of oligopolists. An alternative suggestion is that oligopolists might be required to notify their prices periodically to a central agency and then to adhere to them for a specific time.[15] Although a conduct approach may create a set of *per se* rules that define clear cut illegal forms of oligopolistic markets, it is enormously cumbersome and requires extensive bureaucratic resources. It is also difficult to establish what a competitive or reasonable price should be.

Finally, the performance approach examines the market behaviour of oligopolists and seeks to prevent them behaving in a way that is anti-competitive.[16] Policy makers will have to take into account progress in production and allocating efficiency, full employment and equity, in deciding when a performance is anti-competitive. If the phenomenon of parallelism in oligopolistic markets is to be considered anti-competitive, which is inappropriate as oligopolistic interdependence exists in many cases, then it is extremely difficult to define the desirable performance behaviour of oligopolies. Under an idealistic model such as perfect competition, it can be said that this aim is visible; but under imperfect

---

[12] Scherer, *op.cit.*, Chap. 5.
[13] *ibid.*
[14] see Bishop, *Oligopoly Pricing: a Proposal* (1983) 28 *Antitrust Bulletin*, 311.
[15] *ibid.*; such a system is known as "bid-pricing"; a particular merit of it would be that the firm itself bids for its price rather than a government agency setting it.
[16] Scherer, *op.cit.*, Chap. 5.

competition, which is the most likely situation, performance cannot be predicted—not even conduct. All the policy makers can hope for is the best possible outcome, not the perfect one; and there is no guarantee that there will be an improvement, since subjective judgement and a great deal of discretion on the performance test elements do not ensure that governmental intervention is the appropriate one.[17]

ANTI-TRUST AND MARKET DOMINANCE

Industrial concentration in the Common Market has been increasing for a considerable period.[18] The analysis of the operation of oligopolies suggests that there might be a case for reserving powers to monitor the operation of oligopolistic industries, although the case for a wholesale attack upon them is not proven. EEC competition law lacks the flexibility to achieve this.

In the history of European competition law, the theory of control of oligopolies has always played a rather dubious role. Under the EEC Treaty, the two primary anti-trust provisions are Articles 85 and 86. The former, being characterised as a behavioural remedy, aims at the alleged anti-competitive behaviour of undertakings which enter into agreements, decisions or concerted practices in order to restrict, resort or prevent competition in the relevant market. The latter is a structural remedy which focuses on the structure of the market (market domination) thus condemning specific performance (abuse) by one or more undertakings.[19]

The application of behavioural remedies (Article 85 of the EEC Treaty)

It is possible for collusive price fixing between oligopolists to be caught by Article 85(1). Apart from the clear case of an agreement or a decision between oligopolists, the term *concerted practice* encompasses any knowing substitution of practical co-operation for the risks of normal competition.[20] It has been suggested[21] that this definition of concerted practice is so wide that it could catch conscious parallelism or price leadership, even where there is no collusion between firms. However, this is not entirely convincing as the definition of concerted practice

---

[17] *ibid.*
[18] see "The Problem of Industrial Concentration in The Common Market" in *Competition Series*, Study no. 3 (1966).
[19] Bellamy and Child *op. cit.*, at n. 5, pp. 15–19.
[20] Whish, *op.cit.* at n. 4, p. 498.
[21] Korah, *EEC Competition Law and Practice* (3rd ed., 1986), pp. 18–22.

requires that there should be a deliberate substitution of co-operation for competition,[22] this imports the notion that there must be some mental consensus involving the mutual acceptance of obligations between undertakings, which is distinguished from the "purely" parallel behaviour under the mutual interdependence theory, which lacks the element of obligation. Furthermore, while it is open for the competition authorities (the Commission) to infer from circumstantial evidence that there is a concerted practice, the mere fact of parallelism would not be sufficient.[23]

Interestingly, although the Court held that a parallelism of behaviour by itself cannot be identified with concerted practice, it left a door open,[24] saying that parallelism could be a pointer towards a concerted practice when it leads to conditions of competition which do not correspond to the normal conditions of the market, having regard to the nature of the products, the importance and the number of undertakings and the volume of the market in question. Under such an approach, the Commission (and the Court) should examine the level of price equilibrium of the goods produced in an oligopolistic market and compare it with the equilibrium level which would have resulted from competition.[25]

In practice, the Court does not seem so far to have inferred the presence of a concerted practice simply from economic evidence, but it has based findings of concerted practices on evidence of some conduct between firms.[26] The Commission, on the other hand, in its decision in Zinc Producers Group,[27] attempted to demonstrate its understanding of oligopoly pricing, showing that it appreciated the distinction between collusive and barometric price leadership, thus refraining from condemning parallel action which may be attributable to market forces. The same line was followed in the decision in *Wood Pulp*,[28] although this time the Commission did not rely solely on the economic analysis of the oligopolistic market in question but also on the direct and indirect exchange of information between the competitors.

Article 85(1) may be applied in order to control oligopolies. By definition, its principal application is to prohibit cartel operation. Oligopolies could be considered as cartels if there is evidence for deliberate co-operation among the firms participating in the market in question. Evidence for such a collusion may be relatively easily inferred in case of agreements or decisions among the oligopolists. Problems arise when oligopolistic parallelism (without any circumstantial evidence) is to be

---

[22] Bellamy and Child, *op.cit.* at n. 5, pp. 30–32.
[23] Case 48/69, *ICI v. E.C. Commission*: [1972] E.C.R. 619.
[24] *ibid.*, at para. 66.
[25] Such an approach is found in the *Peroxygen Products* decision [1985] O.J. L35/1.
[26] Case 48/69, *ICI v. E.C. Commission*: [1972] E.C.R. 1663; Case 40/73, *Suiker Unie v. E.C. Commission*: [1975] E.C.R. 1663; Case 100/80, *Musique Diffusion Francaise S.A.; Pioneer High Fidelity (GB) v. E.C. Commission*: [1983] E.C.R. 1825.
[27] [1984] O.J. L220/27.
[28] [1985] O.J. L85/1; on appeal Case 89/85, *Ahlstrom Osakeyhtio v. E.C. Commission*.

regarded as concerted practice. The effort of the Commission to rely merely on economic evidence in order to determine this reveals a structural approach to the whole issue. This structural approach inevitably brings Article 86 into play. The following analysis examines whether the latter could efficiently be used to control oligopolies.

The application of structural remedies (Article 86 of the EEC Treaty)

A question of considerable interest in E.C. competition law has been whether Article 86 could be used to control oligopolistic markets. Its wording reads as follows: "Any abuse of one or more undertakings of a dominant position ..... shall be prohibited." The significance of the reference to more than one undertaking has given rise to controversy as to whether it could bring oligopolists within its scope.

The narrow view of this reference[29] is that it means that the market power and performance of undertakings within the same corporate group or economic unit can be aggregated and dealt with under Article 86. It will be a question of fact in each case whether undertakings in the same group are to be treated as one unit. In *Metro*[30] the Court held that due to lack of evidence concerning co-ordinated policy among undertakings in the same group, they could not be considered as one unit for the purposes of Article 86. Similarly, in *Continental Can*,[31] *Commercial Solvents*,[32] *Hoffman-La Roche*[33] and *Hugin*[34] the policies and conduct in dispute were attributed to the parent companies. In *General Motors*[35] and *Michelin*,[36] the Commission proceeded against the subsidiaries, as they had taken decisions without consultation with their parent companies.

On the other hand, the wide interpretation of the reference[37] to more than one undertaking suggests that independent undertakings might be considered to hold a "collective dominant position" in the market and that their market performance could then be controlled under the heading of abuse. According to this view, parallel pricing, product differentiation, market sharing, and horizontal mergers in oligopolistic markets might be scrutinised. The Commission shared this idea in the

---

[29] Bellamy and Child, *Common Market Law of Competition* (3rd ed.), pp. 188 *et seq.*
[30] Case 26/76, [1977] E.C.R. 1875.
[31] Case 6/72, [1973] E.C.R. 215.
[32] Cases 6, 7/74, [1974] E.C.R. 223
[33] Case 102/77, [1978] E.C.R. 1139.
[34] Case 22/78, [1979] E.C.R. 1869.
[35] Case 26/75, [1976] E.C.R. 1367.
[36] Case 322/81, [1983] E.C.R. 3461.
[37] See Flint, "Abuse of a Collective Dominant Position" [1978] 2 *Legal Issues of European Integration* 21; Lever and Lasok, "Mergers and Joint Ventures in the EEC" (1986) 6 *Oxford Yearbook of European Law* 121, pp. 137–140.

early 1970s[38] but the Court appeared to have rejected it in the case *Hoffman-La Roche v. Commission*[39]; it held that in an oligopoly the courses of conduct interact, while in the case of undertaking(s) which derive(s) profits from a dominant position, the conduct is to a great extent determined unilaterally.[40] Therefore, it seemed to suggest that the problems of oligopoly could not be controlled under Article 86.

In two recent decisions,[41] which were both appealed to the Court, the Commission surprisingly decided to rely on the notion of "abuse of a collective dominant position" in order to condemn the conduct of oligopolists under Article 86. It still remains unclear what factors must be taken into account to establish such abuse when it is committed by several undertakings, as the Commission's decisions rely on divergent definitions of the term "collective dominant position".

In the *Flat Glass* decision, the Commission relied on a structural link-up between the flat glass manufacturers of Italy.[42] In fact, after careful consideration one comes to the conclusion that this structural link was a cartel agreement, as they maintained special and common links with a group of wholesalers, being the main glass distributors in Italy, and had established among themselves a privileged relationship through the systematic exchange of information on flat glass products. However, both kinds of behaviour were judged by the Commission to also fulfil all factual preconditions of Article 85(1), thus being an anti-competitive agreement.

Although the flat glass oligopoly was quite symmetric and the product homogeneous, thus allowing the Commission to define the notion of "collective dominance" as a conduct which involves "methods other than those on which normal competition between economic operators is based, thus further weakening the degree of competition in a market in which, precisely because of the collective dominant position of these undertakings the degree of competition is already reduced",[43] the bringing into play of Article 85(1) created more problems than it was expected to solve. Indeed, the parallel application of Articles 85(1) and 86, namely a behavioural and structural remedy at the same time, is only exceptionally recognised by EEC competition law.[44] It should be recalled that

---

[38] See the Commission's Report on the Behaviour of Oil Companies in the Community during the period from October 1973 to March 1976: Com. (75) 675; also in the Sugar Cartel, [1973] O.J. L140/17, where it held that the two Dutch producers held a joint dominant position. The Court on appeal said nothing about it because there was no abuse by the companies concerned (Case 40/73, *Suiker Unie v. Commission*: [1975] E.C.R. 1942).

[39] [1978] E.C.R. 1139.

[40] *ibid.*, at para. 39.

[41] The Commission *Flat Glass* decision of December 7, 1988, [1989] O.J. L33/44 and the Commission *Magill TV Guide* decision of December 21, 1988, [1989] O.J. L78/43.

[42] [1989] O.J. L33/66, No. 79; also the appeal Case T–68/89, *Societa Italiana Vetro v. Commission*.

[43] *ibid.*, at para. 80.

[44] The exceptional character of a parallel application of Art. 86 and Art. 85 can also be demonstrated by the new regulations concerning the air and sea transport sectors, in particular, Art. 7.2 of Reg. 3976/87 and Art. 5.3(2) of Reg. 3975/87.

under Article 85(3) there is the possibility for the Commission to grant an individual or a block exemption in a case where competition has been restricted, prevented or distorted in the relevant market (provided that certain conditions have been met),[45] whereas under Article 86, such a margin of appreciation is lacking. Furthermore, a *de minimis* rule[46] is applied under the framework of Article 85, although the EEC Treaty requires that the abuse of dominance under Article 86 should occur in a substantial part of the common market and the Court has recognized[47] that where there is no effect on intra-community trade, Article 86 does not apply. From the above mentioned considerations it is evident that the joint application of Articles 85 and 86 in a cartel agreement is undesirable and poses problems as to the coherence of EEC competition law. Of course, even in the case where an exemption under Article 85(3) or a block exemption has been granted and in due course an abuse of dominance occurs, there is the possibility for the Commission to open proceedings under Article 86; but parallel application of Articles 85 and 86 is meaningless.[48]

The view adopted by the Commission that enterprises linked by a cartel agreement can also fulfil Article 86 by abusing their dominant position, may find support in two cases, the *Suiker Unie*[49] and *Ahmed Saeed* Cases,[50] as well as in the mainstream of German doctrine. In *Suiker Unie*, the Court held that parallel application of Articles 85 and 86 in concerted practices could be possible, whereas in the Ahmed Saeed case it stated that certain agreements would only constitute the formal embodiment of an economic reality, characterised by the fact that the undertaking in a dominant position had succeeded in imposing its conditions upon the other participants in the market.

It could be maintained that the real meaning of parallel application of Articles 85 and 86 in the above cases is that where an abuse of a dominant position is carried out through an agreement or concerted practice with other undertakings, Article 85(1) may apply.[51] Of course the Commission has the discretion to proceed the case either under Article 85 or under Article 86.[52] However, a cartel agreement which falls short of Article 85(1) should not be characterised at the same time as an abuse of dominant position, since the standards for the evaluation of the restriction of competition by agreement or concerted practice differ from the standards for the evaluation of an abuse of market power. In both

---

[45] The conditions laid down in Art. 83(3).
[46] *de minimis non curat lex*, or the concept of appreciable effect on competition, established by the Court in Case 5/69, *Volk v. Vervaecke*: [1969] E.C.R. 295.
[47] Case 40/73, *Suiker Unie v. Commission*: [1975] E.C.R. 1663; Case 127/73, *BRT v. SV SABAM*: [1974] E.C.R. 313.
[48] See Schodermaier, "Collective Dominance Revisited" in [1990] 1 E.C.L.R. 29.
[49] [1975] E.C.R. 1663.
[50] Case 66/86, *Ahmed Saeed v. Zentrale zur Bekampfung vor unlauternem*: 4 C.M.L.R. 102.
[51] See Case 172/80, *Zuchner v. Bayerische Vereinsbank*: [1981] E.C.R. 2031.
[52] See Case 85/76, *Hoffman-La Roche v. Commission*: [1979] E.C.R. 461.

Articles, effective competition is to be preserved, but the level of competition which is threatened under each of them is different. Under Article 86, competition is already reduced, as a result of the operation of the dominant firm. An agreement, decision or a concerted practice between undertakings threatens to restrict, distort, or prevent a broader level of competition in the relevant market.

It follows from the foregoing argument that the position taken by the Commission in the *Flat Glass* case is not entirely convincing. It remains to be seen what the Court will decide on this case.[53] However, enterprises linked by a cartel agreement are not at the same time an entity exerting collective market dominance; therefore, the idea of a structural link between enterprises being the decisive element of joint dominance should be refuted.[54]

On the other hand, in the *Magill* decision, the Commission introduced new elements in the concept of collective dominance. In this case the Commission put the emphasis on the fact that the dominating enterprises did not compete with each other and that third parties therefore found themselves in a position of economic dependence.[55] It should be borne in mind that in the early 1970s the Commission adopted the theory of mutual interdependence as an instrument to understand the operation of oligopolies. It has given a practical expression to these thoughts in its *ABG* decision[56] and in the *Alsatel* case.[57] These cases are of fundamental importance in understanding the Commission's approach to oligopoly control. In the former, the Commission held that the parallel behaviour of enterprises must be the decisive element of collective market dominance, whereas in the latter case, its pleadings relied mainly on the fact that the oligopolists concerned had acted in a parallel manner, although a conspiracy between them could not be found.

Therefore, since the *Alsatel* case, the Commission's approach to collective dominance in oligopolistic markets was based on the mutual interdependence theory regarding the mere oligopolistic parallelism as an indication and sufficient evidence of collective dominance. That approach was purely structural, taking into account the very existence of the oligopoly. The concept of dominance was based on the equating of it with an absence of effective competition and the test concerned the ability of the firm(s) to act independently of competitors, customers and consumers, and having the power to exercise an appreciable influence on conditions under which effective competition would develop.[58]

At the same time (during the 1970s), the Court was reluctant to accept the Commission's argument. Although it never spelled out a

---

[53] Case 75/89, *SIV v. E.C. Commission*.
[54] Schodermeier, *op.cit.* at n. 48, p. 29.
[55] [1989] O.J. L78/48, No. 22.
[56] [1977] O.J. L117/1.
[57] Case 247/86, *Alsatel v. Novasam*.
[58] See Cases *Hoffman-La Roche* op. cit. at n. 52, *United Brands Co. and United Brands Continental v. E.C. Commission* (27/76), [1978] E.C.R. 207, *Michelin, op. cit.* at n. 36.

positive definition of joint market dominance, it at least spotlighted the situations where joint market dominance does not exist. In two cases, *Hoffman-La Roche* and the *Suiker Unie*, it did not accept the theory of mutual interdependence and rejected the Commission's arguments that parallelism between undertakings is an indication and sufficient evidence of abusive dominance. It held that the parallel behaviour of oligopolists cannot suffice to put them into a collective dominant position and that EEC competition law does not prevent enterprises from adapting intelligently to the behaviour of their competitors.[59]

This hesitation by the Court to appreciate the theory of oligopolistic interdependence forced the Commission to adopt a new line. This new line was expressed in the *Magill TV Guide* decision and it introduced new elements in the development of the concept of collective dominance.

The starting point is, of course, the mutual interdependence theory. Parallelism in oligopolistic markets is almost the rule and it is accepted that it is the basis of an oligopoly. This parallel behaviour is an economic evidence and by no means should it be transformed into a legal evidence in order to condemn an oligopoly. Thus, further conditions must be met in order for the concept of collective dominance to fulfil the requirements laid down in Article 86 EEC.

It should be mentioned that an attempt to introduce such new elements was made in the *ABG* decision, where the parallel behaviour of the big and fully integrated oil companies as to their refusal to supply ABG, was regarded by the Commission as a discrimination against ABG. Thus, collective dominance might occur when oligopolists perform their parallelism abusively. In the writer's opinion, this approach was founded on an unsound basis. The reason is that the definition of the concept of dominance and collective dominance should derive from the market structure, thus being quantitatively or qualitatively calibrated to market share. If one introduces performance tests (discrimination as an expression of abuse) in order to define dominance,[60] then what would be the test for condemning this dominance? Performance tests must be used to define the abuse of a dominant position.

The Commission in its *Magill* decision[61] did introduce two new structural elements in order to define the concept of collective dominance. Of course, the parallel behaviour of oligopolists constitutes the basis of collective market dominance, but two other findings complete it: (i) that in the relevant market no competition between oligopolists exists and (ii) that potential customers find themselves in a position of economic dependence *vis-à-vis* the oligopolists.

The absence or the reduction of competition between oligopolists requires further analysis. As mentioned above, in oligopolistic markets price competition is minimal, even non-existent. The reason is that the

---

[59] [1975] E.C.R. 1942.
[60] Case 322/81, *Michelin v. Commission*: [1983] E.C.R. 3461, where the Court said that dominance as such is not prohibited.
[61] [1989] O.J. L78/48, No. 22.

relevant product market is, in most cases, homogeneous, thus rendering demand substitutability very low. Homogeneous products in oligopolistic markets meet a price equilibrium which is determined by the oligopolistic market forces (no firm raises or decreases prices independently of its rivals). Therefore, from an economic point of view, price competition is lacking, but this finding is an inherent condition of oligopolies. The oligopolistic market is characterised by a strong tendency to uniformity and stability of prices. What remains is quality competition, innovation and advertising between oligopolists. This kind of competition can only lead to changes of market share within the group of oligopolists, but it cannot guarantee the effective protection of consumers, which is the most important role of competition between oligopolists.[62]

The element of "absence" or "restriction" of competition between oligopolists doesn't appear to be sufficient to support the finding of a collective dominant position in a market. Either reference to structural peculiarities concerning price differentiation (which is the exception in oligopolistic markets) should be made, or competition should be interpreted so broadly that the contours of the element become blurred.[63]

The second new element introduced by the Commission is the notion of dependence. When consumers find themselves in a position of economic dependence *vis-à-vis* the oligopolists, the latter acting in a parallel way, there is strong evidence that the relevant market is collectively dominated. Indeed, this finding was evident in the *Magill TV Guide* case, where BBC, ITV and RTE refused to supply Magill with their weekly programme listings. Magill was in a position of absolute economic dependence upon the former broadcasting companies, as he had no alternative sources of supply.[64]

In fact, the notion of dependence was mentioned by the Commission in the *ABG* decision,[65] where the latter could not find sufficient quantities of oil, as a result of the refusal of the oil companies to supply it. It was this economic dependence that rendered the reduced supply the character of discriminatory practice found under the framework of Article 86 EEC.

What is interesting in the *Magill* case, is the fact that the Commission perceived a dominant position in the case of each oligopolist *vis-à-vis* its customers, which had been abused. The product was homogeneous (TV listings) and the market had almost all the characteristics of a symmetric oligopoly (lack of price competition, barriers to entry by TV broadcasting licences). The case would have been different if, for example, the BBC or another company had unilaterally supplied Magill with its weekly TV listing. Under those circumstances, the relevant market would not have been collectively dominated, since not every oligopolist

---

[62] See Barre, *Economie Politique* (14 ed. 1985) Vol. 1, p. 633.
[63] Schodermeier, *op.cit.* at n. 48, p. 32.
[64] [1989] O.J. L78/48, No. 22.
[65] [1977] O.J. L117/1.

participated in the parallel conduct. In addition, Magill would not have been in absolute economic dependence *vis-à-vis* all oligopolists, since it could, at least, have published one TV guide. In other words, the non-existing demand substitutability would have become very low, but still price elasticity of demand would have been zero, as Magill could not publish a comprehensive weekly TV Guide. It is unclear if the other two companies could exercise a collective dominance in the market, but the crucial point would be their market shares.

It can be concluded from the above mentioned analysis of the element of dependence when assessing collective dominance, that the Commission (and the Court) should examine the degree of demand substitutability in the relevant market. If the product market is homogeneous and the oligopoly symmetric, then no considerable difficulties will arise. When substitutability of demand is very low or non-existent, as a result, mainly, of non-price competition, then the parallel conduct of the oligopolists concerned may constitute collective dominance. On the other hand, if the relevant market is asymmetric and the product itself not homogeneous, the degree of demand substitutability could not be aggregate, as there would be different products and the cross price elasticity of demand would show some movement. In this case, competition may occur and it would be difficult to construe a collective dominance exercised by all oligopolists. The two newly introduced elements in the *Magill* case seem to have added nothing to the evaluation test of dominance, where that collective dominance is to be assessed by applying the same test for the appraisal of dominance under Article 86. To put it another way, the tests of demand substitutability and cross price elasticity of demand will continue to be the decisive factors when the assessment of market dominance (single or collective) is an issue.

THE COMMUNITY'S APPROACH TO COLLECTIVE DOMINANCE

Modern anti-trust laws are faced with insurmountable difficulties in their attempt to control oligopolies, as existing structural remedies cannot deal sufficiently with oligopolistic concentration. These structural remedies aim at the control of market domination by one firm. Competition law attempts to strike at the phenomenon of legal or economic monopoly. In general, this could be seen as an indication of governmental intervention in the market. Policy makers, in their effort to secure a level of effective and workable competition, try to prevent market concentration.

Oligopolies cannot be defined legally; even their economic definition is not a scientific one. Whereas in economic theory one can describe precisely the attributes of monopoly on the one hand and perfect competition on the other, it is not possible to do this in the case of oligopoly. Indeed, there are considerable taxonomic problems in deciding what constitutes an oligopoly. Different concentration ratios reveal symmetric or asymmetric oligopolies, but the question which remains unanswered is how few firms should participate in a market in order for it to be defined as an oligopolistic one.

E.C. competition law does not expressly provide for the necessary instruments to control oligopolies. All it can do is to control collusive behaviour between oligopolists under Article 85(1) and on the other hand prevent a horizontal merger between them, which would result in excess market concentration. Interestingly, the new merger control Regulation 4064/89[66] is a purely structural instrument in that it indicates that dominance and its effects are to be examined from an impersonal perspective of competitive structure, rather than from a perspective of undertakings' ability to pursue a course of conduct insulated from competitive pressures.[67] The Commission, under Regulation 4064/89, may control oligopolies, but only those resulting from the merger.

On the other hand, Article 86 strikes at the abuse of dominance in a relevant market. It is a combination of a structural approach (dominance) under performance test (abuse). The case law of the Court has developed the concepts of "dominance" and "abuse" in relation to a single firm or more than one firm which belong to the same group or economic unit. Oligopolies are comprised of independent firms, none of which has a dominant position in the market. Article 86 cannot catch this situation. The development by the Commission of the concept of "collective dominance", in order to bring oligopolists under the framework of this provision, has not been accepted by the Court.

The practicality of application of Article 86, even with a well developed notion of "collective dominance", as an attempt to control oligopolies remains to be tested. Theoretical models of oligopolies are insufficiently convincing to warrant a major attack on oligopolistic markets; much seems to depend on how particular markets operate and many factors contribute to a failure of the competitive process. An approach to oligopoly that is based on the idea of abuse and threatens fines and actions before courts (domestic courts or the Court of Justice) appears inappropriate. The oligopolistic phenomenon requires a pragmatic approach and, in the writer's opinion, there are two alternatives: either to relax any control on oligopolies, following the recent American, less interventionist approach, or to introduce new instruments that could regulate oligopolistic markets. The United Kingdom's investigative system under the Fair Trading Act 1973 may be used as a good example, since it does not condemn but merely confers power to try to improve competitive conditions prospectively. The *lacuna* in E.C. competition law will perhaps become more evident in due course, as the Community moves towards the creation of a fully fledged common market. Market

[66] [1989] O.J. L395/1.
[67] For a detailed analysis of the control of concentrations through mergers, see Chap. 3, above.

concentration, as a prerequisite of efficiency, will create difficulties in controlling what is to be understood and defined as an oligopoly.

Anti-trust and distribution agreements

The problem of deciding of what is a prohibited and what is a permitted restriction of competition in respect to distribution agreements lies in the vertical character of them. In many cases a manufacturer will be unable to sell his goods at all unless he persuades a distributor to handle them. Building a market for the manufacturer may prove a costly and risky affair for the distributor, unless he is protected from competition by the manufacturer or from other distributors. In particular, the distributor will require protection from "free riders" who, after he has established the market, come into his territory and undercut him with cheaper products of the same brand obtained from other sources. In such a case, certain restrictions on *intra*-brand competition would be acceptable in order to promote more effective *inter*-brand competition.

Such a conclusion gives rise to a further dilemma. The protection sought by distributors may be a legitimate means of enhancing competition by enabling undertakings to enter new markets, but the protected territory allotted to them may partition geographical markets.[68] In particular, distributors may be able to maintain higher prices than those obtaining the same goods from elsewhere, since they are not exposed to competition from parallel imports of those goods originating from sources outside their territory.

The principle of exclusivity

Distribution agreements including exclusivity clauses may give rise to certain problems of competition policy. On the one hand, an exclusive distribution agreement normally prevents the supplier from appointing another distributor in a designated territory or selling in that territory himself, while the distributor undertakes not to sell competing products.[69] Apparently exclusive distribution agreements restrict not only the freedom of the parties involved, but they may have adverse effects on third parties, *e.g.* other distributors who wish to deal with the supplier. On the other hand, there are some considerations that appear to mitigate their anti-competitive effects. First, it is questionable whether competition is restricted if the supplier would not have been able to penetrate the market in the absence of the agreement, because the distributor would

---

[68] See Case 100/80, *Musique Diffusion Francaise v. Commission*: [1983] E.C.R. 1825.
[69] Exclusive distribution is to be distinguished from exclusive purchase agreements in that the former involves a specific territory allotted to the distributor, whereas the latter does not. See Reg. 1984/83 on exclusive purchasing agreements.

not have been prepared to enter into the agreement without the protection of exclusivity.[70] Secondly, exclusive distribution agreements bring a number of benefits: by appointing an exclusive distributor, the supplier avoids having to deal with a large number of traders and is able to intensify his sales efforts and rationalise his distribution, particularly in cases of inter-state trade.[71] Thirdly, inter-brand competition could be intensified by the existence of vertical agreements promoting sales of products; vertical agreements are considered to have pro-competitive effects[72] as constitutes the intermediary stage between production and consumption.

The principle of selectivity

Selective distribution systems are multiple vertical agreements between a supplier and appointed resellers who are forbidden from selling to anyone other than end users or other appointed resellers. Suppliers of sophisticated consumer products often limit the resale of their goods to a number of selected dealers, as they may wish to market them only through outlets that possess at least a minimum of technical expertise or through dealers that are prepared to undertake certain obligations, such as sales promotion, regular ordering or other kind of investment.

Selective distribution agreements may produce pro-competitive effects if the resellers are selected solely on the basis of non-discriminatory qualitative criteria relating to their technical ability to handle the goods and the suitability of their premises; qualitative criteria should be justified by reference to the nature of the product and reasonably necessary to ensure an adequate distribution of them. All suitably qualified resellers should be admitted to the system and the supplier should not obstruct parallel imports or exports.

The supplier in a selective distribution system, in order to entrust a number of selected distributors with the promotion and selling of his products, requires them to provide specialised personnel, sophisticated equipment, suitable trade premises, etc.—conditions that always presuppose a certain turnover. Inevitably, quantitative criteria are indirectly introduced in parallel with the qualitative ones. The supplier is often willing to assist the distributor in providing know-how, technical equipment patented or licensed in his name. The latter co-operation introduces elements of franchise agreements within the distribution system.

---

[70] See the cases before the European Court of Justice: Case 56/65, *Société Technique Miniere v. Maschinenbau Ulm*: [1966] E.C.R. 235 and Case 258/78, *Nungesser v. E.C. Commission*: [1982] E.C.R. 2015.

[71] See Reg. 1983/83, Recitals 5 to 7.

[72] See Case 161/84, *Pronuptia de Paris v. Schillgalis* (the leading case in franchise agreements) and the U.S. Department of Justice Vertical Restraints Guidelines in *Anti-trust and Trade Regulation Report* (1985) Vol 8.

Selectivity in distribution has a reciprocal effect in protecting both parties to the agreement.

Territorial protection in distribution agreements

Distribution agreements include provisions intended to ensure that the distributor will be the only person to market the contract products in the territory assigned to him. In fact, these provisions determine the geographical market of his activities. The means to achieve this aim is to impose export restrictions on other distributors of the same supplier; furthermore, in order to protect distributors in other areas similar restrictions are imposed upon the distributor himself. Further devices for achieving the same end are the exercise of trademark rights, pricing policies designed to make imports and exports between territories uneconomic or a refusal to honour the guarantee for parallel imported products. A distributor who is entirely protected from imports of contract products by third parties enjoys *absolute territorial protection*.[73] Antitrust is ill-disposed to distribution agreements that grant *absolute territorial protection*. "Open" exclusive dealing agreements allowing parallel imports are permitted, other things being compatible with the conditions laid down in Article 85(3). The same approach is followed for *qualified territorial protection* which prevents the distributor from seeking customers, advertising, establishing a branch or maintaining a distribution depot outside the designated territory.

One important aspect of the Community's policy on territoriality is the distinction which has been developed between "active" and "passive" sales. The former indicates the effort of an undertaking to seek customers and promote its sales outside a particular territory by advertising, or establishing distribution agreements with third parties.[74] The latter embraces mere responses to unsolicited orders from customers outside the allotted territory.

In general, the Community's anti-trust policy seeks to ensure that trade flow in the common market is not obstructed by agreements preventing parties from promoting their sales. With respect to exclusive distribution agreements (Regulation 1983/83)[75] and patent licences agreements (Regulation 2349/84),[76] the Commission is prepared to grant exemption to an agreement imposing restrictions on active sales, provided that parallel imports are not obstructed. Passive sales could not be subject to restrictions in a distribution agreement. By this compromise, Community anti-trust policy has preserved a limited degree of territorial protection for distributors, falling short of absolute territorial

---

[73] See Joined Cases 56 & 58/ 64, *Consten and Grundig v. E.C. Commission*: [1966] E.C.R. 299 (the leading cases in absolute territorial protection).
[74] See the Commission's Decision, *Mitchell Colts/Sofiltra*, [1987] O.J. L41/31.
[75] [1983] O.J. L173/1.
[76] [1984] O.J. L219.

protection. Territorial restrictions that prevent parallel imports will preclude an exemption under Article 85(3).

Selective and exclusive distribution agreements[77] under European Community law tend to link the contract territory allotted to a distributor with only that particular undertaking. The argument advanced for this regime is the promotion and enhancement of intra-brand competition, which will be diminished if competing products are promoted through the same undertaking.

The argument holds water only if the distributor/service and maintenance operator can be regarded as a continuation of the intra-structure of the industry. If exclusive or selective agreements combine promotion and service/maintenance activities, then they could be considered as an indispensable stage of the automobile industry and the exclusive link between manufacturers and dealers could be an essential condition for the acquisition of the distribution contract. This scheme, indeed, promotes inter-brand competition (competition between manufacturers), as the dealers have the authority to distribute products and sell them to the final consumer and at the same time provide service and maintenance works. In fact, the dealers substitute the manufacturer and compete alongside him with other manufacturers and their dealers.

If there is to be a separation between promotion and servicing activities, a link which is currently a condition for acquiring the distribution contract, then the restriction on a dealer not to hold different dealerships in the same contract territory should be abolished. The argument that it promotes inter-brand competition could not be substantiated. In fact, the link between sales and services could be considered as the only ground for obliging dealers not to conclude distribution agreements with competing manufacturers within the same contract territory. As service and maintenance facilities require skilled personnel, sophisticated equipment and the relevant premises for conducting the relevant operations, it would be extremely difficult for the same undertaking to hold competing dealerships within the same contract territory, as it would have to meet the qualitative criteria required by different manufacturers. The qualitative criteria required by manufacturers from dealers when combining promotion and servicing/maintenance activities are more complicated, as they constitute a cumulative requirement of marketing and maintenance criteria, with the relevant side effects on turnover. The combination of sales/services as a criterion for acquiring a dealership has already created undertakings with turnovers that could trigger the application of both domestic and Community anti-trust legislation on dominant position.

If the distribution agreements are to allow a distributor to hold several dealerships in the same contract territory, then, indirectly, they would have to require the raising of qualitative criteria to be met by the distributor, in order for competing manufacturers to entrust the latter with the promotion, service/maintenance of their products. It is obvious

---

[77] Regs. 17/62, 19/65, 1983/83, 1984/83, 123/85.

that the side effects of this increased multiple qualitative criteria pre-suppose huge turnovers. Thus, this regime would create space for more dominant undertakings and it would make the monitoring of them from anti-trust authorities more difficult. From a consumer point of view, this regime (several dealerships held by a distributor which combines service and maintenance activities) brings about a theoretical advantage: that of multiple choice and product market information. On the other hand, consumers are in the hands of dominant undertakings, which are prone to abuse their market dominance.

Consumer redress and legal protection

The distribution agreements covered by the Block Exemption Regula-tions provide limited judicial protection to aggrieved consumers. The reason is that they are regarded only as instruments granting exemption from Article 85(1) and (2), although as a directly applicable and directly effective Community legal instrument, they avail individuals of the opportunity to rely upon their provisions before domestic courts. Even in this case, only the parties to a distribution agreement (the dealer and the manufacturer) can rely upon its provisions before national courts.

Aggrieved consumers, as third parties, have no *locus standi* under the regulation either at Community *forum* or at domestic *fora*. Theoretically speaking, they could initiate the fine proceedings under Regulation 17/62, by having recourse to Article 3 of that regulation (complaints procedure). Also, if a distributor/dealer refuses to supply a vehicle to a consumer, this behaviour could constitute abuse of dominance, provided that its market share is high. The consumer could complain to the Commission, which has the exclusive authority and discretion to initiate proceedings before the European Court of Justice, to waive the exemp-tion of the particular distribution agreement from Article 85(1) and (2) and impose fines on the undertakings that violate Community law.

The situation is identical at domestic level. National anti-trust author-ities preclude consumers/third parties from having recourse to remedies before courts or administrative authorities, on the grounds that they lack the required legal interest and do not have *locus standi*. Generally speak-ing, anti-trust law is bi-partite in its application and enforcement. It embraces on the one hand the parties to a cartel agreement or a domi-nant firm and on the other hand the competent anti-trust authorities (E.C. Commission or domestic authorities).

Chapter 5

Doing business with the public sector

GENERAL REMARKS

Public procurement can best be defined as the range of purchasing activities by the state and its authorities in pursuit of public interest. It embraces contractual relationships with the private sector in procuring supplies, construction works and services. Recently, public utilities have been included in the scheme. The stakes behind the regulation of public procurement and the integration of public markets in the European Union appear so high that the whole issue became a priority overnight. The magnitude of public procurement in the Europe of 12 has been estimated at ECU 560 billion, an approximate 15 per cent of the Community's G.D.P.[1] These figures were based on 1988 prices. The reader should not be surprised if the figures approach ECU 750 billion at 1996 prices, with the latest enlargement taken into account. In real terms, public procurement represents a significant amount of the Member States' G.D.P., a fact that has been seen as very important by European institutions. Given the level of infrastructure and the amount spent on it every financial year by contracting authorities of the Member States, the public sector has acquired a significant dimension within the European integration process and the need to regulate it with a view to eliminating market distortions has become urgent.

THE LEGISLATIVE FRAMEWORK OF PUBLIC PROCUREMENT

The Treaty of Rome and its amending Maastricht Treaty on European Union do not contain explicit provisions on public procurement. However, there is no doubt that provisions on non-discrimination (Article 7), on the prohibition of barriers to intra-community trade (Article 30 *et seq.*), on the freedom to provide services (Articles 52, 53) and on the right of establishment (Articles 59, 60), on public undertakings and undertakings to which Member States grant special or exclusive rights

---

[1] Commission of the European Communities, *The Cost of Non-Europe, Basic Findings*, Vol.5, Part.A; *The Cost of Non-Europe in Public Sector Procurement*, (Luxembourg, 1988).

and state monopolies providing services of general economic interest (Article 90), can be applied in order to regulate government purchases and combat discriminatory procurement practices in the Member States. Nevertheless, the diversity of public law systems in the European Union and the peculiarities in existing domestic public procurement rules, would have rendered the regulation of public markets ineffective, if recourse only to primary Community legislation was sought.

In order to regulate public markets, Community institutions have opted for directives, since they are legal instruments which take into account existing national sensibilities and particularities in Member States' legal orders. European directives are flexible legal instruments not only because they leave the choice of the form and methods of their implementation in the hands of Member States, but they also provide for a period within which the latter should implement their provisions. A directive has binding force with respect to the result to be achieved for each Member State to which it is addressed. The fact that the form and methods of its implementation are left to the discretion of the addressee Member States, reveals the unique character of such legal instruments, for which there is no parallel in national or international law.[2]

The public procurement regime can be classified into the public supplies sector,[3] the public works sector,[4] the public utilities sector[5] and the public services sector.[6] The principal objective of all public procurement directives relies on the assumption that transparency and improved market information should enhance market efficiency by ensuring that conditions of competition are not distorted and that contracts are allocated to suppliers and contractors under the conditions which are most favourable for the contracting authorities. The directives are based on three underlying fundamental principles: Community-wide advertising of public contracts above certain thresholds; prohibition of technical specifications capable of discriminating against potential bidders; and application of objective criteria of participation in tendering and award procedures.

The public supplies regime

The transitional period[7] witnessed the first attempts to regulate the public procurement sector. For the purpose of giving guidance to Community Institutions and Member States in the implementation of Articles 52, 53 and 59, 60, in 1962 the Council of Ministers adopted two

---

[2] See Kapteyn and Verloren van Themaat, *Introduction to the Law of the European Communities*, (3rd ed., 1989), pp. 331 *et seq.*
[3] EEC Directive 70/32, 77/62 as amended by Directive 80/767 and 88/295 and consolidated by Directive 93/36, [1993] O.J. L199.
[4] EEC Directive 71/304, 71/305 as amended by Directive 89/440, and consolidated by Directive 93/37, [1993] O.J. L199.
[5] EEC Directive 90/531, as amended by Directive 93/38, [1993] O.J. L199.
[6] EEC Directive 92/50, [1992] O.J. L209.
[7] The period from the establishment of the European Communities until 31/12/1969. See Art. 8(7).

Programmes Generales[8] for the elimination of existing restrictions on interstate trade. Among the restrictions to be abolished were rules and practices of Member States, with respect to foreigners only, which "[e]xclude, limit or impose conditions upon the capacity to submit offers or to participate as main contractors or subcontractors in contract awards by the State or legal persons governed by public law". Both *Programmes* envisaged a gradual and balanced removal of restrictions based on quotas and the co-ordination of national procedures for the award of public contracts to nationals of other Member States through agencies or branches or directly to persons or undertakings established in other member states.

With respect to the prohibition of quotas and measures having an effect equivalent to quantitative restrictions, the Commission in 1966 introduced Directive 66/683[9] requiring the elimination of measures prohibiting the use of imported products or prescribing that of domestic products, thus favouring them. However, public supplies contracts were exempted pending the adoption of a specific directive. Four years later, in 1970 the Commission introduced Directive 70/32[10] on the basis of Article 33(7) EEC, applying the prohibition of measures having an equivalent effect to public procurement. This directive applied to all products of whatever description which were admitted to free circulation within the Community by virtue of Articles 9 and 10. These were products originating in a Member State and third country products admitted to free circulation in a Member State. It indicated two barriers posed by the state, its territorial authorities or other public corporate bodies, upon procurement of public supplies (Articles 3(1) and 3(2), as well as the preamble)—those preventing or inhibiting the supply of imported products and those favouring the supply of domestic products or granting preferential treatment (other than state aids which must be assessed under the framework of Article 92 and taxation) to domestic suppliers. In addition, the directive (Article 3(3)) listed a number of forms of discrimination against foreign goods. Among those were technical specifications, which though applicable to both domestic and imported products, had restrictive effects on trade. The *ratione* and the aim behind it was the same with that of Directive 66/683, but the very first Community instrument to regulate public supplies contracts (Directive 70/32) came into force when the transitional period had virtually expired, thus rendering Article 30 directly effective. One might question the logic behind that decision.

A possible answer could be that having Article 30 directly effective, after the elapse of the transitional period, the whole directive would have been better implemented into national legal orders; thus Article 30 could have served as a yardstick for its incorporation by Member States. On the other hand, this delay on the part of the Community in adopting an

---

[8] [1962] J.O. 36 and [1962] J.O. 32.
[9] [1966] J.O. 37.
[10] [1970] J.O. L13/1.

instrument regulating public supplies, revealed a highly complicated and sensitive regime that was related not only to the free movement of goods, but expanded further covering aspects in the field of competition and common commercial policy. The most difficult obstacle appeared to be the regulation, under the same legal instrument, of intra-territorial and extra-territorial aspects of the principle of free movement of goods with reference to public supplies. The expiry of the transitional period helped the Communities as to the former; having established direct effectiveness of Article 30, within the common market, the effort was focused on the latter, and that was the extra-territorial application of Community law in respect to public supplies.

In 1977, the Council adopted Directive 77/62[11] pursuant to Articles 30 and 100 EEC, concerning the co-ordination of procedures for the award of public supply contracts. This instrument, which came into force in 1978, was designed to ensure a more effective supervision of compliance with the negative obligations of Article 30 and Directive 70/32 by means of the imposition of a number of positive obligations on purchasing bodies (Article 1(b): contracting authorities specified in Annex I).

The imposition of a positive obligation on a Member State by a directive reveals that a margin of appreciation as to the forms and methods of the result to be achieved is allotted to it. Of course, there is no doubt that directives are binding only with respect to the result to be achieved,[12] thus requiring Member States to opt for the appropriate methods and forms to implement their provisions into domestic law, but the fact that a directive imposes a positive obligation may affect the direct effectiveness of its provisions, in case of wrongful or non implementation. Positive obligations, in contrast to negative ones, allot to Member States a greater margin of discretion. Member States should abstain from action that hinders a Community aim, but, in addition, they must take all the appropriate measures to enhance the function and operation of that aim. A positive obligation seems to contain two subsequent requirements: that of abstention and that of introduction of further measures to secure the results of the former.

With respect to direct effectiveness of provisions of directives imposing positive obligations on Member States, initially the Court was reluctant[13] to accept that the margin of appreciation derived from a positive obligation was capable of rendering the provision in question directly effective. Interestingly, in two cases[14] it ruled that even positive obligations contained in a directive may produce direct effect, but the situation is far from clear.

---

[11] [1977] O.J. L13/1.
[12] Art. 189 EEC Treaty.
[13] See Case 57/65, *Alfons Luttucke v. Hauptzollampt Saarlouis*: [1973] E.C.R. 57.
[14] Case 28/67, *Molkerei-Zentrale Westfalen/Lippe GmbH v. Haupzollampt Pederborn*: [1968] E.C.R. 143; Case 13/68, *SpA Salgoil v. Italian Ministry for Foreign Trade*: [1968] E.C.R. 453.

The fact that Directive 77/62 imposed a number of positive obligations on Member States raised a number of questions as to the direct effectiveness of its provisions. The aim of the directive was that transparency and improved market information should enhance market efficiency by ensuring that conditions of competition were not distorted and that contracts were allocated to suppliers and contractors under the most favourable conditions for the contracting authorities. The co-ordination was based on three basic principles: (1) Community-wide advertising of contracts; (2) prohibition of technical specifications capable of discriminating against potential bidders; and (3) application of objective criteria of participation in tendering and award procedures. However, the scope of the directive was rather limited. It excluded public supplies contracts by transport authorities, the production, distribution and transmission of transport services for water or energy and telecommunications services. Apparently the main legal reason for that exclusion was that these entities had different legal statuses and operated under different regimes in Member States. Some of them were completely covered by public law, others governed by private law, while some were in the process of privatisation, although the essential control remained in the hands of the State. On the other hand, it could be argued that this was not a valid argument, since the instruments employed for the regulation of these sort of entities were directives, which implement Community envisaged standards into national law, taking into account existing national sensibilities. It appears that the regulation of the public utilities in respect to their purchasing had been rather premature for the time.

Directive 77/62 contained a sort of *de minimis* rule; it was applicable only to public supply contracts estimated net of VAT 200,000 EUA (European Unit of Account) plus.[15] Its legal basis (Articles 30 and 100 EEC) rendered it inapplicable to products originating in and supplied by third countries. The directive was also inapplicable to public supplies contracts awarded pursuant to

(i) an international agreement between a Member Sate and one or more non-Member countries;

(ii) an international agreement relating to the stationing of troops between undertakings in a Member State or a non-Member country; and

(iii) a particular procedure of an international agreement.[16]

In 1980 Directive 77/62 was amended by Directive 80/767[17] in order to take account of the 1979 GATT agreement on government procurement.[18] The agreement committed the Community to grant to suppliers

---

[15] Art. 5(1)(a) Directive 77/62.
[16] This may be the case of supplies under ECSC and Euratom Treaties.
[17] [1980] O.J. L215/1.
[18] [1980] O.J. L75/1.

from third countries better access, through the application of lower thresholds, to central government purchasing and to some defence procurement, than suppliers from the Community enjoyed under Directive 77/62. That agreement became part of Community law as it was approved by Council Decision 80/271.[19]

In 1984 the Commission's communication to the Council on Public Supply Contracts[20] revealed an unsatisfactory situation with respect to the implementation of the supplies directives in the legal orders of Member States. The list of factors responsible for the lack of success includes *inter alia*:

— failure to advertise contracts in the Official Journal, as a result of splitting up of contracts, although improvements had been made in the retrieval of information as the result of the establishment of the Data Bank TED (Tenders Electronic Daily)[21];

— ignorance of the relevant rules on the part of contracting authorities or deliberate omission of these rules;

— excessive use of the exceptions permitting non-competitive tendering (negotiated procedures) instead of open or restricted procedures;

— discriminatory requirements posed by contracting authorities by means of compliance with national technical standards, to the exclusion of European standards or equivalent standards of other countries.

— unlawful disqualification of suppliers or contractors or discriminatory use of the award criteria.

The Commission's White Paper on the completion of the internal market[22] reiterated that there was a serious and urgent need for improvement and elaboration of the relevant public procurement directives. In accordance with the Commission's action programme, the Council in 1988 adopted Directive 88/295[23] amending all previous supplies directives. The main improvements are:

— with open tendering procedures as the norm, negotiated ones were allowed in exceptional circumstances[24];

---

[19] [1980] O.J. L215/1.
[20] Com. (84) 717 final.
[21] It is anticipated that Directive 83/189, [1983] O.J. L165/1, enacted in order to assist suppliers to fulfil the requirements of norms and standards referred to in Directive 77/62 will help to eliminate discrimination arising through their use.
[22] Com. (85) 310 final.
[23] [1988] O.J. L127/1.
[24] Art. 7(2) of Directive 88/295.

— the definition of the types of supplies contracts was widened[25] and the method of calculation of the thresholds was clarified[26];

— the exempted sectors were more strictly defined[27];

— purchasing authorities had to publish in advance information on their annual procurement programmes and their timetable, as well as a notice giving details of the outcome of each decision of award.[28]

— the rules on technical standards were brought in line with the new policy on standards which is based on the mutual recognition of national requirements, where the objectives of national legislation are essentially equivalent, and on the process of legislative harmonisation of technical standards through non-governmental standardisation organisations (CEPT, CEN, CENELEC).[29]

In an attempt to consolidate all previous legislation relating to public supplies and align it in conformity with the relevant directives on public works[30] and public services[31] and the utilities sector,[32] Directive 93/36[33] was adopted in June 1993. The consolidated directives aim at introducing a similar procedural regime in their relevant sectors and at enhancing the clarity of some of the previously existing provisions.[34]

The public works regime

The two general programmes adopted by the Council for the purpose of guiding the Community institutions in the implementation of the provisions of Articles 52, 53, 59 and 62, took account of the special features of public works contracts. A gradual and balanced removal of restrictions based on quotas and the co-ordination of national procedures for awarding public works contracts to nationals of other Member States were the main aims envisaged therein.

The issue of public sector activities related to construction contracts after the transitional period was addressed by Directive 71/304,[35] which required Member States to abolish restrictions on participation of non-

---

[25] Art. 1(a) of Directive 88/295.
[26] Art. 6(1)(c) of Directive 88/295.
[27] Art. 3(2)(a)(b)(c) of Directive 88/295.
[28] Art. 9 of Directive 88/295.
[29] Art. 7 of Directive 88/295. See the White Paper *Completing the Internal Market*, paras. 61–79; also Council Resolution of May 7, 1985, [1985] O.J. C136, on a new approach in the field of technical harmonisation and standards.
[30] Directive 93/37, [1993] O.J. L199.
[31] Directive 92/50, [1992] O.J. L209.
[32] Directive 93/38, [1993] O.J. L199.
[33] Directive 93/36, [1993] O.J. L199.
[34] See Birkinshaw and Bovis *Public Procurement: Legislation and Commentary* (1992).
[35] [1971] O.J. L185/1.

nationals in public procurement contracts. However, it came into force after the completion of the transitional period, when Articles 59 and 60 concerning the freedom to provide services became directly effective, thus leaving few aspects to be implemented by Member States. It now serves mainly to list professional trade activities which constitute public works.

The aims envisaged in Articles 52 *et seq.* on the right of establishment and Articles 59 *et seq.* on the freedom to provide services were further enhanced by the adoption of Directive 71/305,[36] which was the primary vehicle for the opening up of the public works contracts. Based on the prohibition of discriminatory technical specifications, adequate advertising of contracts, the fixing of objective participation criteria and a joint supervision procedure both by Member States' authorities and the E.C. Commission to ensure observation of these principles,[37] it sought the co-ordination of national procedures in the award of public works contracts. The directive's major objective was the establishment and enhancement of a transparency regime in the public works sector, where conditions of undistorted competition would ensure that contracts were allocated to contractors under the most favourable terms for the contracting authorities. Like the supplies Directive 77/62, Directive 71/305 had a limited aim. It did not introduce new tendering procedures nor were existing national procedures and practices replaced by a set of Community rules. Member States remained free to maintain or adopt substantive and procedural rules on condition that they comply with all the relevant provisions of Community law and in particular, the prohibitions following from the principles laid down in the Treaty in regard to the right of establishment and the freedom to provide services.[38]

The concept of contract under the first works directive was very extensive[39] and covers those contracts concluded in writing between a contractor and a contracting authority for pecuniary interest concerning either the execution or both the execution and design of works related to building or civil engineering activities listed in class 50 of the NACE Classification,[40] or the execution by whatever means of a work corresponding to the requirements specified by the contracting authority. The above formula was wide enough to embrace modern forms of contract such as project developing contracts, management contracts and concession contracts.[41] The initial works Directive 71/305 did not apply to concession contracts, except where the concessionaire was a public

---

[36] [1971] O.J. L185/5.

[37] See the preamble of Directive 71/305.

[38] See Joined Cases 27–29/86, *CEI v. Bellini*: [1987] E.C.R. 3347.

[39] Art. 1(a) of Directive 71/305 as amended by Directive 89/440.

[40] General Industrial Classification of Economic Activities within the European Communities, see Annex II Directive 71/305.

[41] Concession contracts are public works projects under which the consideration for the works consist in a franchise (concession) to operate the completed works or in a franchise plus payment. For more details see the *Guide to the Community Rules on Opening Government Procurement*, [1987] O.J. L358/1 at 28.

authority covered by the directive. In such a situation, the works subcontracted to third parties would be fully subject to its provisions. In any other case, the only provisions of the directive were that the concessionaire should not discriminate on grounds of nationality when it awarded contracts to third parties itself.[42] The regulation of concession contracts was introduced almost two decades later by Directive 89/440, amending Directive 71/305. In fact, it incorporated the Voluntary Code of Practice, which was adopted by the representatives of Member States meeting within the Council in 1971.[43] The code was a non-binding instrument and contained rules on the advertising of contracts and the principle that contracting authorities awarding the principal contract to a concessionaire were to require them to subcontract to third parties at least 30 per cent of the total work provided for by the principal contract. Obviously, these requirements could not easily be incorporated in a binding instrument such as Directive 89/440; thus a relaxation of Member States' commitments occurs therein. As a result, the co-ordination rules of the latter apply to concession contracts only in respect of advertising. The directive's rules on tendering procedures, suitability criteria and award procedures and technical specifications were inapplicable. Interestingly, Article 3(3) of Directive 71/305 on the prohibition of discrimination on grounds of nationality by a concessionaire awarding subcontracts has disappeared from the text of the amending Directive 89/440. The reason could be that by the end of the transitional period Articles 7, 48, 52, 59 and 119 were directly effective and in addition, their horizontal direct effect had been pronounced by the European Court of Justice.[44]

The definition of contractors comprised any legal or natural person involved in construction activities and for the purposes of the directive, the contracting authority might impose a requirement as to the form and legal status of the contractor that won the award.[45] As far as contracting authorities were concerned, their definition was very wide and covers bodies governed by public law which is defined as being any body "established for the specific purpose of meeting needs in the general interest and not having an industrial or commercial character, which has legal personality and is financed for the most part by the State or is subject to management supervision by the latter.[46] There is a list of such bodies in Annex I of Directive 71/305, which is not an exhaustive one like that in the supplies directive, and Member States were under an obligation to notify the Commission of any changes in that list.

---

[42] Art. 3(3) Directive 71/305.
[43] [1971] O.J. C82/13.
[44] See Case 36/74, *Walrave and Koch v. Association Union Cycliste Internationale*: [1974] E.C.R. 1405; Case 43/75, *Drefenne v. SABENA*: [1976] E.C.R. 455.
[45] Art. 21 of Directive 71/305 as amended. The same requirement is found also in the Supplies Directive (Art. 18 of Directive 77/62).
[46] This definition resembles the Court's ruling on state controlled enterprises in Case 152/84, *Marshall v. Southampton and South West Hampshire Area Health Authority*: [1986] E.C.R. 723.

Works contracts in the utilities and defence sectors and those awarded in pursuance of certain international agreements were explicitly excluded by virtue of Articles 4 and 5 of the directive. These provisions were identical in effect to the corresponding ones of the supplies directive.[47] This revealed the fact that public contracts under the framework of the works directive covered mainly construction projects in the education, health, sports and leisure facilities sectors, inasmuch as the State or regional or local authorities undertake such projects. In case the entities involved in this sort of activity (*e.g.* a hospital or a university) enjoyed considerable independence from the State or local government regarding the undertaking of works contracts, Directive 71/305 was inapplicable to them, since they were not included in its Annex I as bodies governed by public law for the purposes of the directive in question. This seems to have limited the scope of the directive only to cases where the State or local government had direct control over the above mentioned entities. Given the fact that works contracts in the utilities sectors were also excluded from the framework of the directive, its applicability covered a rather modest portion of the construction sector. In order to moderate this apparently undesirable result, the amending Directive 89/440[48] provides for an obligation upon Member States to ensure compliance with its provisions when they subsidise directly, by more than 50 per cent, a works contract awarded by an entity involved in activities relating to certain civil engineering works and to the building of hospitals, sports recreation and leisure facilities, school and university buildings and buildings used for administrative purposes. These conditions seem not to impose a heavy duty on Member States, as only direct subsidies trigger the applicability of the directive. Indirect ways of subsidising the entities in question, such as tax exemptions, guaranteed loans, or provision of land free of charge, render it inapplicable.

It should be noted that under both the original supplies and works directives, preference schemes in the award of contracts were allowed. Such schemes required the application of award criteria based on considerations other than the lowest price or the most economically advantageous tender, which are common in both regimes.[49] However, preferences could only be compatible with Community law in as much as they did not run contrary to the principle of free movement of goods (Article 30 *et seq.*) and to competition law considerations in respect of state aids.[50] Preference schemes have been abolished since the completion of the internal market at the end of 1992.

In 1993, the Council enacted a Directive with a view to consolidating all existing legislation in the field of public works. The consolidated

[47] Art. 3 of Directive 77/62 as amended by Directive 88/295.
[48] Art. 2 Directive 71/305 as amended by Directive 89/440.
[49] See Arts. 29(4) and 29(a) of Directive 71/305; also Art. 26 of Directive 77/62.
[50] See the Commission's communication *Regional and Social Aspects of Public Procurement*, where it gives an overview of the preference schemes still existing in Member States, Com.(89) 400 final.

Directive 93/37[51] has embraced all relevant Community legislation relating to public works with some minor amendments and clarifications of existing provisions of Directive 89/440.

The public utilities regime

As previously mentioned, both supplies and works contracts in the transport, water, energy and telecommunications sectors were excluded from the relevant supplies and works directives.[52] The exclusion of the above mentioned sectors from the framework of supplies directives (Directives 77/62 and 88/295) had been attributed to the fact that the authorities entrusted with the operation of public utilities had been subject to different legal status in Member States, varying from completely state controlled enterprises to privately controlled ones. With respect to works directives, the above justification appears valid, although the apparent connection between construction projects and the excluded sectors leads to the conclusion that Directives 71/305 and 89/440 have very limited application.

As far as supplies contracts were concerned, a convincing reason behind the exclusion of these sectors is that the projects covered therein could not fall within the thresholds of Directives 77/62 and 88/295. Energy, telecommunications, transport and, to a lesser extent, the water industry, are technical sectors requiring state-of-the-art technology (especially telecommunications and energy). The prices in the contracts are very high, in comparison with (simple) supplies ones, so the only way these sectors could be brought within Directive 77/62 would have been either to increase the thresholds (ECU 200,000) of the supplies contracts to such a level as to catch a substantial amount of contracts of the excluded sectors, or on the other hand, to lower the envisaged thresholds of contracts in telecommunications, energy, transport and water industry sectors[53] to the level of the (simple) supplies ones (ECU 200,000). Either option would have resulted in a very undesirable situation; if the first option was chosen, the bulk of supplies contracts would have escaped from the framework of Directive 77/62. On the other hand, squeezing the thresholds of the excluded sectors to ECU 200,000 would have eliminated the *de minimis* rule for those sectors. A *de minimis* rule is a *conditio sine qua non* where quantitative criteria for regulation of a sector are chosen.

With respect to works contracts, the exclusion of the telecommunications, transport, energy and water industry sectors from Directives 71/305 and 89/440 could be justified, rather, due to the different legal status of the entities in question in the Member States. If a privately controlled entity operating in the above sectors were to be involved in a

[51] Directive 93/37, [1993] O.J. L199.
[52] Art. 2 of Directive 77/62 as amended; Art. 3 of Directive 89/440.
[53] Art. 12 of Directive 90/531; ECU 400,000 for water, energy and transport supplies and ECU 600,000 for telecommunications supplies.

construction project, works directives would be inapplicable, as the former was not included among the contracting authorities specified in Annex I (bodies governed by public law). To cover both private and public controlled entities operating in the relevant utilities sectors, the works directives should have expanded the definition of contracting authorities; but this would have resulted in an internal disturbance of the operation of the directives, which are envisaged as regulating construction project awards exclusively by the state or local government or bodies governed by public law. Thus, the only viable and reasonable solution was to introduce a separate instrument, applying the same principles as those found in Directive 77/62, in order to regulate the transport, telecommunications, energy and water sectors.

The Commission was requested by the Council to follow the progress of the CEPT proceedings[54] on harmonisation in the field of telecommunications and to submit to the latter a timetable for measures ensuring effective competition in the field of supply contracts awarded for telecommunications services. The Commission, in its recommendations on telecommunications[55] also expressed its desire to ensure that the objective of an open market, in particular for suppliers within the Community, was being achieved without undesirable consequences for the pattern of Community trade with non-Member countries. In its 1984 communication to the Council on public supply contracts[56] and its White Paper on the completion of the internal market,[57] the Commission reiterated the need to liberalise the so far excluded sectors, particularly telecommunications.

The European Parliament's Committee on Economic and Monetary Affairs and Industrial Policy presented a report in the European Parliament[58] stressing the need for extension of the scope of the supplies directives to cover excluded sectors. In its resolution[59] the Parliament approved all the Commission's and Council's actions so far, and called on them to submit a proposal for a directive to govern the excluded sectors. The Council, in its Recommendation 84/550[60] shared the Commission's considerations as to the opening of access to public telecommunications contracts, providing that governments of Member States offer opportunities for Community undertakings to tender on a non-discriminatory basis for the supply of specified telecommunications equipment and should also report to the Commission on implementing measures and practical effects. In 1988 the Commission issued Directive

---

[54] CEPT is the European Conference of Postal and Telecommunications Administrations, established in Montreux in 1959 and aiming at closer relabetween member administrations to improve their administrative and technical services, [1977] O.J. C11/3.
[55] Com.(80) 422 final.
[56] Com.(84) 717 final.
[57] Com.(85) 310 final.
[58] See *von Wogau report*, DOC.A2–38/85.
[59] [1985] O.J. C 175/241.
[60] [1984] O.J. L289/51.

88/301[61] on competition in the markets in telecommunications terminal equipment.

Finally, in 1990 the Council adopted Directive 90/531[62] on the procurement procedures of entities operating in the water, energy, transport and telecommunications sectors. The regime imposed is rather similar to the supplies directives with some important differences as to the flexibility given to the contracting authorities over the choice of methods to be used to make the award process competitive.[63] The utilities directive has been amended by Directive 93/38,[64] which mainly incorporates the newly enacted public services Directive 92/50[65] into the utilities regime.

The legislative background of the utilities directive and the ordeal of the regulation of public utilities procurement justify the high complexity of the regime. The fact that public utilities often have an unclear legal status or their legal nature varies within the Member States' legal systems has obviously rendered it difficult to introduce a single legal instrument to regulate their purchasing, although such a prolonged delay should be attributed to other factors. It may be recalled that public utilities absorb the vast majority of high technology equipment designated to the public sector. Protectionism in strategic industrial sectors has been pursued through preferential purchasing with a view to either sustaining the relevant industries or to assisting the development of infant industries in Member States. The regulation of utilities purchasing not only had to overcome the significant legislative barriers accountable to their nature but also the abandoning of individual industrial policies of Member States through strategic procurement. In addition to these constraints, the fear of an uncontrolled flow of direct investment which would target vulnerable European-based high technology industries and the subsequent possible increase in takeovers and acquisitions, mainly from Japanese and American predators, poured cold water on the attempts of European Institutions to integrate the utilities procurement within the common market.

The utilities directive has been the most radical approach to the public sector integration in Europe and its enactment coincided with the envisaged international liberalisation of public procurement during the Uruguay GATT negotiations. One could question such a strategy by European institutions, particularly bearing in mind the vulnerability of Europe's high-tech industry in comparison to that in the U.S. and Japan. However, the GATT regime has introduced a new era in the sense that

---

[61] [1988] O.J. L131/73.
[62] [1990] O.J. L297.
[63] The directive provides different implementing periods for Spain, Greece and Portugal. Spain has to implement its provisions by January 1, 1996, Greece and Portugal by January 1, 1998. The delay in the uniform implementation of the utilities directive could be attributed to the preparations needed for the integration of the public utilities sectors in the respective countries.
[64] [1993] O.J. L199.
[65] [1992] O.J. L209.

highly protectionist countries like the U.S. and Japan must now abolish their "buy national" laws and policies and open, on a reciprocal basis, their public markets to international competition.

The ambit of the utilities directive and its field of application appear more complicated than those in the supplies and works directives, although the internal legal structure among the three directives is very similar. Articles 1 and 2 form the broad framework of the directive's application, by providing various definitions and the scope of some preliminary exemptions. The utilities directive devotes a substantial amount of provisions to an attempt to exempt from its application certain contracts or activities that have been deemed ineligible for community-wide regulation.

Apart from the normal exemptions under the grounds of defence, security and confidentiality, the major exemptions are provided for under Articles 1 and 2. Radio and television broadcasting have not been classified as telecommunication activities and have been specifically excluded from the ambit of the directive by virtue of Article 2. Also, bus transport services to the public are excluded on condition that their providers operate under a regime of competitive conditions, which means that other potential contractors or suppliers of similar services are allowed to enter the relevant geographical and product markets and compete against the existing utilities provider (Article 2 (4)). A similar rule applies to telecommunication services which operate within a competitive market.[66]

Under the same Article 2, special exemptions are also provided to private entities supplying gas, heat, drinking water and electricity. Although the wording and spirit of the directive covers private entities operating under exclusive and special rights in the utilities sectors, nevertheless, under certain conditions these entities can be exempted from the application of the rules of the directive. In the case of the production of drinking water and electricity, if a private entity is able to show that it does so for its own purposes, which are not related to the provision of drinking water or electricity to the public, it is exempt. Similarly, if a private entity is able to show that it supplies to the public network drinking water or electricity which is destined for its own consumption, and that the total so supplied to the network is not more than 30 per cent of the total produced by that network in any one year over a three year period, it is also exempt.[67]

In the case of gas and heat supplies, if the production by a private entity is related to an activity other than the supply to a network for public consumption, then these entities are also exempt. In the same way, if the supply of gas and heat by a private entity to a public network relates to economic exploitation only and does not exceed 20 per cent of the firm's turnover in any one year, taking an average of the preceding

---

[66] Art. 2(4) and Art. 8 of the utilities directive amended by Directive 93/38.
[67] Art. 2(5)(a) of the utilities directive amended by Directive 93/38.

three years and the current year, then such an entity is also exempt.[68] These exemptions predominantly cover entities which have research and development as their main objective in the relevant utilities sector, or do not play a major role in supplying public networks with water or energy.[69]

There are also exemptions for entities exploring for gas, oil, coal and other solid fuels under Article 3. Entities operating in these sectors will not be regarded as having an exclusive right provided that certain conditions are fulfilled. These conditions are cumulative and stipulate that, when an exploitation right is granted to the entity in question, the latter is exempt from the utilities directives provided that:

— other bodies are able to compete for the same exclusive rights under free competition;

— the financial and technical criteria to be used in awarding rights are clearly spelt out before the award is made;

— the objective criteria are specified as to the way in which exploitation is to be carried out;

— these criteria are published before requests for tenders are made and applied in a non-discriminatory way;

— all operating obligations, royalty and capital and revenue participation agreements are to be published in advance; and finally,

— contracting authorities are not required to provide information on their intentions about procurement except at the request of national authorities.[70]

Furthermore, Member States have to ensure that these exempted bodies apply, at least, the principles of non-discrimination and competition. They are obliged to provide on request a report to the E.C. about such contracts. However, this requirement is less stringent than the mandatory reporting rules in the supply and works directives. It should be mentioned that the utilities directive does not apply to concession contracts granted to entities operating in utilities sectors prior to the coming into force of the directive. All exemption provisions within the utilities directive are subject to assessment in the light of the four year overall review of the process.[71]

Other exemptions cover entities in the relevant sectors which can demonstrate that their service and network associated contracts are not

---

[68] Art. 2(5)(b) of the utilities directive amended by Directive 93/38.

[69] see O'Loan, "Implementation of Directive 90/531 and Directive 92/50 in the United Kingdom", [1993] 2 *Public Procurement Law Review* 29. Also, Cox, *Public Procurement in the European Community: The single market rules and the enforcement regime after 1992* [1993] 2 P.P.L.R.

[70] Art. 3(1) of the utilities directive amended by Directive 93/38.

[71] Art. 3(2) to (4) of the utilities directive amended by Directive 93/38.

related to the specific supply and works functions specified in the Directive, or if they are related, that they take place in a non-Member State and they are not using a European public network or physical area.[72] The Member States are under an obligation to inform the European Commission, on request, of the cases when these exemptions have been allowed. There are also provisions which allow for resale and hire contracts to third parties to be exempt when the awarding body does not possess an exclusive or special right to hire or sell the subject of the contract, and there is already competition in the market from other suppliers or producers to provide the commodity or service to third parties.[73] Similar relaxed reporting and monitoring requirements are found in Article 8, which applies to telecommunication exemptions.[74]

Another set of significant exemptions is provided for water authorities under Article 9. Under this provision water authorities specified in Annex I are specifically exempt from the rules when they purchase water. They are however covered by the Directive when they purchase other supply and construction products.[75] Similarly, there are specific exemptions for the electricity, gas and heat, oil and gas and coal and other solid fuels entities outlined in Annex II, III, IV and V, but only when they award contracts for the supply of energy or for fuels for the production of energy. For all other relevant contracts these bodies are included in the rules. These exemptions were provided because of the need to allow contracting authorities to buy from local sources of supply, which may not always be the cheapest, but which are important on the basis of regional development policies or environmental grounds, and because these purchases are central to the entities' operations and not part of normal supply and works procurement process.[76]

Finally, specific exemptions under the utilities directive provide for those carriers of passengers and providers of transport services by air and by sea. In the preamble of the directive it is stated that, under a series of measures adopted in 1987 with a view to introducing more competition between firms providing public air services, it was decided to exempt such carriers from the scope of the legislation. Similarly, because shipping has been subject to severe competitive pressures, it was decided to exempt certain types of contracts from the Directive.[77]

The utilities directive intends to open up procurement practices in the four previously excluded sectors mainly to E.C.-wide competition. With respect to goods (and services) originating in third countries, things are more complicated. A product outside the Community, in order to be

---

[72] Art. 6(1) of the utilities directive amended by Directive 93/38.

[73] Art. 7(2) of the utilities directive amended by Directive 93/38.

[74] Art. 8(2) of the utilities directive amended by Directive 93/38.

[75] Art. 9(1) (a) of the utilities directive amended by Directive 93/38.

[76] It has been considered that these exemptions might be the appropriate framework to introduce a common energy policy.

[77] In the future sea ferry operators would be excluded, but their position has been kept under review. Inland water ferry services and river ferry services operated by public authorities were to be brought within the rules.

subject to a public contract regulated by one of the E.C. public procurement directives, must lawfully be put in free circulation in at least one Member State.[78] Except where there has been an international agreement which grants comparable and effective access for Community undertakings to public markets of a third country (reciprocity principle), Article 29 renders it possible for European contracting authorities in the utilities sector to reject offers from outside the Community and requires Community preference where Community offers are equivalent to offers from third countries (where the price difference does not exceed 3 per cent). With reference to international agreements granting access to public markets, the utilities directive opens the door for the application of the GATT agreement on government procurement in the utilities sector.

The public services regime

Whilst the liberalisation of trade, as envisaged in international agreements such as GATT or in supranational organisations such as the European Communities, primarily embraces the free movement of goods, provisions regulating the provision of services are often described as inadequate. Modern economies have witnessed a shift in trade patterns from product manufacturing industries to markets where the provision of services is the predominant sector of the industry. The lack of regulation of services at a global level has given rise to economic controversies. Trade wars have been taking place and the international legal community currently attempts to adopt measures towards regulation of trade in services within the context of the GATT Uruguay round of multilateral trade negotiations.

In line with the above considerations European institutions enacted Directive 92/50,[79] on the award procedures relating to public services contracts, attempts to pave the way for liberalisation of services in public markets. The directive follows the same principles as the rest of the Community's legislation on public procurement, that is, compulsory Community-wide advertising of public contracts, prohibition of technical specification capable of discriminating against potential bidders and uniform application of objective criteria of participation in tendering and award procedures. The services directive has introduced a special type of award procedure, namely *design contests,* with reference to planning projects. According to Article 1 (g), *design contests* are those national procedures which enable the contracting authority to acquire in the fields of area planning, town planning, architecture and civil engineering, a plan

---

[78] For the concept of origin of goods and their lawful free circulation in the Common Market see Regulation 802/68, [1968] O.J. Spec. Ed. 165.
[79] [1992] O.J. L209.

or a design selected by a jury, after being put out to competition with or without the award of prizes.

Under the services directive, public services contracts are contracts which have as their object the provision of services classified in the Common Product Classification (CPC) nomenclature of the United Nations, as a nomenclature for Classification of Services at Community level is lacking. The United Nations Common Product Classification covers almost every conceivable service an undertaking may provide, although the services description is rather plain.

The services directive is the first legal instrument which attempts to open the increasingly important public services sector to intra-community competition. It should be mentioned that the directives on public supplies, public works and utilities contain provisions where the provision of services is regarded as ancillary to the main contract under their regime, provided the value of the services is less than the value of the supplies or works. Such services are covered by the relevant directive.

Specific services contracts are excluded from the scope of the services directive. It should be mentioned that not all of these specific exclusions are listed in the amended utilities Directive 93/38, because they would not, in any event, fall within the ambit of a defined activity. Apart from those contracts which are covered by the relevant provisions of the works, supplies and utilities directives, and therefore not considered as services, the other contracts excluded from the services directive and amended utilities Directive 93/38 are:

(i) contracts for the acquisition or rental, by whatever financial means, of land, existing buildings, or other immovable property or concerning rights thereon. However, financial service contracts concluded at the same time as, before or after the contract of acquisition or rental, in whatever form, will be subject to the directive;

(ii) contracts for the acquisition, development, production or co-production of programme material by broadcasters and contracts for broadcasting time[80];

(iii) contracts for voice telephony, telex, radiotelephony, paging and satellite services[81];

(iv) contracts for arbitration and conciliation services;

---

[80] This includes the purchase of, on the one hand, services producing audio-visual works such as films, videos and sound recording, including advertising and, on the other hand broadcasting time (transmission by air, satellite or cable). In principle, these services would be covered but are given derogations in so far as they are connected with broadcasting activities; see Armin-Trepte, *Public procurement in the EC* (1993), p. 101.

[81] These have been excluded because they are not part of the Community liberalisation package for the telecommunications services market.

(v) contracts for financial services in connection with the issue, sale, purchase or transfer of securities or other financial instruments, and central bank services[82];

(vi) employment contracts;

(vii) research and development service contracts other than those where the benefits accrue exclusively to the contracting authority for its use in the conduct of its own affairs, on condition that the service provided is mostly remunerated by the contracting authority.

Research and development services contracts are covered in identical terms in both. The exclusion of such contracts under both the services and the utilities directives lies in the assumption that research and development projects should not be financed by public funds.[83] However, where research and development contracts are covered by the procurement rules, a provision in the utilities directive allows a contracting entity to award a contract without a prior call for competition where it is purely for the purpose of research, experiment, study or development and not for the purpose of ensuring profit or of recovering research and development costs and in so far as the award of such a contract does not prejudice the competitive award of subsequent contracts which have in particular these purposes.[84]

Interestingly, service concessions, although included in the draft directive,[85] have been excluded from the provisions of Directive 92/50. The exclusion of service concessions falls short of the aspirations to regulate concession contracts for the public sector under the works directive and breaks the consistency in the two legal instruments. The reasons for the exclusion of service concessions from the regulatory regime of public procurement could be attributed to the different legal requirements in Member States to delegate powers to concessionaires. The delegation of services by public authorities to private undertakings in some Member States runs contrary to constitutional provisions.

---

[82] This refers to contracts which constitute transactions concerning shares, for example. In the public sector, it will also include within the derogation contracts awarded to financial intermediaries to arrange such transactions because these are specifically excluded from the scope of investment services (Category 6 of Annex IA). However, this exclusion does not appear in the utilities directive so that contracts for the services of intermediaries who will make the arrangements for such transactions wfll be subject to the provisions of the utilities directive; see de Graaf, "The political agreement on a common position concerning the utilities services Directive" (1992) 1 P.P.L.R. 473. The choice of such intermediaries is often difficult in practice since it is quite often made on the basis of the perceived quality of the intermediary or on references from existing clients and past experience. This choice will be made no easier by the application of the procurement rules which do not necessarily best fit such services; see Armin-Trepte, *op. cit.*, p. 101.

[83] See de Graaf, and Armin-Trepte, *op. cit.*

[84] Article 20(2)(b) of amending utilities directive 93/38.

[85] see Com.(90) 372 final, Syn 293 and Com.(91) 322 final, Syn 293.

The Directive adopts a two-tier approach in classifying services procured by contracting authorities. This classification is based on a "priority"[86] and a "non-priority"[87] list of services, according to the relative value of such services in intra-community trade. The division is not permanent and the European Commission has the situation under constant review by assessing the performance of "non-priority" services sectors. The two-tier approach, in practical terms, means that the award of "priority" services contracts are subject to the rigorous regime of the public procurement directives (advertisement, selection of tenderers, award procedures, award criteria), whereas the award of "non-priority" services contracts must follow the basic rules of non-discrimination and publicity of the results of the award.

COMPLIANCE AND ENFORCEMENT OF PUBLIC PROCUREMENT LEGISLATION

The compliance directives

In the absence of specific primary Community legislation laying down remedies available to individuals at national level in case of infringement of Community law, two questions arise: the first is whether an infringement of a directly effective primary or secondary Community provision may be used by individuals before national courts as grounds for an action for damages against the state; the second question approaches the problem from a slightly different perspective: that the infringed provision

---

[86] "Priority" services include: maintenance and repair services, land transport services (except for rail transport services, including armoured car services and courier services, except transport of mail); air transport services of passengers and freight, except transport of mail; transport of mail by land and by air, telecommunications services (except voice telephony, telex, radiotelephony, paging and satellite services); financial services including (a) insurance services, (b) banking and investment services (except contracts for financial services in connection with the issue, sale, purchase or transfer of securities or other financial instruments, and central bank services); computer and related services; research and development services; accounting, auditing and book-keeping services; market research and public opinion polling services; management consultant services (except arbitration and conciliation services) and related services; architectural services; engineering services and integrated engineering services; urban planning and landscape architectural services; related scientific and technical consulting services; technical testing and analysis services; advertising services; building-cleaning services on a fee or contract basis; publishing and printing services on a fee or contract basis; sewage and refuse disposal services; sanitation and similar services.

[87] "Non-Priority" services include: hotel and restaurant services; rail transport services; water transport services; supporting and auxiliary transport services; legal services; personnel placement and supply services; investigation and security services; education and vocational education services; health and social services; recreational, cultural and sporting services.

does not produce direct effect. Is, then, the state liable toward individuals? Can they seek compensation from the state for its infringement and its wrongful implementation of Community law?

In public procurement cases, Article 30 establishing the free movement of goods and Article 52 concerning the right of establishment, both have direct effect.[88] Also, the Court of Justice has recognised that specific (substantive) provisions of the relevant directives produce direct effect. There are also cases in which national courts have awarded compensation to individuals who suffered damages due to a mere breach of Community law.[89] More intriguing are those cases before national courts where infringement of Community law has already been pronounced directly by the Court of Justice (the Court) through a proceeding under Article 169. In these cases, national courts are confronted with state legislation, the incompatibility of which with Community law has unequivocally and authoritatively been declared by the Court. Is the existence of incompatible state legislation grounds for an action for damages before national courts?

The whole matter goes further to the question as to whether the Court can require the courts of the Member States to make declarations of invalidity in respect of national legislation found to infringe Community law or to make declaration of awards of damages to the victims. By virtue of Article 171, the Court said in the *Waterkeyn* case[90] that national courts are bound to draw the *"necessary inferences"* from judgements under Article 169. What is meant by this term is not clear. In the *Waterkeyn* case, the Court did not expressly require national courts to declare invalid a national law or administrative rule that violates directly effective primary or secondary Community legislation. On the other hand, there is a strong suggestion, in the same case, that such measures should be considered as invalid.

The assertion of a national rule that violates Community law as valid, probably justified by public interest, would leave individuals with the possibility of being compensated only through judicial review based on the system of non-fault liability, where a wrongful act is not required. This appears contrary to the principles of good faith and legitimate expectation and far beyond the spirit of the Treaty.[91] On the other hand, if national courts recognise the unlawful nature of an infringement of

---

[88] This occured at the end of the transitional period (31/12/69); see also Cases 2/74, *Reyners v. Belgian State*: [1974] E.C.R. 631 and Case 33/74, *Van Binsbergen v. Bestuur van de Bedrijfsvereninging voor de Metaalnijverheid* : [1974] E.C.R. 1299.

[89] Case 213/89, *R. v. Minister of Agriculture Fisheries and Food*: [1990] E.C.R. I–2433; also Case 14/68, *Wilhem v. Bundeskartellamt*: [1969] E.C.R. 1 at 27; Case 78/70, *Deutsche Grammophon GmbH v. Metro-SB Grossmarkte GmbH*: [1971] E.C.R. 1 at 31; Case 44/84, *Hurd v. Jones (Inspector of Taxes)* [1986] E.C.R. 29.

[90] Cases 314–316/81, 82 & 83, *Procureur de la Republique et al. v. Waterkeyn*: [1982] E.C.R. 4337.

[91] All the above mentioned principles, legal certainty, legitimate expectation, Community loyalty and Community solidarity are inherent in the fundamental provision of Article 5.

Community law as such, they would, normally, open the door for compensation on the basis of fault.

As far as the Community's non-contractual liability is concerned, the Court of Justice seems to be reluctant to consider that the unlawfulness of the Community Institutions' decisions is, in itself, sufficient to establish the Community's liability. Indeed, the criterion for Community institutions to be held liable for compensation, apart from the actual damage suffered by an individual and the causal link between that damage and the alleged unlawful act of the institution in question,[92] is the sufficiently flagrant violation of a superior rule of law for the protection of individuals.[93]

In the light of the Court's approach towards the Community's non-contractual liability, national courts face the dilemma of whether to limit their protection to individuals to the unenforceability and the setting aside of national legislation inconsistent with the Rome Treaty, and to the making of an order for the restitution of sums exacted in breach of Community law, or to expand the above mentioned protection by recognising the right to receive compensation for damage sustained as a result of an infringement of Community law.

With respect to the second question, that of the possibility of relying upon a provision of Community law that does not have direct effect, as grounds for an action for damages against the state before national courts, the Court in one of its most important recent judgments[94] answered it in the affirmative. The cases referred to it concerned the non-implementation by Italy of an EEC directive on the protection of employees in the event of the insolvency of their employer and reached the Court through a reference under Article 177. The questions the Court faced, at the request of national courts, were:

(i) whether provisions of the directive in question (80/987) were capable of producing direct effect, thus being relied upon by individuals; and

(ii) the above being answered in the negative, whether individuals had a right to receive compensation from the Member State for the negative effects of its failure to implement the directive.

The Court found that the provisions of the directive were not sufficiently clear, precise and unconditional to produce direct effect, thus answering the first question in the negative. In considering whether an individual has a right to be compensated by a state that has failed to implement a directive, the Court held that in principle, an individual is entitled to

---

[92] Case 4/69, *Alfons Lutticke v. E.C. Commission*: [1971] E.C.R. 325; [1996] C.M.L.R. 378.

[93] Case 5/71, *Aktien-Zuckerfabrik Schoppenstedt v. E.C. Council*: [1971] E.C.R. 975 at 984.

[94] Judgment on the Joined Cases 6/90 & 9/90, (*Francovich and Bonifaci v. Italian Republic*).

compensation in such circumstances.[95] In order to found state liability, it relied on Article 5 of the EEC Treaty, the principle of Community loyalty and solidarity, which provides that Member States are under an obligation to take all the necessary measures to ensure that Community law is properly applied. It has been held by the Court[96] that Article 5 (especially its negative obligation) is capable of producing direct effect, but only in conjunction with other substantive Treaty provisions or in circumstances in which this obligation is further developed in implementing legislation or through case law. Based on the above considerations, as well as on the doctrine of the useful effect (*effet utile*) of Community rules and the rights being acknowledged therein, which would be weakened if individuals were not provided with the possibility of compensation in the case of their rights being affected by a violation of Community law by a Member State, the Court proceeded further and examined the specific conditions that should be met in order for an individual suffering damages to be entitled to compensation by the defaulting state.

Three conditions should be fulfilled: first, the result required by the directive must involve the granting of rights to individuals; secondly, these rights must be identifiable on the basis of the provisions of the directive and thirdly, there must be a clear causal link between the breach of its obligations by the Member State and the damage suffered by the individual concerned. The above conditions being met, an individual may benefit from a right to compensation at national level based on Community law which is not directly effective. The amount of compensation payable should be determined by national courts in accordance with relevant domestic legislation. The *Francovich* judgment was a landmark decision with respect to state liability under Community law. Individuals may rely upon Community law which does not produce direct effect before their national courts. The Court of Justice laid down the required conditions for the admissibility of an action for damages before national courts submitted by an individual claiming damages against a Member State which has failed to implement a directive, hereby injuring a right conferred therein. How strict the national courts will be when confronted with such actions remains to be seen. Obviously, harmonisation of domestic provisions on awards of compensation will be required.

What appears to be common in the two systems of liability (Community non-contractual and state liability) is the importance that is given to the individual. According to the judgment of the Court in the *Francovich* case,[97] the individual must be granted rights conferred by the directive

---

[95] See also Case 213/89, *R. v. Minister of Agriculture Fisheries and Food*: [1990] E.C.R. I-2433.

[96] Case 14/68, *Wilhem v. Bundeskartellampt*: [1969] E.C.R. 1 at 27; Case 78/70, *Deutche Grammophon GmbH v. Metro-SB Grossmarkte GmbH*: [1971] E.C.R. 1 at 31; Case 44/84, *Hurd v. Jones* [1986] E.C.R. 29.

[97] See Joined Cases 6/90 & 9/90, *Francovich and Bonifaci v. Italian Republic*: [1993] E.C.R. 61.

itself. This means that Member States and their competent national authorities must not have any discretion in determining the content and extent of such rights. Here, it should be recalled that lack of discretion in the hands of a Member State is perhaps the most fundamental condition for the direct effect of provisions of directives. Thus, the relevant provisions of the directive should be close to producing direct effect, being deprived of it due to their conditionality or to their insufficient clarity and precision. On the other hand, Community liability occurs when a rule of law for the protection of individuals has been violated. The latter condition indicates the extent of the legal interest of the individual seeking compensation by the Community. That interest approaches the individual and direct concern required in Article 173(2), when individuals seek judicial review of regulations *stricto sensu* and directives. The Court of Justice is extremely strict when considering an action for damages brought by an individual against a Community institution under Article 215(2). Community liability must fulfil the draconian condition of a sufficiently flagrant violation (mostly a qualitative criterion indicating the manifest and grave disregard of the limits of a state's powers)[98] of a superior rule of law for the protection of individuals. Furthermore, the injury resulting from that violation must involve particular economic policy choices.

As many provisions of Community legislation concerning public procurement (directives) are deemed to produce direct effect, the question of whether an infringement of them can be considered as sufficient grounds for an action for damages at national level, combines with the duty of national courts to afford an effective protection mechanism (remedies) of the rights conferred on individuals by directly effective Community law.

In an attempt to give an answer to these questions, the Council enacted a directive on the harmonisation of laws, regulations and administrative provisions relating to the application of review procedures to the award of public works and public supply contracts.[99] In addition, Directive 92/13[1] extends the remedies and review procedures covered by Directive 89/665 to the water, energy, transport and telecommunication sectors.

Both directives have been based on Article 100A. Some questions arise as to whether this article is the proper legal basis. The first question is whether Article 100A covers approximation of procedural remedies. It could be argued that it is not necessary to harmonise or to approximate procedural remedies since it is the general duty of Member States under Article 5 to ensure the fulfilment of Community obligations. On the other hand, Article 100A contains no express or implied limitation to the

---

[98] Joined Cases 83 & 94/76 & 4, 15, 40/77, *Bayerische HNL Vermehrungsbetreibe GmbH v. Council and Commission*: [1978] E.C.R. 1209 at 1224–1225.
[99] Directive 89/665, [1989] O.J. L395.
[1] [1992] O.J. L76/7.

approximation of substantive rules of law, in the framework of the completion of an internal market.

The second question relates to the power of national courts or administrative bodies to suspend a procedure or to set aside a decision in respect of the award of a contract. It is not clear whether these tasks and powers can be granted through Article 100A without requiring the addition of Article 235. However, it should be admitted that the unanimous decision making required therein, could not be easily achieved and from a practical political point of view, the qualified majority provided for in Article 100A appears much more desirable.

The scope of the compliance directives

According to Article 1 of Directive 89/665 and Article 1 of Directive 93/13, Member States shall ensure effective and rapid review of decisions taken by contracting authorities which infringe public procurement provisions. Undertakings seeking relief from damages in the context of a procedure for the award of a contract, should not be treated differently under national rules implementing European public procurement laws and under other national rules. This means that the measures to be taken concerning the review procedures should be similar to national review proceedings, without any discriminatory character.

Any person having or having had an interest in obtaining a particular public supply or public works contract and who has been or risks being harmed by an alleged infringement of public procurement provision shall be entitled to seek review before national courts. This is laid down in the third para of Article 1 of Directive 89/665 and Article 3 of Directive 92/13 and in both cases is followed by a stand-still provision concerning the prior notification by the person seeking review to the contracting authority of the alleged infringement and of his intention to seek review. However, with respect to admissibility aspects, there is no qualitative or quantitative definition of the interest of a person in obtaining a public contract. As to the element of potential harm by an infringement of public procurement provisions, it should be cumulative with the first element, that of interest. The prior notification should intend to exhaust any possibility of amicable settlement before the parties have recourse to national courts.

Where the compliance directive in the utilities sectors[2] is really novel is in Chapter Two. Member States are required to give the contracting entities the possibility of having their purchasing procedures and practices *attested* by persons authorised by law to exercise this function. Indeed, this attestation mechanism may investigate in advance possible irregularities identified in the award of a public contract and allow the contracting authorities to correct them. The latter may include the

[2] Directive 92/13, [1992] O.J. L76/7.

attestation statement in the notice inviting tenders published in the Official Journal. The system appears flexible and cost-efficient and may prevent wasteful litigation. Quite promisingly, the attestation procedure under Directive 92/13 will be the essential requirement for the development of European standards of attestation.[3]

THE OPERATION OF THE PUBLIC PROCUREMENT DIRECTIVES

The applicability of the directives: definitions

Contracting authorities

Under the supplies, works and services directives, the term contracting authorities includes the state and its organs interpreted in functional terms. It also covers bodies governed by public law, a legal category which must satisfy a set of cumulative criteria for a contracting authority to be characterised as such.[4] The body must be established for the specific purpose of meeting needs in the general interest, not having an industrial or commercial character; it must have legal personality; it must be financed, for the most part, by the state or regional or local authorities; it must be subject to management and supervision by those bodies. The utilities directive also uses the term "bodies governed by public law" for the contracting entities operating in the relevant sectors.[5] A second category of contracting authorities under the utilities directive includes public undertakings.[6] The terms indicate any undertaking over which the state may exercise direct or indirect dominant influence by means of ownership, or of financial participation therein, or of laws and regulations which govern it. Dominant influence can be exercised in the form of majority holding of the undertaking's subscribed capital, in the form of majority controlling of the undertaking's issued shares or finally, in the form of the right to appoint the majority of the undertaking's management board. Under the GATT agreement on government procurement, the term public authorities confines itself to central governments and their agencies only.[7]

Public contracts

Public supplies contracts[8] are contracts for pecuniary consideration concluded in writing between a supplier (natural or legal persons) and

---

[3] see Art. 7 of Directive 92/13.
[4] Art. 1(b) of Directive 93/36 and Art. 1(b) of Directive 93/37.
[5] Art. 1(1) of Directive 93/38.
[6] Art. 1(2) of Directive 93/38.
[7] Council Decision 87/565, [1987] O.J. L345.
[8] Art. 1(a) of Directive 93/36.

public authorities, which include the state, local and regional authorities and bodies governed by public law, having as their objective the purchase and delivery of goods.

Public works contracts[9] are contracts for pecuniary consideration concluded in writing between a contractor (natural or legal persons) and public authorities, which include the state, local and regional authorities and bodies governed by public law, having as their objective the completion of works/construction projects.

Public services contracts[10] are contracts for pecuniary consideration concluded in writing between a service provider (natural or legal persons) and public authorities, which include the state, local and regional authorities and bodies governed by public law, having as their objective the provision of services, as defined in the United Nations nomenclature of product and service classification.

Public contracts in the utilities sector[11] embrace supplies and works contracts between natural or legal persons and entities operating in transport, water, energy and telecommunications sectors.

Specific types of contracts under the public procurement directives

Concession contracts

A public works concession is defined by the works directive[12] as a written contract between a contractor and a contracting authority concerning either the execution or both the execution and design of a work and for which the consideration consists at least partly in the right to exploit the construction. As will be explained below, the directive contains a mitigated regime with respect to a public works concession contract only having to comply with the common rules on advertising.

Subsidised works contracts

Works contracts which are subsidised directly by more than 50 per cent by the states, can still fall within the scope of the directive.[13] Works which are not subsidised directly, or for less than 50 per cent, fall outside this anti-circumvention provision. Not all subsidised works fall within the scope of the directive: only civil engineering works, such as the construction of roads, bridges and railways, as well as building work for hospitals, facilities intended for sports, recreation and leisure and university buildings; buildings used for administrative purposes are referred to as subsidised works contracts.[14] This list is exhaustive.

[9] Art. 1(a) of Directive 93/37.
[10] Art. 1(a) of Directive 92/50.
[11] Art. 1(4)(a),(b),(c) of Directive 93/38.
[12] Art. 1(d) of Directive 93/37.
[13] Art. 2(1) of Directive 93/37.
[14] Art. 2(2) of Directive 93/37.

Framework agreements

The utilities directives have introduced a new selection and tendering procedure, namely framework agreements, which is influenced to a large extent by the benefits of chain supply management and partnership schemes. The supplies, works and services directives do not refer to framework agreements. A framework agreement is an agreement between a contracting authority and one or more suppliers, contractors or service providers the purpose of which is to establish the terms, with particular regard to prices and, where appropriate, the quantity envisaged, governing the contracts to be awarded during a given period.[15] A framework agreement does not posses binding character and should not be considered as a contract between the relevant parties.[16] In practical terms it represents a sort of a standing offer which remains valid during its time span. Within the provisions of the utilities directive, when a contracting authority awards a framework agreement under the relevant procedures which are common to other public contracts covered therein, subsequent individual contracts concluded under the framework agreement may be awarded without having recourse to a call for competition.[17] Individual contracts which have been awarded under a framework agreement are subject to the requirement of the publication of a contract award notice in the Official Journal. The directive specifically stipulates that misuse of framework agreements may distort competition and trigger the application of the relevant rules, particularly with reference to concerted practices which lead to collusive tendering.

In-house contracts and contracts to affiliated undertakings

Article 6 of the services directive provides for the inapplicability of the directive to service contracts which are awarded to an entity which is itself a contracting authority within the meaning of the directive on the basis of an exclusive right which is granted to the contracting authority by a law, regulation or administrative provision of the Member State in question.[18] Article 13 of the utilities directive provides for the exclusion of certain contracts between contracting authorities and affiliated undertakings.[19] These are service contracts which are awarded to a service provider which is affiliated to the contracting entity and service contracts

---

[15] Art. 1(5) of Directive 93/38.
[16] Framework agreements should not be confused with framework contracts, the latter producing binding effects; see Armin-Trepte, *op. cit.* at n. 80, p. 93.
[17] Art. 20(2)(i) of Directive 93/38.
[18] This practice resembles the market testing process often employed in the U.K. between a contracting authority and an in-house team; see Harden, "Defining the range of application of the public sector procurement Directives in the United Kingdom", (1992) 1 P.P.L.R. 362.
[19] An affiliated undertaking, for the purposes of Art. 1(3) of the Utilities Directive, is one the annual accounts of which are consolidated with those of the contracting entity in accordance with the requirements of the seventh company law Directive (Council Directive 83/349, [1983] O.J. L193/1)).

which are awarded to a service provider which is affiliated to a contracting entity participating in a joint venture formed for the purpose of carrying out an activity covered by the directive.[20] The exclusion from the provisions of the directive is subject, however, to two conditions: the service provider must be an undertaking affiliated to the contracting authority and at least 80 per cent of its average turnover arising within the European Community for the preceding three years, derives from the provision of the same or similar services to undertakings with which it is affiliated. The Commission is empowered to monitor the application of this Article and require the notification of the names of the undertakings concerned and the nature and value of the service contracts involved.

Secret public works contracts

The works directive does not apply to works contracts which are declared secret or the execution of which must be accompanied by special security measures[21] in accordance with the laws, regulations or administrative provisions in force in the Member State concerned; nor does the directive apply to works contracts when the protection of the basic interests of the Member States' security so requires it.

Construction projects under international agreements

The works directive does not apply to public works contracts awarded in pursuance of certain international agreements[22]; nor does the directive apply to public works contracts awarded pursuant to the particular procedure of an international organisation.[23] Several international organisations, such as NATO, have their own rules on the award of public works contracts.

Size of public contracts under the public procurement directives

Thresholds

The European rules of public procurement and all the requirements laid down in them are triggered only if certain value thresholds are met. The thresholds laid down are as follows:

---

[20] see the explanatory memorandum accompanying the text amending the utilities Directive (Com.(91) 347 Syn 361) which states that this provision relates, in particular, to three types of service provision within groups. These categories, which may not or may not be distinct, are: the provision of common services such as accounting, recruitment and management; the provision of specialised services embodying the know how of the group; the provision of a specialised service to a joint venture.

[21] Art. 4(b) of Directive 93/37.

[22] Art. 5(a) of Directive 93/37.

[23] Art. 5(c) of Directive 93/37.

— ECU 5 million for all work and construction projects.[24]

— ECU 200,000 for supplies contracts within the European Union[25] and ECU 136,000 for supplies contracts from third countries[26] which participate in the GATT agreement on government procurement (USA, Canada, Japan, Singapore, Hong Kong, Norway, Switzerland and Israel).

— ECU 600,000 for supplies of telecommunication equipment under the utilities directive[27] and ECU 400,000 for all other supplies contracts awarded by public utilities.[28]

— ECU 200,000 for services contracts.[29]

Estimation of contract value

The way in which the value of a contract is calculated is crucial for the application of the relevant directive. To ensure that identical calculation methods are used throughout the European Community and to prevent intentional avoidance of the procurement directives by artificially low contract valuations, the directives lay down specific rules.[30]

Where the contract is to be concluded in the form of a lease, rental or hire-purchase agreement, the calculation method varies according to the contract's duration.

The estimated value is to be calculated on the basis of:

— where its term is 12 months or less, the total value for the contract's duration;

— where its term exceeds 12 months, the total value for the contract's duration, including the estimated residual value of the products;

— where the contract is concluded for an indefinite period or where its term cannot be defined, the monthly value multiplied by 48;

— where contracts are of a regular nature or are to be renewed over a given period, the following must be taken into account:

(i) either the actual aggregate value of similar successive contracts awarded over the previous 12 months or accounting period, adjusted where possible for anticipated changes in quantity or value over the subsequent 12 months;

---

[24] Art. 3(1) of Directive 93/37; Art. 14(c) of Directive 93/38.
[25] Art. 5(1)(a) of Directive 93/36.
[26] Art. 5(1)(c) of Directive 93/36.
[27] Art. 14(b) of Directive 93/38.
[28] Art. 14(a) of Directive 93/38.
[29] Art. 7(1) of Directive 92/50.
[30] Art. 5(2) to (6) of Directive 93/36; Art. 6(1) to (5) of Directive 93/37; Art. 14(4) to (13) of Directive 93/38; Art. 7(2) to (8) of Directive 92/50.

(ii) or the estimated aggregate value of the successive contracts concluded during the 12 months following the initial delivery or accounting periods where this exceeds 12 months.

In any event, the choice between these two valuation methods must not be made with the intention of keeping contracts outside the scope of the directive.

If a proposed procurement of supplies of the same type may lead to contracts being awarded at the same time in separate lots, the estimated value of all the lots must be taken into account. If it reaches the relevant threshold, all the lots must be awarded in compliance with the directive. The same rules apply when estimating the value of leasing, rental or hire-purchase contracts. Where provision is explicitly made for options, the basis for calculating the estimated contract value must be the highest possible total permitted for the purchase, lease, rental or hire options included.

When calculating the value of a public works contract, account has to be taken of the estimated value of the works and of the estimated value of the supplies needed to carry out the works, even if these supplies are made available to the contractor by the contracting authorities.

The estimated value of work which the contracting authority intends to have carried out at a later date by the contractor awarded the current contract, and which consists of a repetition of the work to be carried out under the current contract, must be included in the contract value.

The works directive provides for special rules when a contract is subdivided into several lots. When the aggregate value of the lots is over five million ECU, the provisions of the directive apply to all lots. A work or a contract may not be split up with the intention of avoiding the applicability of the directive. However, lots with a net value of less than one million ECU may be exempted from the scope of the Directive, provided that the total estimated value of all the lots exempted does not exceed 20 per cent of the total estimated value of all lots.

THE PRINCIPLES OF THE DIRECTIVES

Mandatory advertisment and publication of public contracts

One of the most important principles of the public procurement directives is the principle of transparency. Transparency is achieved through community wide publicity of public procurement contracts over the relevant thresholds via the publication of three kinds of notices in the Official Journal of the European Communities:

(i) Periodic Indicative Notices (PIN). Every contracting entity must notify its intentions for public procurement contracts within the forthcoming financial year.[31]

(ii) Invitations to tender. All contracts above the relevant thresholds should be tendered and the notice containing the invitation to tender must include the award procedures and the award criteria for the contract in question.[32]

(iii) Contract Award Notices (CAN). This is a form of notification after the award of the contract of the successful tenderer and the price of its offer, as well as the reasons for its selection by the contracting authority.[33]

Notices are published by the publications office of the European Communities. Within twelve days (or five days in the case of the accelerated form of restricted or negotiated procedures), the publications office publishes the notices in the Supplement to the Official Journal and via the TED (Tenders Electronic Daily) database. Two notices are published in full in their original language only and in summary form in the other Community languages. The publications office takes responsibility for the necessary translations and summaries. The cost of publishing notices in the Supplement to the Official Journal are borne by the Community.

Selection and qualification criteria

Selection criteria are determined through two major categories of qualification requirements; legal, and technical/economic. Contracting authorities must follow objectively determined and homogeneously specified selection criteria for enterprises participating in the award procedures of public procurement contracts. This would eliminate potential grounds for discrimination on the grounds of nationality and in combination with the prohibition of technical specifications which are capable of favouring national undertakings, it will eventually provide for the required background for the liberalisation of the Community's public markets.

Legal requirements

The definition of a contractor wishing to submit a tender for the award of a public contract comprises any legal or natural person involved in

---

[31] Art. 9(1) of Directive 93/36; Art. 11(1) to (3) of Directive 93/37; Art. 22(1)(a) to (c) of Directive 93/38; Art. 15(1) of Directive 92/50.

[32] Art. 9(2) of Directive 93/36; Art. 11(2) of Directive 93/37; Art. 21 of Directive 93/38; Art. 15(2) of Directive 92/50.

[33] Art. 9(3) of Directive 93/36; Art. 11(5) of Directive 93/37; Art. 24 of Directive 93/38; Art. 16(1) of Directive 92/50.

supplies, construction or services activities. It also includes private consortia, as well as joint ventures or groupings. Contracting authorities may impose a requirement as to the form and legal status of the contractor that wins the award.[34] This requirement focuses only on the post selection stage, after the award of the contract and indicates the need for legal certainty. Specific legal form and status required by contracting entities facilitates monitoring of the performance of the contract and allows better access to justice in case of a dispute between the contracting entity and the undertaking in question. The successful contractor should also fulfil certain qualitative requirements concerning his eligibility and technical capacity[35] and his financial and economic standing.

Eligibility requirements

In principle, there are automatic grounds for exclusion when a contractor, supplier or service provider[36]:

   (i) is bankrupt or is being wound up;

  (ii) is the subject of proceedings for a declaration of bankruptcy or for an order for compulsory winding up;

 (iii) has been convicted for an offence concerning his professional conduct;

 (iv) has been guilty of grave professional misconduct;

  (v) has not fulfilled obligations relating to social security contributions;

 (vi) has not fulfilled obligations relating to the payment of taxes.

Financial and economic standing

Evidence of financial and economic standing may be provided[37] by means of:

   (i) appropriate statements from bankers;

  (ii) the presentation of the firm's balance sheets or extracts from the balance sheets where these are published under company law provisions;

---

[34] Art. 21 of Directive 71/305 as amended by Directive 89/440 and Art. 18 of Directive 77/62 as amended by Directive 88/295. The same regime is followed in the utilities Directive 90/531, Art. 26, and the services Directive 92/50, Art. 26.

[35] Arts. 20–23 of Directive 77/62; Arts. 23 et seq. of Directive 71/305; Arts. 29 et seq. of Directive 90/531; Arts. 29 et seq. of Directive 92/50.

[36] Art. 20 of Directive 93/36; Art. 24 of Directive 93/37; Art. 31 of Directive 93/38; Art. 29 of Directive 92/50.

[37] Art. 22 of Directive 93/36; Art. 26 of Directive 93/37; Art. 31(b) of Directive 93/38; Art. 31 of Directive 92/50.

(iii) a statement of the firm's annual turnover and the turnover on construction works for the three previous financial years.

Technical capacity

The technical knowledge and ability of a contractor

In construction projects, the references which the contractor may be required to produce must be specified in the notice or invitation to tender.[38] They include:

— the contractor's educational and professional qualifications or those of the firm's managerial staff, and, in particular, those of the person or persons responsible for carrying out the works;

— a list of the works carried out over the past five years, accompanied by certificates of satisfactory execution for the most important works. These certificates shall indicate the value, date and site of the works and shall specify whether they were carried out according to the rules of the trade and properly completed. Where necessary, the competent authority shall submit these certificates direct to the authority awarding the contracts;

— a statement of the tools, plant and technical equipment available to the contractor for carrying out the work;

— a statement of the firm's average annual manpower and number of managerial staff for the last three years;

— a statement of the technicians or technical divisions which the contractor can call upon for carrying out the work, whether or not they belong to the firm.

The technical capacity of a supplier

In supplies contracts, the references which may be requested[39] must be mentioned in the invitation to tender and are the following:

— a list of the principal deliveries effected in the past three years, with the sums, dates and recipients, public or private, involved:
  (i) where to public authorities awarding contracts, evidence to be in the form of certificates issued or countersigned by the competent authority;
  (ii) where to private purchasers, delivery to be certified by the purchaser or, failing this, simply declared by the supplier to have been effected;

[38] Art. 27 of Directive 93/37 and Art. 31 of Directive 93/38.
[39] Art. 22 of Directive 93/36.

— a description of the undertaking's technical facilities, its measures for ensuring quality and its study and research facilities;

— indication of the technicians or technical bodies involved, whether or not belonging directly to the undertaking, especially those responsible for quality control;

— samples, descriptions or photographs of the products to be supplied, the authenticity of which must be certified if the contracting authority so requests;

— certificates drawn up by official quality control institutes or agencies of recognised competence attesting conformity to certain specifications or standards of goods clearly identified by references to specifications or standards;

— where the goods to be supplied are complex or, exceptionally, are required for a special purpose, a check carried out by the contracting authorities (or on their behalf by a competent official body of the country in which the supplier is established, subject to that body's agreement) on the production capacities of the supplier and, if necessary, on his study and research facilities and quality control measures.

List of recognised contractors

Registration in lists of recognised contractors that exist in various Member States may be used by contractors as an alternative means of proving their suitability, also before contracting authorities of other Member States.[40] Information deduced from registration in an official list may not be questioned by contracting authorities. Nonetheless, the actual level of financial and economic standing and technical knowledge or ability required of contractors is determined by the contracting authorities. Consequently, contracting authorities are required to accept that a contractor's financial and economic standing and technical knowledge and ability are sufficient for works corresponding to his classification only in so far as that classification is based on equivalent criteria with respect to the capacities required.

THE AWARD OF PUBLIC CONTRACTS

Tendering procedures

Participation in tendering procedures is channelled through open, negotiated or restricted procedures;

---

[40] Art. 25 of Directive 93/36; Art. 29 of Directve 93/37; Art. 35 of Directive 92/50.

— *Open procedures* are those where every interested supplier, contractor or service provider may submit an offer.[41]

— *Negotiated procedures*[42] are such procedures for the award of public contracts whereby contracting authorities consult contractors of their choice and negotiate the terms of the contract with one or more of them. In most cases they follow restricted procedures and they are heavily utilised under framework agreements in the utilities sectors.[43] There are two different kinds of negotiated procedures: (i) negotiated procedures with prior notification and (ii) negotiated procedures without prior notification;

  (i) Negotiated procedures with prior notification[44] provide for selection of candidates in two rounds. In the first round, all interested contractors may submit their tenders and the contracting authority selects, from the candidates, those who will be invited to negotiate. In the second round, negotiations with various candidates take place and the successful tender is selected. In principle, the minimum number of candidates to be selected is three, provided that there is a sufficient number of suitable candidates.

  (ii) Negotiated procedures without prior notification[45] are the least restrictive of the various award procedures laid down in the directive and may be conducted in one single round. Contracting authorities are allowed to choose whichever contractor they want, begin negotiations directly with this contractor and award the contract to him. The directive provides for only a few rules with which this procedure must comply. A prior notice in the Official Journal is not required.

— Finally, restricted procedures[46] are those procedures for the award of public contracts whereby only those contractors invited by the contracting authority may submit tenders. The selection of the winning tender takes place in two rounds. In the first round, all interested contractors may submit their tenders and the contracting authority selects, from the candidates, those who will be

[41] Art. 1(d) of Directive 93/36; Art. 1(e) of Directive 93/37; Art. 1(7)(a) of Directive 93/38; Art. 1(d) of Directive 92/50.
[42] Art. 1(f) of Directive 93/36; Art. 1(g) of Directive 93/37; Art. 1(7)(c) of Directive 93/38; Art. 1(c) of Directive 92/50.
[43] See the section on framework agreements above: *Specific types of contracts under the public procurement directives*, pp. 123 *et seq.*
[44] Art. 6(2) of Directive 93/36; Art. 7(2) of Directive 93/37; Art. 20(1) of Directive 93/38; Art. 11(2) of Directive 92/50.
[45] Art. 6(3) of Directive 93/36; Art. 7(3) of Directive 93/37; Art. 20(3) of Directive 93/38; Art. 11(3) of Directive 92/50.
[46] Art. 1(e) of Directive 93/36; Art. 1(f) of Directive 93/37; Art. 1(7)(b) of Directive 93/38; Art. 1(d) of Directive 92/50.

invited to tender. In principle, the minimum number of candidates to be selected is five. In the second round, bids are submitted and the successful tender is selected.

An accelerated form of restricted or negotiated procedure may be used[47] where, for reasons of urgency, the periods normally required under the normal procedures cannot be met. In such cases, contracting authorities are required to indicate in the tender notice published in the Official Journal the grounds for using the accelerated form of the procedure. The use of an accelerated procedure must be limited to the types and quantities of products or services which it can be shown are urgently required. Other products or services must be supplied or provided under open or restricted procedures.

The directives stipulate that open procedures, where possible should constitute the norm. Open procedures increase competition without doubt and can achieve better prices for the contracting authorities when purchasing goods in large volumes. Price reduction based on economies of scale can bring about substantial cost savings for the public sector. Open procedures are mostly utilised when the procurement process is relatively straightforward and are combined with the lowest price award criterion. On the other hand, competition in tendering procedures is limited by using the restricted and negotiated procedures. By definition, the number of candidates that are allowed to tender is limited (five in restricted, three in negotiated procedures), therefore the directives have attached a number of conditions for the contracting authorities to justify when they intend to award their contracts through restricted or negotiated procedure. Restricted and negotiated procedures are utilised in relation with the most economically advantageous offer award criterion and suited for more complex procurement schemes. Although contracting authorities can freely opt for open or restricted procedures, the latter should be justified by reference to the nature of the products or services to be procured and the balance between contract value and administrative costs associated with tender evaluation. A more rigorous set of conditions apply for the use of negotiated procedures. When negotiated procedures with prior notification are used, they must be justified on grounds of irregular or unacceptable tenders received as a result of a previous call. Negotiated procedures without prior notification are restrictively permitted in absence of tenders, when the procurement involves manufactured products or construction works purely for research and development, when for technical or artistic reasons or reasons connected with the protection of exclusive rights a particular supplier or contractor is selected, in cases of extreme urgency brought by unforeseeable events not attributable to the contracting authorities,

---

[47] Art. 12 of Directive 93/36; Art. 13 of Directive 93/37; Art. 26(2) of Directive 93/38; Art. 19(4) of Directive 92/50.

when additional deliveries and supplies or works would cause disproportionate technical operational and maintenance difficulties.

Prohibition of post-tender negotiations

All negotiations with candidates or tenderers on fundamental aspects of contracts, in particular on prices, are prohibited in open and restricted procedures; discussions with candidates or tenderers may be held, but only for the purpose of clarifying or supplementing the content of their tenders or the requirements of the contracting authorities and provided this does not involve discriminatory practices.[48] The need for such a prohibition is clear, since the possibility to negotiate may allow the contracting authority to introduce subjective appraisal criteria.

Tendering procedures for concession contracts

The works directive has adopted a special, mitigated regime for the award of concession contracts.[49] The provisions of the directive only apply to concession contracts when the value is at least ECU 5 million. No rules are given as to the way in which the contract value must be calculated.

Design contests

Where the services directive[50] is particularly novel is in Article 1(g), where provision has been made therein for a fourth type of award procedure, namely design contests, with reference to planning projects. According to Article 1(g), design contests are those national procedures which enable the contracting authority to acquire in the fields of area planning, town planning, architecture and civil engineering, a plan or a design selected by a jury, after being put out to competition with or without the award of prizes. The award of design contests, according to the services directive, must follow specific rules. The admission of participants to the contest shall not be limited either by reference to the territory or part of a Member State, or on the grounds that under the law of the Member State in which the contest is organised, participants would have been required to be either natural or legal persons. Furthermore, where design contests are restricted to a limited number of participants, the contracting authorities must lay down clear and nondiscriminatory selection criteria which ensure sufficient and genuine

---

[48] Art. 24 of Directive 93/36.
[49] Art. 3 of Directive 93/37.
[50] Directive 92/50.

competition among the participants. The jury shall be composed exclusively of natural persons who are independent.

Award criteria

In principle, there are two criteria laid down in the public procurement directives for awarding public contracts:

— the lowest price;

— the most economically advantageous offer.

The lowest price criterion is self-explanatory.[51] The tenderer who submits the cheapest offer must be awarded the contract. Subject to the qualitative criteria and financial and economic standing, contracting authorities do not rely on any other factor than the price quoted to complete the contract. The reasons for utilising the lowest price criterion are: simplicity, speed, less qualitative consideration during the evaluation of tenders.

The appreciation of what is the most economically advantageous tender offer[52] is to be made on a series of factors and determinants chosen by the contracting entity for the particular contract in question. These factors include: price, delivery or completion date, running costs, cost effectiveness, profitability, technical merit, product or work quality, aesthetic and functional characteristics, after sales service and technical assistance, commitments with regards to spare parts and components and maintenance costs, security of supplies.

The award of concession contracts

For the award of concession contracts, contracting authorities must apply similar rules on advertising as the advertising rules concerning open and restricted procedures for the award of every works contract. Also, the provisions on technical standards and on criteria for qualitative selection of candidates and tenderers also apply to the award of concession contracts. The directive does not prescribe the use of specific award procedures for concession contracts. The directive presupposes the concession contracts are awarded in two rounds, such as in the case of restricted procedures or negotiated procedures for works contracts. Nothing, however, prevents contracting authorities from applying an open—one round—procedure. The directive contains no rules on the minimum number of candidates which have to be invited to negotiate or

---

[51] Art. 26(1)(a) of Directive 93/36; Art. 30(1)(a) of Directive 93/37; Art. 34(1)(b) of Directive 93/38; Art. 36(1)(b) of Directive 92/50.
[52] Art. 26(1)(b) of Directive 93/36; Art. 30(1)(b) of Directive 93/37; Art. 34(1)(a) of Directive 93/38; Art. 36(1)(a) of Directive 92/50.

to submit a tender. It would seem that a contracting authority may limit itself to selecting only one single candidate, provided the intention to award a concession contract has been adequately published. A contracting authority may under no circumstances refrain from publishing a notice.[53]

Additional award criteria

Subcontracting and public procurement

Subcontracting plays a major role in the opening up of public markets as it is the most effective way of small and medium sized enterprises' participation in public procurement. All directives on public procurement, influenced by the Commission's communications on subcontracting and small and medium enterprises, encourage the use of subcontracting in the award of public contracts. Particularly in public supplies contracts, the contracting entity in the invitation to tender may ask the tenderers on their intention to subcontract to third parties part of the contract.[54] This reveals the importance of subcontracting for regional development in public procurement. In public works contracts, contracting authorities awarding the principal contract to a concessionaire may require him to subcontract to third parties at least 30 per cent of the total work provided for by the principal contract.

Local labour employment and public procurement

Contracting authorities are often posed with the dilemma of utilising public procurement contracts, particularly in construction, as a tool for combating long-term unemployment within their region. Although at first instance, local labour clauses appear to fall foul of the relevant Treaty provisions on non-discrimination (Article 7) and right of establishment (Article 52), the European Court of Justice in a seemingly important case[55] on public procurement pronounced that the utilisation of local labour clauses could be included in the non-exhaustive list of factors determining award criteria, especially the most economically advantageous offer, if they did not have discriminatory effects. The Court apparently rejected the possible utilisation of local labour clauses as a selection criterion, a decision which runs in consistency with previous case law, recognising the exhaustive character of selection criteria stipulated by the public procurement directives.

---

[53] Art. 11(3)(4) and Art. 16 of Directive 93/37.
[54] Arts. 17 and 20 of the public supplies (93/36) and public works (93/37) directives, Directive 93/36 and Directive 93/37 respectively.
[55] Case 31/87, *Gebroeders Beentjes B.V. v. State of Netherlands*: [1988] E.C.R. 4635.

The award of public housing schemes

The award of public housing contracts[56] may deviate from the normal regime of the directive for the purpose of selecting a contractor who meets the requirements specified by the public authority. The design and construction of a public housing scheme, as well as the size and complexity of the project, as well as the estimated duration of the work involved, require that planning be based from the outset on close collaboration within a team comprising representatives of the contracting authorities, experts and the contractor to be responsible for carrying out the works. In these cases, the contracting authorities have to apply the advertising rules and the criteria for qualitative selection relating to the restricted procedure. Moreover, the contracting authorities have to include in the contract notice as accurately as possible, a description of the works to be carried out. With respect to quantitative selection, no restrictions apply. Hence, there is no obligation for the contracting authorities to select more than one single contractor to negotiate admission to the building team.

EXTRA-TERRITORIAL EFFECTS OF THE PUBLIC PROCUREMENT REGIME

The legal procurement regime of the European Union has been extended in order to cover signatories to the GATT agreement on government procurement.[57] Foreign firms (from third countries) can participate in tendering procedures for the award of public contracts from public entities in the common market and vice versa, European firms can participate in tendering procedures in foreign public markets. The GATT agreement on government procurement embraces the following countries: USA, Canada, Japan, EFTA countries, Singapore, Hong Kong and Israel and promises considerable improvement in reciprocal market access.

The first public procurement directives were inapplicable to products originating in and supplied by third countries. In practical terms the meaning of this limitation was that a product outside the Community, in order to be subject to a public contract regulated by one of the directives, had to be lawfully put in free circulation in at least one Member State.[58] The Council, being conscious of the above limitation adopted a Resolution[59] concerning access to Community public supply contracts for

---

[56] Art. 9 of Directive 93/37.
[57] See E.C. Council Regulation 1461/93 ([1993] O.J. L146) and E.C. Council Decision 93/324 ([1993] O.J. L125).
[58] For the concept of origin of goods and their lawful free circulation in the Common Market see Regulation 802/68, [1968] O.J. Spec. Ed. 165.
[59] [1977] O.J. C11/1.

products originating in non-member states. At the same time, negotiations in the international framework were being carried under the GATT Tokyo round (1973–1979). Finally, on April 12, 1979, the GATT agreement on government procurement (AGP) was concluded and became part of the Community's legal order by virtue of Article 228(2) EEC Treaty and Council Decision 80/271.[60]

The agreement on government procurement

The primary aims of the AGP were similar to those of supplies Directive 77/62, namely transparency of laws and procedures on government procurement and elimination of protection for domestic suppliers and discrimination between foreign suppliers.[61] However, the AGP provisions went further than those of Directive 77/62 by introducing more favourable conditions for tenders from outside the Community; the AGP was envisaged as the vehicle for establishing an international framework of rights and obligations with respect to government procurement with a view to achieving liberalisation and expansion of world trade. As a consequence, third country signatories to the AGP are under the obligation to provide for the same opportunities for access to Community tenderers in their respective public markets, as those provided for by E.C. Member States to undertakings from these countries.

Due to the above modifications, Directive 77/62 was amended. The result of this amendment is that the AGP rules are now incorporated in the supplies regime,[62] which is the only regime in the public procurement sector, the application of which produces extra-territorial effects.

The situation under the AGP (Tokyo round) rules, which have been incorporated in Directive 88/295 is the following: foreign undertakings (from third countries) which have subsidiaries within the Common Market will have the same access to public supplies contracts as European undertakings and can invoke and enforce Community law both at Community and (mainly) at national level. Obviously, it is required that undertakings from outside the Community must have an economic presence in it. Subsidiaries should take the form of a corporate personality subject to tax laws of the Member State within which they operate. It should also be noted that under all public procurement directives, contracting authorities have the right to impose an obligation on one or more undertakings awarded a contract, that the latter take a specific legal form. Suppliers, signatories to the GATT, but not established in the Community, will still be subject to the AGP, although they cannot invoke and enforce Community law. They cannot even enforce GATT rules, unless the competent forum (E.C. Member State or third state GATT signatory) provides for the appropriate remedies. The AGP lays down a

---

[60] [1980] O.J. L215/1.
[61] See Weiss, "Public Procurement in the EEC—Public Supply Contracts", (1988) 13 E.L.R. pp. 318–334.
[62] Directives 80/767 and 88/295, above.

rather inoffensive dispute settlement and enforcement procedure, where consultation and conciliation between the aggrieved contractor and the contracting authority play the dominant role. With respect to enforcement of the AGP rules, the Committee on Government Procurement (composed of representatives from each of the parties), as the body responsible for consultation on matters relating to the operation of the AGP or the furtherance of its objectives, has the right to authorise any measure adopted by a party aiming at suspending the reciprocity principle, between that party and a party that refuses access to public markets for undertakings of the former. State retreat represents a very interesting compliance method of international trade, which, however, may result in unsatisfactory consequences, as it represents a complex interrelation of private and public law rights. Undertakings which are non-signatories to GATT may face trade restrictions by Member States according to Article 115 EEC, which governs the Community's common external policy.

Despite its promising aims and purposes,[63] the AGP-EC regime on public supplies contracts has had a rather limited application as (i) it embraced only its signatories, (ii) it covers only the supply of products and services that are incidental to the supply contract and not services contracts *per se* and (iii) it applied only to centrally controlled authorities, thus leaving local or regional authorities outside its scope.

The above mentioned regime has left large areas of procurement activity unregulated by the GATT or by E.C. secondary legislation. Works and utilities contracts and supply of services have been excluded. Both Community and global public procurement markets are very promising business fields. The Council in its 1977 resolution[64] noted that the opening up of the public procurement market in respect of non-Community countries could only be accomplished through reciprocity in treatment and mutual balance of advantages. The reciprocity doctrine or the "mirror principle" requires that non-member states provide in their domestic markets similar opportunities to those provided by the European Member States to undertakings coming from those countries. This means that the element of reciprocity should occur between all European Member States and the third country in question. This is a rather unlikely situation, so the Commission in its statement in 1977 concerning Article 115[65] was prepared to permit a limited and controlled use of it by individual Member States, which have established economic and commercial relations with non-member countries in the field of public procurement. During the Tokyo round negotiations, the Council noted also that Community undertakings were participating in contracts awarded in third countries. This reveals that reciprocity was a

---

[63] See the FIDE Congress on Application in the Member States of the directives on public procurement", Madrid 1990.
[64] [1977] O.J. C11/1.
[65] [1977] O.J. C11/2.

bilateral phenomenon in economic activities between a Member State and a third country. At first sight, this appears contradictory with the centralised policy that Community institutions seek to apply in the public procurement sector. In this regard, the Commission stated that, in order to prevent deflection of trade between a Member State and a third country, it would authorise the former, under Article 115, to exclude from public contracts certain products, originating in third countries, which are in free circulation in another Member State, where similar arrangements (reciprocity effects) have been made for products imported directly. In other words, it was thought that the use of Article 115 might eliminate the "free rider" phenomenon and "protect" the benefits gained through a bilateral trade flow between a Member State and a third country. From an economic point of view, this tactic may prevent deflection and diversification of trade, but on the other hand, it creates what is sometimes more serious: non-tariff barriers to intra-Community trade. It is difficult, in the framework of an economic union such as the E.C., to strike the balance between a common external tariff and individual commercial policies pursued by one or more Member States.

One could question the reason that the AGP did not extend its scope to cover works contracts also. It should be recalled that supplies and works contracts were the only regimes covered by public procurement Community legislation during the GATT Tokyo round (1979). A possible answer could be that supply of products was the maximum that could be agreed, at least at the first stage in the cumbersome and laborious negotiations between the European Communities and GATT signatories. Like the EEC Treaty, GATT does not prohibit discrimination by government purchasing agencies in favour of national products. Under the E.C. regime, discrimination based on economic reasons is justified. National authorities may justify their discriminatory purchasing practices by invoking concerns for employment and social equity, under the broader goal of promoting greater economic efficiency and industrial adjustment. Under the GATT regime, Article III 8(a) excludes government procurement from the principle of national treatment regarding its regulation. Thus, free movement of goods was considered, with respect to public procurement, to be the first step under the framework of the multilateral agreements between the E.C. and GATT signatories, with a view to liberalising trade and preventing non-tariff barriers arising from national procurement policies.

Another possible justification of the limitation of the AGP rules to supplies of goods only could have been that works and construction contracts involve further aspects that must be taken into account in an attempt to liberalise their regime. They involve social and regional policy, short and long term employment considerations, peripheral development of the E.C. regions, etc. Liberalising the public works regime between the Community and third countries will not only bring into play not only free trade area considerations (free movement of goods), but will also go further, trespassing on the field of economic union, where labour, capital, payments and services need also to circulate freely.[66]

The utilities Directive 90/531 intends to open up procurement practices in the four previously excluded sectors—water, energy, telecommunications and transport—mainly to E.C. wide competition. With regard to goods (and services) originating in third countries, things are more complicated. A product outside the Community, in order to be subject to a public contract regulated by one of the E.C. public procurement directives, must lawfully be put in free circulation in at least one Member State.[67] Except where there has been an international agreement which grants comparable and effective access for Community undertakings to public markets of a third country (reciprocity principle), Article 29 of Directive 90/531 renders it possible for E.C. contracting authorities in the utilities sector to reject offers from outside the Community and requires Community preference where Community offers are equivalent to offers from third countries (where the price difference does not exceed 3 per cent). With reference to an international agreement granting access to public markets, Directive 90/531 opens the door for the application of the AGP in the utilities sector, concluded between the European Community and 11 GATT signatories during the GATT Tokyo round in 1979. The AGP embraces only supplies contracts, which are currently the only public sector regime open to international competition. The European Union's commitment towards international liberalisation of public markets has been demonstrated by its offer to the GATT AGP signatories during the Uruguay round, to eliminate all discrimination regarding contracts in urban transport, ports, airports, heavy electrical and telecommunications equipment.[68]

Expansion of the AGP framework to embrace supplies and works contracts in the utilities sector and services contracts was pursued during the GATT Uruguay round.[69] The new regime introduced substantial changes in the application of the AGP with respect to types of contracts and coverage of contracting authorities as well as remedies. Works and services contracts are now covered and the list of contracting authorities embraces not only central government departments and their agencies but regional and local authorities and some utilities in the form of public authorities or public undertakings. Certain exemptions between the signatories do apply, but based on bilateral agreements, the new regime

---

[66] See Gormley, "Some reflections on Public Procurement in the EEC", (1990) 2 E.B.L.R. pp. 143–145.

[67] For the concept of origin of goods and their lawful free circulation in the Common Market see Regulation 802/68, [1968] O.J. Spec. Ed. 165.

[68] See Council Regulation 1461/93, [1993] O.J. L146, on access to public contracts for tenderers from the United States; Council Decision 93/323, [1993] O.J. L125, on the conclusion of agreement between the EEC and USA on government procurement.

[69] Art. XXIV 1 AGP, signed on April 15, 1994 by all the previous signatories exept Hong Kong and Singapore.

promises a significant expansion of the existing European procurement legislation.[70]

With respect to EFTA countries, the E.C. reached an agreement on October 22, 1991 with the seven states (European Economic Area) to participate in the Single Market from January 1, 1993. This will change the so far existing framework under the preferential agreement regime existing until 1991[71] to a free trade area, as the EFTA states will be required to implement Community law, and of course E.C. public procurement directives in their national legal orders. The regime applies also to Hungary and Poland, by virtue of their association agreements.[72]

[70] The applicability of the new AGP by its signatories is subject to its ratification before January 1, 1996.
[71] See Weiss, "The law of public procurement in EFTA and the EEC; The legal framework and its implementation", (1987) Yearbook of European Law, pp. 59–111.
[72] [1993] O.J. L347/36 and [1993] O.J. L348/36.

Chapter 6

The financial services sector

GENERAL REMARKS

The Treaty of Rome establishing the European Community as amended by the Single European Act and the Maastricht Treaty on European Union was intended to create an internal market encompassing a whole range of services including financial services such as banking, insurance and the markets in stocks, securities and related products. Primary Community legislation stipulates the parameters of the principle of free movement of capital as an essential element for the creation of the common market. The Court of Justice has recognised the free movement of payments as an additional freedom to the four fundamental freedoms of the European Community. The services sectors have seen a dramatic expansion in recent years in contrast with manufacturing, which has reached over capacity levels throughout the world. Although the provision of services could be regarded as an ancillary activity to the manufacturing industry, contemporary growth patterns support the view that services have acquired a more autonomous dimension in economic orders. A shift, in terms of relative importance with reference to a country's GDP form traditional manufacturing to services has occurred. Although the European integration process achieved considerable progress in liberalising the services sector in the common market, the goals set out in the Treaty had still not been fully achieved by 1985. In that year the European Commission published the White Paper on the completion of the internal market, calling for a new impetus to integration. The aim was to integrate national economies into a single market by the end of 1992. The White Paper programme was incorporated into the Community legal order in 1986 by virtue of the Single European Act amending the E.C. Treaties, which defined the internal market as "*an area without internal frontiers in which the free movement of goods, services, persons and capital is ensured*". The White Paper made the point that a common market for goods was already to a large extent in place and that it was important to make similar progress in the area of services, particularly financial services, in the light of their vital role in the European economy.

THE FINANCIAL SERVICES SECTOR IN EUROPE

The financial services sector has been an increasingly important part of the Community economy. In terms of output it accounts for about 70 per cent of gross domestic product (GDP) for the Twelve as a whole, while in employment terms it provides over 3 million jobs—or about 2 per cent of the E.C. total. Financial services also provide a major input into the rest of the Community economy, with nearly half of the total profits earned by credit and insurance institutions being reinvested in other industries. Yet for many years they were unable to benefit to the same extent as the manufacturing industry from the progress made towards dismantling trade barriers between the Member States.

The completion of the single market in financial services marks the culmination of a process that has been under way for some time. Highly integrated markets already exist in reinsurance (insurance of insurers) and transport insurance, while many banks have branches in the Community's main financial centres, and a large number of securities are listed on the stock exchanges of more than one member country. In the past, however, national regulations imposed mainly for prudential reasons have hampered financial institutions in their attempts to set up in other Member States or offer services there. Open markets, free competition and cost efficiency have not always proved attainable.

For some time, too, changes have been taking place in the environment in which European financial institutions operate. The market has become a global one, increasingly integrated across the world. Financial services companies can now transfer capital very quickly from one continent to another. The development of new telecommunications and information technologies has reinforced the globalisation process and ensured the rapid spread of innovation and new financial products. Interestingly, wider competition between different kinds of financial institutions as well as competition between European financial institutions and their American and Japanese counterparts tends to blur the distinctions between banking, insurance and securities firms. With world financial markets rapidly moving to continuous 24-hour trading centred on three principal time zones in the USA, Europe and the Far East, it is essential for the European integration process to accomplish not only a single market of services but also to be able to compete on the world stage. The case for an integrated European financial services market offers many advantages. National laws on their own no longer offer an adequate framework for the future development of the sector, especially in the light of the pace at which globalisation is moving. If Europe is not to lose its share of the business and of the employment which is associated with it, the Community has to develop an efficient and open market in financial services. From the consumer's point of view, there are great benefits to be reaped from having access to a wide range of competitive financial products irrespective of nationality. For the competitiveness of the manufacturing industry too, it is vital for the financial sector to be as competitive as possible.

A report prepared for the Commission in 1988 on the cost of "non-Europe" in financial services showed significant potential gains to be made from completing the internal market. It estimated that the overall benefit to the consumer could amount to anything between ECU 11 billion and ECU 33 billion, with further gains likely to result from more closely aligned interest rates. The report also pointed out that the benefits of the internal market were expected to extend beyond simply eliminating the extra costs due to trade barriers affecting financial services, since there would also be an added boost to trade itself. This would mean more competition, generating wider opportunities for the financial services industry and lower costs for the consumer. It would also mean greater freedom of choice for consumers, allowing them to go to service suppliers from other Member States to obtain the best terms and conditions on offer.

The foundations of an integrated financial services market can be found in three fundamental freedoms for the establishment of the common market. The freedom of establishment, the freedom to provide services and the free movement of capital represent the parameters for the European-wide fully integrated financial services market. Freedom of establishment denotes freedom for all financial institutions to base their head offices and to set up branches anywhere inside the Community. The freedom to provide services indicates freedom for all financial institutions to offer their own particular products across frontiers in other Member States without having to set up offices there. Finally, there should be freedom of capital movements throughout the Community, without any legislative or administrative obstacles aimed at the protection of domestic economic or monetary policies.

A legislative programme drawn up by the European Commission and adopted by Member States was designed to remove all restrictions and obstacles that interfere with these freedoms. It should be noted that the freedom of capital movements represents the catalyst of the Community's approach to the liberalisation of financial services. Already in the early 1960s, direct investment and portfolio investment in quoted shares and bonds were liberalised. In 1986 the Council adopted a directive extending the list of liberalised transactions to include long-term loans, unquoted securities and the issuing of foreign securities on domestic markets. In 1988 the Council approved a directive to liberalise all other transactions: short-term monetary instruments, current and deposit account operations, financial loans and credits. The above legal framework obliges Member States to ensure that their residents have access to the financial systems in other Member States and to all the financial products available there. It also abolishes all restrictions on capital transfers and any other discriminatory measure that could hinder or distort the free movement of capital.

Despite its undoubtedly crucial role, the liberalisation of capital movements is not sufficient in itself to ensure effective integration of the financial services markets. Its function should be considered within the framework of the freedom of establishment and the freedom to provide services. Even after the lifting of all restrictions on capital movements, inconsistent national regulations could pose barriers restricting freedom of establishment and hampering free trade in financial services. Without common rules for the supervision of financial institutions, business would tend to migrate to centres where supervision is most lax. There also have to be equivalent standards for protection of investors. Based on the basic principles of the Treaty and on the legislation already in place, the White Paper set out a general strategy for achieving the Community's objectives, involving the harmonisation of basic standards for supervising financial institutions and protecting investors, depositors and consumers; mutual recognition by the supervisory authorities in the Member States of the way in which they each apply those standards; and based on these first two elements, "home country control and supervision" of financial institutions (*i.e.* by the country where they are based) covering all their operations throughout the Community, whether through branches or in direct services across frontiers. As far as banking operations and dealings in securities are concerned, the key element of the system is a single licence issued by the Member State where an institution is based, allowing it to market services in other member countries either through branches or directly across frontiers, provided it is allowed to market those same services in its home country. In the insurance sector, on the other hand, supervisory control was divided for a time between the Member State where a company is based and those where it has agencies or branches, before the system eventually switched over to the same pattern as for other financial institutions in 1994.

THE INTEGRATION OF THE BANKING SECTOR

The European banking Directives

— Council Directive 73/183 on the abolition of restrictions on freedom of establishment and freedom to provide services in respect of self-employed activities of banks and other financial institutions ([1973] O.J. L194);

— First Council Directive 77/780 on the co-ordination of the laws, regulations and administrative provisions relating to the taking up and pursuit of the business of credit institutions ([1977] O.J. L322);

— Second Council Directive 89/646 on the co-ordination of laws, regulations and administrative provisions relating to the taking up and pursuit of the business of credit institutions and amending Directive 77/780 ([1989] O.J. L386);

— Directive 94/19 of the European Parliament and the Council on deposit guarantee schemes ([1994] O.J. L135);

— Council Directive 89/299 on the own funds of credit institutions ([1989] O.J. L124);

— Council Directive 89/647 on a solvency ratio for credit institutions ([1989] O.J. L388);

— Commission Directive 91/31 adapting the technical definition of "multilateral development banks" in Council Directive 89/647 on a solvency ratio for credit institutions ([1991] O.J. L17);

— Council Directive 92/302 on the supervision of credit institutions on a consolidated basis ([1992] O.J. L110);

— Council Directive 86/635 on the annual accounts and consolidated accounts of banks and other financial institutions ([1986] O.J. L372);

— Council Directive 89/117 on the obligations of branches established in a Member State of credit institutions and financial institutions, having their head offices outside that Member State, regarding the publication of annual accounting documents ([1989] O.J. L44);

— Council Directive 91/308 on prevention of the use of the financial system for the purpose of money laundering ([1991] O.J. L168);

— Council Directive 92/121 on the monitoring and control of large exposures of credit institutions ([1992] O.J. L29).

The First banking co-ordination Directive was adopted in 1977 and achieved three main goals. The first was to abolish most of the obstacles to freedom of establishment for banks and other credit institutions within the common market. The second goal consisted in laying down common standards for granting banking licences in European Member States. Finally, the third and most important goal was to introduce the basic principle of home country control, where home regulatory and supervisory authorities have responsibility for the activities of banking institutions operating in different Member States. The latter principle indicated advanced co-operation between domestic supervisory authorities in an attempt to avoid duplication of regulation and reduce unnecessary bureaucracy. The First banking Directive was a genuine legal instrument which intended to harmonise the divergent field of banking and related services in the common market and achieve a common platform of operational parameters for the industry. However, a number of obstacles still needed to be removed before a genuinely unified Community banking market could become fully operational. The most important ones reflected the bureaucratic and somehow protectionist environment in different Member States. Banks or credit institutions still had to obtain prior authorisation from 11 different supervisory authorities to set up branches in other Member States. On the other hand, it was impossible to offer banking services across the frontiers in some Member States, a fact which epitomised the closed and highly segmented domestic banking sectors across Europe. Finally, a problem inherent to the directive created some degree of legal uncertainty; banking activities had not been precisely defined in the directive itself.

As a response to the above shortcomings, the Second banking co-ordination Directive, adopted in 1989, abolished all these barriers. It consolidated the principle of a single banking licence, valid throughout the European Community, authorising a bank or credit institution to operate anywhere in the common market either through branches or directly. National supervisory authorities were obliged to recognise licences issued in other Member States. It also set out a list of banking activities, including not only the main traditional services but also some that were new for certain Member States, such as trading in securities. Finally, it laid down a minimum capital requirement of ECU 5 million in order to establish a new bank. Supervisory rules were also introduced covering, among other things, internal management and audit systems.

Further legislation was needed to ensure equal competition between banks and other credit institutions and to forestall a migration of banks to countries with less strict supervision. Of paramount importance were consumer protection considerations resulting from the integration of the banking sector in Europe. To eliminate uncertainty and establish a concrete basis for European banking services, a directive on the bank's *own funds* defined the bank's own funds and formed a numerator of a solvency ratio applicable to banking and credit institutions operating within the common market. The own funds directive complements the solvency ratio directive, which set high capital adequacy standards in the industry. The directive applies a solvency ratio (8 per cent) between assets and off-balance sheet items, which are adjusted to reflect different degrees of risk, and own funds available to cover those risks. The bank's own funds have been divided into two tier systems, which are supposed to cover the bank's risks on an equal basis; for example, tier one own funds include capital reserves and reserves for general banking risks which shall represent at least 4 per cent of the solvency ratio. Every other item shall fall within the remaining 4 per cent.

The protection of the consumer and the general public were the main objectives behind two recommendations relating to the protection of depositors' interests and to limiting the size of exposure risks undertaken by credit institutions. The uniform control of large exposures of credit institutions and the monitoring of their risk concentrations were the subjects of the large exposure Directive, which defined as large exposure an exposure to a particular client or a group of connected clients of more than 10 per cent of the bank's own funds. The limit of large exposures was set to 25 per cent of own funds (20 per cent for intra-group credits of which the bank or the credit institutions is part). Regarding deposit protection schemes, Directive 94/19 introduced compulsory membership of such schemes for all credit institutions operating in the common market. Interestingly, there is a considerable margin of discretion in the hands of Member States to determine whether such schemes should be publicly or privately organised.

Rules on the annual and consolidated accounts of banks were enacted by virtue of Directive 86/635 and transparency and disclosure requirements of foreign branches were introduced through Directive 89/117. Moreover, in line with the consolidated accounts directive, supervision of banking and credit institutions on a consolidated basis was introduced. The banking sector often operates under complex group and control structures and since 1983 legislation has been introduced to harmonise supervision of banking groups on a consolidated basis, provided that the parent undertaking was a credit institution or a bank itself. Supervision at a group level, with particular reference to solvency and risk exposure, was hindered by the relevant provisions of the 1983 directive which excluded its application from groups controlled through holdings or non-financial institutions. The latter situation was changed by virtue of Directive 92/30, which consolidated supervision to groups controlled through financial holding companies and to groups where the parent undertaking is neither a credit nor a financial institution, but the group as a whole contains at least one banking or credit institution. The consolidated supervision Directive follows a principle similar to the home control approach found in the banking co-ordination directives. In terms of competence, by mutual agreement between the relevant national authorities, consolidated supervision should be exercised by authorities of the Member State in which the group concentrates most of its activities. Such a principle could produce extra-territorial effects to the extent that consolidated supervision in non-Member States would be achievable.

Another initiative in the banking sector was the adoption of legislation concerning common rules for consumer credit operations. Two directives (Directive 87/102 as amended by Directive 90/88) have been adopted. It is worth noting that freedom of establishment and the freedom to provide services across frontiers also extends to mortgage credit. This will allow the various forms of credit available from national institutions that specialise in this area to be marketed throughout the Community. Finally, action was needed to prevent disreputable operators from taking advantage of the opening up of the banking and financial markets to exploit potential loopholes in the supervisory arrangements. The outcome was the adoption in 1991 of a directive (91/308) aimed at preventing the use of financial institutions to launder the proceeds of criminal activities.

Complementing the integration of the banking sector, the creation of an *integrated payment system* has been pursued by European Institutions which have reiterated the importance of a rapid and simple process of payments within the European Community. Modern technology and to a large extent the results of the integration process in the banking sector have resulted in simplifying intra-E.C. cross-border payments by means of electronic transfer between banks, by cheque or by payment card. Despite the effort which has been invested in creating a single market for banking services, non-tariff barriers still exist in cross-border payments. Transfers of small sums by individuals and businesses from one Member

State to another has been considered as a complicated, expensive and slow exercise. The European Commission has taken radical steps in improving a uniform payments system. A 1987 recommendation incorporating a code of conduct for relations between banks and retailers with regard to electronic fund transfers as a result of sales transactions envisages the creation of an unobstructed payments system for businesses, particularly small and medium sized enterprises which engage in cross border trade. The code provides for prompt transfers and addresses the issue of delays in payments as a serious threat to the viability of small companies. The European Commission, in its 1988 recommendation setting out minimum terms and conditions for the protection of the holders of payment cards, has provided for minimum standards for consumers using credit and payment cards. Credit cards, as a method of payment, have been increasingly utilised by European consumers and the need for protection against fraud is pressing. Finally, a 1990 recommendation dealing with bank transfers, in particular with the information to be given to the customer, the time transfers should take and the possibilities of redress in the event of complaint, completes the picture of the exercise aimed at the establishment of a uniform payments system in Europe.

In 1990 the Commission published a discussion paper on possible improvements to the integration of the banking sector, which has been looked into by two advisory groups set up in 1991 (one representing banks and central banks, the other bringing together various users). Most of the suggested improvements can be achieved through self-regulation or other voluntary action by the banking industry, although a few areas remain where legislation may be necessary or more effective. In particular, the advisory groups have suggested that improvements should produce clear benefits for users of payment systems. Also, customers should be given clear information on the various ways of making a payment in or to another Member State and the costs involved (including exchange costs). There should be no hidden charges for individuals when exchanging cash at banks or 'bureaux de change' for foreign currency. Furthermore, new legislation should aim at encouraging banks and payment system providers to make payment instruments increasingly inter-operable and to link the payment and clearing systems of different Member States.

A European Banking Standards Committee (EBSC) has been fully operational since 1993. It was established by the three European Credit Associations (The European Banking Federation, the European Savings Bank Group and the Association of Co-operative Banks of the European Community). The EBSC has an advisory but influential role in setting strict standards for the banking sector of the European Community. Its agenda includes certain legal aspects of payment systems which need to be harmonised. Priority has been given to the harmonisation of legal regimes covering payment cards, cross-border transfers, electronic data interchange, securities and cryptographic security.

THE INTEGRATION OF THE INSURANCE SECTOR

The non-life insurance Directives

— Council Directive 64/225 on the abolition of restrictions on freedom of establishment and freedom to provide services in respect
of reinsurance and retrocession ([1964] O.J. Spec. Ed. 131);

— First Council Directive 73/239 on the co-ordination of laws,
regulations and administrative provisions relating to the taking-
up and pursuit of the business of direct insurance other than life
assurance ([1973] O.J. L228);

— Council Directive 73/240 abolishing restrictions on freedom of
establishment in the business of direct insurance other than life
assurance ([1973] O.J. L288);

— Council Directive 78/473 on the co-ordination of laws, regulations and administrative provisions relating to Community
co-insurance ([1978] O.J. L151);

— Council Directive 87/344 on the co-ordination of laws, regulations and administrative provisions relating to legal expenses
insurance ([1987] O.J. L185);

— Second Council Directive 88/357 on the co-ordination of laws,
regulations and administrative provisions relating to direct insurance other than life assurance and laying down provisions to
facilitate the effective exercise of freedom to provide services
amending Directive 73/239, ([1988] O.J. L172);

— Council Directive 92/49 on the co-ordination of laws, regulations
and administrative provisions relating to direct insurance other
than life assurance and amending Directives 73/239 and 88/357
(third non-life insurance directive), ([1992] O.J. L228).

The life assurance Directives

— First Council Directive 79/267 on the co-ordination of laws,
regulations and administrative provisions relating to the taking up
and pursuit of the business of direct life assurance ([1979] O.J.
L63);

— Council Directive 90/619 on the co-ordination of laws, regulations and administrative provisions relating to direct life assurance, laying down provisions to facilitate the effective exercise of
freedom to provide services and amending Directive 79/267
([1990] O.J. L330);

— Council Directive 92/96 on the co-ordination of laws, regulations
and administrative provisions relating to direct life assurance and

amending Directives 79/267 and 90/619 (third life assurance directive) ([1992] O.J. L380);

— Council Directive 77/92 on measures to facilitate the effective exercise of freedom of establishment and freedom to provide services in respect of the activities of insurance agents and brokers (ex. ISIC Group 630) and, in particular, transitional measures in respect of those activities ([1977] O.J. L26);

— Council Directive 91/674 on the annual accounts and consolidated accounts of insurance undertakings ([1991] O.J. L374);

— Council Directive 91/675 setting up an insurance committee ([1991] O.J. L374).

Freedom of establishment for insurance companies was introduced in the 1970s by the first E.C. directives on non-life insurance and life assurance. Motor insurance directives were also adopted, abolishing frontier checks on international insurance cards (green cards) and reducing differences in compulsory third party insurance cover. However, progress towards ensuring full freedom to provide services in the insurance sector was not satisfactory. In 1986, the Council adopted a second directive on non-life insurance to secure some harmonisation of national laws in this area. In particular, a wide range of freedom to provide services in connection with major risks in the industrial, commercial and transport sectors as well as free access to the Community market for large policy holders were set out. The same principle of freedom to provide services (implying free access for policy holders to the whole Community market) also applies to life assurance and motor insurance, and in 1990 the Council adopted directives on them as well.

The life and non-life assurance directives provided for a broad framework of freedom to provide services and hence free access to the whole Community market for customers to take out policies in other Community Member States, either directly or through an intermediary. Consumer protection was guaranteed by a rule under which the law of the policy holder's home country would normally apply. The operational framework for insurance services on non-life insurance and life assurance has established:

— a single licence issued in the country where the insurance company is based, along the lines of the system already adopted for banking;
— greater freedom for the insurer in drawing up new contracts;
— common rules on the assets which insurers are required to set aside to meet their commitments;
— provisions to ensure that inspectors from the country of a policy holder will be able to secure adequate protection for him and to monitor compliance with any rules of general interest in force in his country;

— full information for the policyholder about his insurer and the content of his policy.

The First non-life Directive and First life Directive achieved four objectives: they provided common conditions for authorisation of insurance companies enabling E.C. insurers wishing to operate in other E.C. states to set up branches or agencies in those states without being subject to more onerous restrictions than their local competitors; they laid down common solvency regulations; they established a minimum guarantee fund—non-life generally ECU 400,000 and life ECU 800,000; and finally they established a system whereby each state became responsible for ensuring that an authorised insurer has sufficient technical reserves. It should also be mentioned that the First life Directive restricted composites from opening new branches or agencies to transact life business in E.C. states when they were not already established in 1979.

The Second non-life Directive accomplished three objectives, alongside the provisions of the First non-life Directive. It established freedom for insurers to supply non-life insurance for large risks across frontiers without the need for authorisation in the host state; it provided that the notification of policy conditions, premium rates and documents relating to large risks would be allowed on a non-systematic basis only; and finally, it provided rules governing choice of law applicable to insurance contracts in order, in particular, to favour the consumer.

The Second life Directive introduced freedom of services for life insurance companies. In addition, the host country cannot require authorisation for contracts taken out on the consumer's own initiative. The "own initiative" test will be applied by reference to public policy in the host country.

The Third non-life and the Third life Directive expanded the principles of their predecessors and complement the framework of freedom to provide life and non-life insurance services within the common market. In particular, the Third life and non-life insurance Directives have been influenced by the relevant directives in the banking sector.

The new regime established home country control and mutual recognition, along the lines of the banking directives. It provided a formal framework of co-operation between the supervisory authorities of member states and obliged the home country to verify the suitability of the insurers' management and controllers. The directives also provided for a common basis for calculation of technical reserves and a system to limit the control of policy conditions or premium rates by home or host country. Finally, they lifted the restrictions on new authorisations for composite insurers.

The most important element still to come is the liberalisation of insurance services for mass risks. Although the Second non-life Directive has released the large risk insurance services from host country control, mass risk insurance are still subject to the restrictions of the state where the risk or the policyholder is located. It should be mentioned here that "large" risk insurance services cover two main categories of insurance:

the first is marine, aviation or transit insurance, whereas the second relates to fire, property damage, general liability or financial loss insurance for a large policyholder (principally those having more than two hundred and fifty employees and annual turnover in excess of twelve million ECU).

The Third life and non-life Directives explicitly exclude reinsurance. Due to the fact that reinsurance has largely international dimensions and effects and encroaches upon little of the consumer, there were generally few national regulations. Therefore there was little difficulty in agreeing the Reinsurance and Retrocession Directive which abolished restrictions on the freedom of establishment and freedom to provide reinsurance and retrocession services. However, it only established equality of treatment in local regulations. Hence, reinsurers will be subject to restrictions not applying to their associated companies writing direct business.

As insurance companies are free to provide services in different countries of the European Community, in 1991 for reasons relating to openness and transparency of their operations, the Council adopted a directive on the harmonisation of the annual accounts of insurance companies to facilitate the comparison and monitoring of the accounts of insurers in different countries. Also in 1991 the Commission adopted a recommendation on insurance intermediaries (brokers, agents), with the twofold aim of setting a minimum level of qualifications for them all and of clarifying the distinction between dependent and independent intermediaries. Finally, also in 1991, the Commission sent the Council a proposal for a directive on the freedom of pension funds to manage and invest their assets.

The motor vehicle insurance Directives

— Council Directive 72/166 on the approximation of the laws of Member States relating to insurance against civil liability in respect of the use of motor vehicles, and to the enforcement of the obligation to insure against such liability ([1972] O.J. L103);

— Second Council Directive 84/5 on the approximation of the laws of the Member States relating to insurance against civil liability in respect of the use of motor vehicles ([1984] O.J. L8);

— Third Council Directive 90/232 on the approximation of the laws of the Member States relating to insurance against civil liability in respect of the use of motor vehicles ([1990] O.J. L129);

— Council Directive 90/618 amending, particularly as regards motor vehicle liability insurance, Directive 73/239 and Directive 88/357 which concern the co-ordination of laws, regulations and administrative provisions relating to direct insurance other than life assurance ([1990] O.J. L330).

The motor insurance directives set out to secure wide freedom for major policy holders. But in the interests of insured parties and accident victims, insurers providing services outside their home country must designate representatives responsible for settling claims in the country or countries where they operate. Representatives should normally be insurance companies themselves or intermediaries covered by the law of the particular Member State where an insurance claim is made. The reason for such provision is to ensure access to justice for claimers or victims in case an out-of-court settlement is not possible.

THE INTEGRATION OF STOCK EXCHANGE AND SECURITIES MARKETS

The stock exchange and securities markets directives

— Council Directive 79/279 co-ordinating the conditions for the admission of securities to official stock exchange listings ([1979] O.J. L86);

— Council Directive 80/390 co-ordinating the requirements for the drawing up, scrutiny and distribution of the listing particulars to be published for the admission of securities to official stock exchange listing ([1980] O.J. L100);

— Council Directive 82/121 on information to be published on a regular basis by companies the shares of which have been admitted to official stock exchange listing ([1982] O.J. L48);

— Council Directive 87/345 amending Directive 80/390 co-ordinating the requirements for the drawing-up, scrutiny and distribution of the listing particulars to be published for the admission of securities to official stock exchange listing ([1987] O.J. L185);

— Council Directive 88/627 on the information to be published when a major holding in a listed company is acquired or disposed of ([1988] O.J. L348);

— Council Directive 89/298 co-ordinating the requirements for the drawing-up, scrutiny and distribution of the prospectus to be published when transferable securities are offered to the public ([1989] O.J. L124);

— Council Directive 89/592 co-ordinating regulations on insider dealing ([1989] O.J. L334);

— Council Directive 90/211 amending Directive 80/390 in respect of the mutual recognition of public offer prospectuses as stock exchange listing particulars ([1990] O.J. L112);

— Council Directive 85/611 on the co-ordination of laws, regulations and administrative provisions relating to undertakings for collective investment in transferable securities (UCITS) ([1985] O.J. L375);

— Council Directive 93/6 on the capital adequacy of investments firms and credit institutions ([1993] O.J. L141);

— Council Directive 93/22 on investment services in the securities field ([1993] O.J. L141).

The Commission's overall objective is to create a unified securities market enabling issuers to raise capital on a Community-wide basis, allowing intermediaries to offer services and create branches in other Member States as easily as in their own, and offering investors a wide range of competing investment products to choose from. A number of directives have been adopted towards this end. The three stock exchange directives, although adopted at different times, contributed towards constructing a single package with the same implementation deadline for all three.

The first directive which was adopted in 1979, co-ordinated the conditions for the admission of securities to official stock exchange listings (*e.g.* minimum size, minimum period of existence, distribution of securities among the public, etc.) and imposed permanent obligations on issuers. In particular they had to publish information on any new developments likely to have a substantial effect on the price of their securities. The second directive, dating from 1980, dealt with stock exchange admission prospectuses and co-ordinated the information to be disclosed so as to enable investors to make an informed assessment of the assets and liabilities, financial position, profits and losses, and prospects of the issuer and of the rights attaching to the securities. Finally, the third one which was adapted in 1982, required listed companies to publish half-yearly reports giving turnover and profit and loss figures for the first six months of the financial year.

In addition to the above package, a number of directives have been enacted with a view to complementing the process of integrating the securities and stock exchanges markets. A 1985 directive on open ended undertakings for collective investment in transferable securities (*Ucits*: these include unit trusts and investment funds) laid down common rules, with provision for home country control. Once such an undertaking has been licensed in its home country, it is able to market its units in other Member States without having to reapply for a licence each time, since all the Member States recognise the rules and controls of the home country. A 1987 directive amended the 1980 directive on stock exchange listing prospectuses so as to provide mutual recognition here as well. A prospectus approved in the home country no longer needs separate approval in others and can be issued without any change in content (except, of course, that it may have to be translated). A 1989 directive allows issuers to use the prospectus approved in their home country when securities are offered for the first time to investors for a simultaneous public offer in other Member States. The standard of disclosure must be at least the same as that required by the 1980 directive. A 1990 directive further amended the 1980 legislation to allow issuers to use a single prospectus approved in their home country both for public offers and for admission to stock exchange listings anywhere in the Community. A 1989 directive on insider trading required all the Member States to introduce similar rules, so as to safeguard the smooth operation of the unified market and ensure investor confidence in it. A 1988 directive dealt with the information to be published when major holdings in listed companies are acquired or disposed of. Anyone buying or selling a major shareholding must notify the company in question of their new number of voting rights if any of the thresholds laid down in the directive are exceeded. The company must then publish the information in compliance with its obligations under the 1979 directive.

Two further directives complete the picture of an integrated securities market. An investment services directive aims to bring in a "European passport" for anyone wishing to carry out investment business in securities and related instruments, subject to home country authorisation, regulation and supervision. It extends the right to provide such services (already enjoyed by banks under the second banking Directive) to non-bank firms and will allow all investment firms, banks and non-bank companies, to have access to stock exchange membership in all the Member States and to set up branches or subsidiaries there. Also, a directive on capital adequacy will require investment firms to meet certain conditions designed to ensure that they have sufficient capital to cover a range of risks, although it does not set a binding minimum level of financial resources. The intention is to ensure adequate investor protection and rough equivalence between bank and non-bank investment firms, while enabling the Community's financial centres to remain competitive compared to rival financial markets outside the Community.

Chapter 7

Social policy within the framework of European business law

GENERAL REMARKS

The regulation of industrial relations, both at Community and at national levels, reveals the social dimension of the European integration process and predicates the need to integrate the Community's social patterns with particular reference to labour relations. One of the most important objectives of the European Community's social policy has been the provision of a framework of equality of opportunities between men and women and the progressive integration of women into the workforce of contemporary labour markets. Alongside the above objective, the Community's social policy has focused on the promotion of improved working conditions and standards of living, through harmonised measures relating to employment law, vocational training, health and safety at work, working conditions, social security and last but not least the fundamental right of association and the freedom of collective bargaining between management and labour. Although within the framework of the EEC Treaty and the primary provisions on social policy (Articles 117–122) there is only one specific article referring to equality between men and women, which is related to equal pay (Article 119), a range of secondary Community legislation, particularly directives, have attempted to include many aspects of labour integration in European markets and furthermore, to establish a structure in equality of opportunities and treatment. Such an attempt requires the maximum degree of co-operation between Member States, as national divergences and social sensibilities at domestic level should be taken into account when seeking harmonisation of national social policies in order to conform with Community envisaged standards. European directives, as legal instruments binding only in respect to the result to be achieved and leaving a great deal of discretion in the hands of Member States, have been adopted for the accomplishment of that aim.

The existing legal framework of the European Community aiming at the integration of labour forces and the elimination of sex discrimination

(Articles 117–122) and the set of secondary legislation (Directive 75/117 on equal pay, Directive 76/207 on equal treatment, Directive 79/7 on state social security, Directive 86/378 on occupational social security, Directive 86/613 on equal treatment for the self-employed and finally Directive 92/85 on pregnancy and maternity) has been tested on grounds of efficiency and effectiveness by the European Court of Justice and national courts. The European Court of Justice has played a most significant role, through a large body of case law, in interpreting the above-mentioned legal framework. Judicial interpretation at Community level was, and still is indispensable for the establishment, function and maintenance of a homogeneous industrial relations system among the Member States and the social partners.

THE PRINCIPLE OF EQUALITY: THE FUNCTION OF ARTICLE 119 OF THE EEC TREATY

Article 119 of the EEC Treaty stipulates the principle that men and women should receive equal pay for equal work. It reflects the terms of Article 2(1) of the International Labour Organisation (ILO) Convention No. 100, concerning equal remuneration for men and women workers for work of equal value.[1] Although it provides for a partial definition of the term "equal pay", it gives no definition of the notion of "equal work", of which the precise meaning has been the subject of controversy in the context of European law and policy making.

It has been recognised by the European Court of Justice[2] that Article 119 EEC has a dual function; an economic and a social one. With respect to the former, the historical background of the inclusion of an equal pay principle in the context of the Treaty of Rome reveals the interrelation of social and economic aspects of the European integration process. France, prior to the conclusion of the Treaty, had legislation which provided for equality in pay between men and women workers in the textile industry.[3] To ensure effective and undistorted competition in the relevant market, France insisted on including the equal pay principle in the Treaty, as a primary provision. Indeed, the socio-economic dimension of sex discrimination and its labour market implication, may give rise to non-tariff barriers, which in turn may distort competition throughout the Community and endanger the completion of the common market.[4] In close relation with the above-mentioned considerations, the initially very restrictive interpretation of the scope of the equality principle has gradually been replaced by the view that, in substance

---

[1] This is more obvious in the French context of the EEC Treaty.
[2] See Case 43/75, *Drefenne v. Sabena*: [1976] E.C.R. 445.
[3] See Kapteyn and Verloren van Themaat, *Introduction to the Law of the European Communities* (2nd ed., 1989), pp. 632–638.
[4] White Paper (1994), *Growth, Competitiveness and Employment* [1993] E.C. Bull. 12.

Article 119 means that the sex of an employee may play no part in the configuration of salaries and all other benefits whether in cash or in kind, present or future, paid by the employer.

As far as the social function of Article 119 is concerned, according to the European Court of Justice,[5] it encompasses part of the social objectives of the Community, which is not merely an economic union, as its ultimate objective is to ensure social progress and to seek constant improvement of the living and working conditions of its peoples.[6] It could also be examined in conjunction with the recent developments regarding observance of fundamental rights.[7] Accepting that sex equality is a fundamental right which the European Community has an obligation to observe, Article 119 receives a more dynamic interpretation to embrace all matters which may influence the position of women in the labour market.

THE EQUAL PAY PRINCIPLE AND ITS COMPONENTS

The European Court of Justice has played a very important role in the elaboration of the precise determination of the equal pay principle, providing at the same time the impetus for the Community institutions to develop a more comprehensive programme of equality policy and legislation.[8]

According to Article 119, pay not only embraces the ordinary basic minimum wage or salary, but it also incorporates any other considerations, whether in cash or in kind, which the employee receives, directly or indirectly, with respect to his/her employment relation. To understand and appreciate the broad meaning of the term "equal pay", the European legal framework on equality between men and women (Article 119 and the directives implementing its letter and spirit) should be considered as complementary. In the *Drefenne v. Sabena* case,[9] the European Court of Justice stated that the meaning of "pay" in Article 119 covers all emoluments in cash or kind, paid or payable by the employer, as a result of the worker's employment. Furthermore, in *Garland v. British Rail Engineering Ltd*,[10] the Court adopted a broad interpretation of the concept of pay, so as to cover any special travel facilities granted by an employer to the families of former employees after retirement, even though the employer was under no obligation to do so. The latter consideration, according to the Court's judgment, was immaterial. With

---

[5] See *op. cit.* at n. 2.
[6] Arts. 117 and 118.
[7] Community Charter on the Fundamental Social Rights of Workers (1989); see also European Commission, *Social Action Programme* Com. (89) 568.
[8] European Commission, *Social Action Programme* Com. (89) 568; European Commission, Medium-term Social Action Programme 1995–97.
[9] See above n. 2.
[10] Case 12/81, [1982] E.C.R. 359.

respect to contributions to pension schemes, the Court ruled in the *Drefenne* case that the part due from the employers in the financing of state pension schemes does not constitute a direct or indirect payment to workers. However, in the *Worringham & Humphreys v. Lloyds Bank Ltd*[11] case, it held that the contributions paid by the employer to an occupational pension scheme on the employee's behalf fell under the meaning of "pay", because the higher gross salary payable to men affected the calculation of other financial advantages linked to that salary, for example, redundancy payments and credit facilities.[12] Additionally, the refunding to the employee of extra payments or excess contributions seems to be of particular importance and the Court based its judgments upon that criterion.

Interestingly, the Court pronounced in the *Newstead v. Department of Transport* case,[13] that contributions paid by an employee to an occupational pension scheme, which is substitute for the state scheme, are not covered by Article 119. The contribution to such a scheme was compulsory for men and voluntary for women. The crucial criterion in that case was that the gross salary was the same for men and women, whilst in the former cases the gross salary was higher for men.

Finally, with relation to the equal access to pension schemes, the Court in *Bilka-Kaufhaus v. Weber*,[14] ruled that the exclusion of part-timers from occupational schemes was not contrary to Article 119, provided objectively justified factors unrelated to sex differentiations are present. The above mentioned ruling was of particular significance, since pursuant to the Council directive on occupational pension schemes (Directive 86/378), part-timers seem to be excluded from its application; in practice, part-timers are excluded from most occupational schemes. Given that part-time employment is dominated by women, the above exclusion had an indirect discriminatory effect on them. As a result, the Court's decision was welcome. The uncertainty, however, of "objective economic reasons" (which may render Article 119 inapplicable) does leave the door open for indirect discrimination. It has been argued[15] that the discriminatory treatment of women under occupational pension schemes falls outside the scope of Article 119, if it is objectively justified by reference to actuarial data. Here, it should be mentioned that Council Directive 86/378[16] insists on different actuarial tables. Consequently, the Court must clarify what economic reasons might be justifiable.

---

[11] Case 69/80, [1981] E.C.R. 767.
[12] A similar approach was adopted in *Liefting*, Case 23/83, [1984] E.C.R. 3225, which to a certain extent could be considered as having overruled the *Drefenne* judgment.
[13] Case 192/85, [1988] C.M.L.R. 219.
[14] Case 170/84, [1986] E.C.R. 1607.
[15] See Arnull, "Sex discrimination in occupational schemes" [1986] 11 E.L.R. 363; Curtin, "Scalping the Community legislator: Occupational pensions and the Barber case" [1987] 28 C.M.L.R. 476; Fitzpatrick, "Equality in occupational pensions: the new frontiers after Barber" (1991) 54 M.L.R. 274.
[16] [1986] O.J. L225/40.

From the above analysis, the conclusion which could be drawn is that any facilities in kind may constitute "pay", as well as pension schemes to the extent that they form part of an employee's "pay package", and are considered to have been made in respect of employment.

RELIANCE UPON ARTICLE 119 AT NATIONAL LEVEL

The question of whether individuals may rely on the requirement of receiving equal pay for work of equal value before national courts was considered in the *Drefenne*[17] case. The Court also drew up a distinction between direct and overt discrimination on the one hand, and indirect and disguised discrimination on the other. The former could be identified simply by applying the criteria laid down in Article 119, whereas the latter could only be identified with reference to domestic provisions.[18] Among the forms of direct discrimination, the Court specified those forms of discrimination which originate in legislative provisions or in collective labour agreements and which may be detected on the basis of a pure legal analysis of the situation and where men and women receive unequal pay for equal work carried out in the same establishment or service. In the above mentioned forms the European Court of Justice has recognised the direct effect of Article 119.

The Court repeated that formula in the *Macarthys, Worringham* and *Jenkins* cases,[19] omitting only the reference to the distinction between "direct/overt" and "indirect/disguised" discrimination, thus following the opinion of Advocate General Warner, who pointed out that the distinction created ambiguity and confusion. It should be noted that two cases (*Jenkins* and *Garland*[20]), in which the Court pronounced the direct effect of Article 119, concerned a classical example of indirect discrimination (part-time employment dominated by women).

It could be inferred from the above mentioned cases that Article 119 has direct effect horizontally and vertically to both types of discrimination (direct and indirect) provided that they are judicially determined. Given the fact that the equal work requirement in Article 119 is broadly interpreted by the Court in conjunction with Article 1 of Directive 75/117,[21] so as to embrace the concept of work of equal value, the spatial scope of the comparison is a *conditio sine qua non* for giving Article 119 direct effect. However, this may give rise to controversy, as the Court

---

[17] *op. cit.* at n. 2 above.
[18] So far only Ireland (Employment Equality Act 1977), the Netherlands and the U.K. (Sex Discrimination Act 1975) have introduced statutory definitions of the concept of indirect discrimination.
[19] Case 129/79, *Macarthys Ltd v. Smith*: [1980] E.C.R. 1275 at 1289; Case 69/80, *Worringham & Humphreys v. Lloyds Bank Ltd*: [1982] E.C.R. 767; Case 96/80, *Jenkins v. Kingsgate Ltd*: [1981] E.C.R. 911.
[20] See n. 10 and n. 19 above.
[21] [1975] O.J. L45/9.

seems to be reluctant to take a more positive action, which might result in interfering with national labour markets.

THE PRINCIPLE OF EQUAL TREATMENT: THE STRUCTURE OF THE EQUALITY DIRECTIVES

As mentioned above, secondary Community legislation, particularly directives, have been adopted with a view to supplementing the equality principle stipulated in Article 119. Community institutions have opted for that type of legal instrument, since directives are the optimum legal instrument for harmonisation of national laws.

Equality in pay

Adopted in 1975, Council Directive 75/117[22] on equal pay was one of the earliest measures for the approximation of the laws of the Member States relating to the application of the equal pay principle. It extends the concept of equal pay in order to incorporate the elimination of discrimination on grounds of sex with regard to all aspects and conditions of remuneration for the same work or for work of equal value. According to the historical background of this directive,[23] the E.C. Commission's intention was not to clarify or expand the concept of equal pay contained in Article 119. However, under the influence of the Economic and Social Committee and the opinion of the European Parliament,[24] the Commission re-drafted the final version of the directive so as to incorporate the concept of equal value. The directive also provides for the elimination of discrimination arising in particular from the terms of collective agreements or the provisions of legal or administrative regulations.[25] Furthermore, when a job classification system is used in order to determine pay, it should be based on the same criteria for both men and women and should be drawn up so as to exclude discrimination on grounds of sex.

One of the primary objectives for enacting a directive which includes the concept of equal pay for work of equal value is the elimination of the continuing wage gap between men and women. Despite enjoying full access to paid employment since the end of the Second World War, women consistently earn less than men, not just in Europe but worldwide. It has been argued that in the United Kingdom, women on average are still only earning 66 per cent as much as men.[26] This is mainly due

---

[22] [1975] O.J. L45/9.
[23] See [1973] O.J. C114/46.
[24] [1974] O.J. C88/7.
[25] See Arts. 3 and 4 of Directive 75/117.
[26] Bradley, *Men's Work, Women's Work* (1st ed., 1989), p. 11.

to the concentration of women into sex-defined occupational categories such as nursing, retail sales, restaurant and catering, secretarial and child care, which are relatively low paying occupations. The equal pay directive was designed to alleviate the problem of lower financial compensation for women which results from the sex segregation of the workforce. It should be mentioned here that the concentration that occurred in certain types of employment, usually low paid, could be attributed to individual choices rather than labour market structures.[27] However, irrespective of the origin of this phenomenon, the result is sex segregation of the labour market and equality legislation, amongst other things, could facilitate its dismantling.[28]

Equality in treatment

One year later in 1976, the Council, in order to enhance the status of working women as regards entry opportunities in the labour market, introduced Directive 76/207[29] on the implementation of the principle of equal treatment for men and women in relation to access to employment, vocational training, promotion and general working conditions. The principle of equal treatment, as it is provided in this directive, requires that there should be no discrimination whatsoever on grounds of sex, either directly or indirectly.[30] Also, Member States, in order to eliminate discrimination in access to employment and to all levels of vocational training, are obliged *inter alia* to ensure the abolition of legal and administrative provisions contrary to the principle of equal treatment, and the nullity or amendment of offending provisions in individual or collective agreements. Finally, similar steps are required to be taken in order to ensure equality in working conditions. The above mentioned directive provides for some exemptions to the principle of equal treatment. This has resulted in restricting the scope of the equality principle, thus leaving room for deviations. Therefore, the role of the European Court of Justice in the precise determination of the concept of "determining factor"[31] is of extreme importance. Also the directive requires Member States to provide recourse to judicial remedies for persons alleging an infringement of the principle of equal treatment.[32] It does not, however, provide for any criterion regarding the appropriate sanctions and remedies in case of discrimination.

Again here, the role of the Court, through its judicial interpretation, would close the *lacuna*. An indication of how the Court understands the

---

[27] Lacey, "From Individual to Group", in *Discrimination: the limits of the law* (Hepple and Szyszczak ed., 1992).

[28] For an interesting discussion see Conaghan, "The Invisibility of Women in Labour Law: Gender-neutrality in Model Building" (1986) 14 *International Journal of Social Law* 384.

[29] [1976] O.J. L39/40.

[30] See Art. 2(1) of Directive 76/207.

[31] See Art. 2(2) of Directive 76/207.

[32] See Art. 6 of Directive 76/207.

above mentioned sanctions could be found in its judgments in the *Von Colson* and *Harz* cases.[33] According to these judgments an appropriate system of sanctions must be established to ensure real equality of opportunities. Furthermore, the Court has specified the requirements which must be fulfilled by the sanctions in order to ensure the effectiveness of the national implementing measures. These must be such as to guarantee "real and effective judicial protection" and also must have a real deterrent effect on the employer. According to the Court's decisions, although the victim of sex discrimination is entirely dependent on national law in relation to the award of compensation, as well as to the choice of suitable remedies, the award of compensation by the national judge must be adequate regarding the damage sustained and must therefore amount to more than purely nominal compensation. However, the extension of that compensation does not go so far as to confer a right to engagement for the victim of discrimination.

Equality in social security schemes

Two more directives complete the framework of the E.C. secondary legislation on equal treatment: Council Directive 79/7,[34] which concerns the progressive implementation of the principle of equal treatment in matters of social security, and Council Directive 86/378,[35] on the implementation of the principle of equal treatment in occupational pension schemes. The latter directive was adopted two months after the European Court ruled that the word "pay" in Article 119 also embraces the benefits paid to employees under occupational pension schemes. It is, therefore, obvious that Article 4(a) of Directive 86/378 overlaps to some extent Article 119. Both directives are dealing with the whole working population, whether wage earners or self-employed, including pensioners, the unemployed, the sick and the disabled. Unfortunately, it appears that both social security directives exclude from their scope part-time workers, temporary workers and those working at home. At this point it should be noted that most part-time workers and those working at home are women, so it is they who are mainly affected by that omission. Consequently, it appears to be another failure by the Community to establish real equality in this particular labour market.

Excluding part-time workers from equal treatment under Directives 79/7 and 86/378 results in indirect discrimination against women, something that Article 119 and the related equality directives have tried to eliminate, or at the very least alleviate. This indirect discrimination against women is due to the fact that part-time employment is located predominantly in service sectors, such as sales and food and beverage provision. The service sector, and therefore part-time work itself, are

[33] Case 14/83, *Von Colson & Kamann v. Land Nordhein Westfalen*: [1984] E.C.R. 1891; Case 79/83, *Harz v. Deutche Tradax GmbH*: [1984] E.C.R. 1921.
[34] [1979] O.J. L6/24.
[35] [1986] O.J. L225/40.

areas that are occupied predominantly by women workers. A 1984 Labour Force Survey found that 88 per cent of part-time workers in the United Kingdom are women.[36] The reluctance of European legislation to include part-time workers under the auspices of equality directives has had the opposite effect of the directives' and Article 119's original intentions; to eliminate indirect sex discrimination. A number of cases have followed the *Bilka* judgment, all based on the same rationale of the nature of part-time employment.[37]

Another shortcoming of the above social security directives appears to be that they exclude from their application the determination of pensionable age for the purpose of granting retirement pensions as well as survivor's pensions. With respect to retirement age, divergency among national statutory schemes constitutes an excuse for the existence of unequal treatment. Also, both directives include security schemes that provide for protection against illness, invalidity, old age, accidents at work, occupational diseases and unemployment. However, it has been argued[38] that provisions which regulate widows' pensions and children in social security schemes for the self-employed are beyond the scope of Directive 86/378. Furthermore, dealing separately with the above mentioned two social security directives, it should be mentioned that Directive 79/7 covers statutory social security schemes or social assistance, where this is intended to supplement or replace any such statutory schemes. The discrimination which must be eliminated concerns, in particular, the scope of the schemes and the conditions of access to them, as well as the obligation to contribute and the calculation of contribution and benefits (including increases due to the existence of spouse and dependants) and finally the conditions governing the duration and continuance of entitlements to benefits. Directive 86/378 covers schemes which supplement or replace benefits provided by statutory social security schemes, irrespective of the compulsory or optional nature of membership of such schemes. These are considered to fall between statutory social security and purely private insurance contracts. However, individual contracts, schemes having only one member, insurance contracts (to which the employer is not party) and optional provisions of schemes (which guarantee participants individually) are unfortunately excluded from the scope of application of this directive. Also, the purchase of added years, commutation, surrender options and additional voluntary contributions are excluded. Considering the insistence of the directive on different actuarial tables, the above-mentioned flaws are very disappointing, because they leave virtually intact many spheres of the social security area in which a large number of sexual

---

[36] Bradley, *op. cit.* at n. 57 above, p. 10.

[37] Case 171/88, *Rinner-Kuhn v. FWW Spezial-Gebaudereiningung GmbH*: [1989] E.C.R. 2743; *Kowalksa v. Freie und Handestadt Hamburg*: [1990] E.C.R. I–2591; *Nimz v. Freie und Hansestadt Hamburg*: [1991] E.C.R. I–297; *Arbeiterwohlfahrt der Stadt Berlin EV v. Boetel Monika*: [1992] 3 C.M.L.R. 423.

[38] See Curtin, "Occupational pension schemes and Article 119: beyond the fringe" [1987] 5 C.M.L.Rev. 215.

inequalities actually occur. Finally, it is worth mentioning Directive 86/613,[39] which provides for the application of equal treatment between men and women engaged in a self-employed capacity (including agriculture) and the protection of self-employed women during pregnancy and motherhood, and Directive 92/85[40] on the introduction of measures to encourage improvements in the safety and health of pregnant workers and workers who have recently given birth or are breastfeeding.

Equality in job evaluation schemes: equal pay for work of equal value

Article 1 of Directive 75/117 provides that the principle of equal pay covers the same work or work to which equal value is attributed. The whole directive complements Article 119 and according to the Court's judgment in *Jenkins v. Kingsgate*,[41] the equal pay directive is principally designed to facilitate the practical application of the principle of equal pay outlined in Article 119 and does not alter the content or scope of that principle as defined in the Treaty. Also, in *Worringham & Humphreys v. Lloyds Bank*[42] it was held that in Article 1 of the directive the concept of "same work" (contained in the first paragraph of Article 119) includes cases of work to which equal value is attributed. In *Commission v. Denmark*[43] it was held that the directive lays down detailed rules regarding certain aspects of the scope of Article 119. The above mentioned judgments indicate that the Court, adopting a teleological approach to the interpretation of Article 119, broadened the scope of that Article so as to cover not only identical or broadly similar work, but also work to which equal value is attributed. So the application of the equal pay principle presupposes a comparison between the work done by a woman and that done by a man. Consequently, the scope and limits of such comparison should be examined.

In the *Macarthys* case,[44] the Court held that comparisons are confined to parallels which may be drawn on the basis of concrete appraisals of work actually done by employees of a different sex within the same establishment or service. Also, in the same case, it was decided that the principle of equal pay is not confined to situations in which men and women are contemporaneously doing equal work for the same employer. So a job evaluation scheme is needed, drawn up either by the authorities or by the employers to assess jobs. This scheme, according to the Court's judgment in the *Rummler* case,[45] should be based on gender neutral criteria and not on the average capabilities of workers of a particular sex.

[39] [1986] O.J. L359/56.
[40] [1992] O.J. L348/1.
[41] Case 96/80: [1981] 3 E.C.R. 911.
[42] Case 69/80: [1981] E.C.R. 767.
[43] Case 143/83: [1985] E.C.R. 427.
[44] Case 129/79: [1980] E.C.R. 1275.
[45] Case 237/85: [1987] E.C.R. 127.

Also, although the criteria on which such schemes are based must genuinely represent the nature of the work in question, they have to take into account other factors for which workers of both genders are particularly suited, if the nature of the work permits. Also, according to the Court's practice, a woman has a legal right to challenge the findings of a scheme and have her work assessed by a competent authority. The rationale behind this practice could be that the definition of the value of jobs is agreed between management and union. Presuming that female employees have a disproportionate representation and so less weight than their male counterparts in the decision-making process of unions, the firm's job evaluation scheme could disguise and reinforce gender bias. However, job evaluation schemes are only one of several ways in which the Member States can assess jobs and the principle of equal pay cannot be rendered inapplicable because there is no scheme at all and the employer refuses to introduce one.

The European Court of Justice has introduced the principle of proportionality in cases concerning sex discrimination. In the *Jenkins* and *Bilka* cases[46] it held that a defence of an equal pay claim may be admissible under Article 119 if an employer can objectively justify the differential treatment of women; the above treatment might be reasonably necessary to achieve some objective other than those related to sex discrimination. The use of the principle of proportionality and the strictness of the interpretation of the defence's requirements are welcome. However, in so far as the Court and the Community institutions are bound to respect and observe human rights, it should be mentioned that economic growth should not be an end *per se*, so as to outweigh the right of equal treatment, but only the medium for achieving the well-being of individuals. The question that arises here, is how could differential treatment be compatible with human rights by reason only that it is objectively justified under economic considerations? Although it should be expected that the Court would reject as inadmissible any defence put forward by an employer based on economic criteria, its practice does not conform to this. Finally, the comparison that a woman has to make in order to satisfy an equal pay claim deserves some comments. The rejection of the autonomous legal character of the equal pay directive, as well as the imposition of limits on the spatial scope of comparisons, could actually be a drawback to the equal value claim. If there is an absence of a male comparator or a valid job evaluation scheme, a woman whose work is of greater value than that of the only available male comparator does not have any chance of establishing a claim that her work has been undervalued without using the hypothetical male formula.

Unfortunately, the equality directives and Article 119 have failed to provide for the equal treatment of women, in this instance in the area of equal pay for work of equal value. If there is no male comparator or a valid job evaluation scheme, a woman's chances of establishing a claim

---

[46] See n. 19 and n. 14 above.

of unequal treatment are hampered. And, as stated previously, because of the sex segregated nature of the workforce, many women are employed in female dominated fields for which there are no comparable male equivalents on which claims can be established and evaluated against. For women employed in nursing and child care, though they are paid the same as men employed in these fields, they are paid significantly less than men employed in the health care and education sectors as a whole, *i.e.* doctors and teachers. As there are no formal schemes in place with which to evaluate occupations for which there are no readily apparent male equivalents, women are again being indirectly discriminated against while male/female wage differences continue to persist. The gender stratification of the workforce into male dominated and female dominated occupations impedes the actualisation of the equal pay for work of equal value principle established by Directive 75/117, while the inability of the E.C. Commission, and the individual Member States to formulate and implement schemes which would alleviate the problem described above further delays the equal treatment and equal pay for women.

However, given the fact that there is widespread occupational segregation in the Community, male earnings in these female dominated occupations are lower than in male dominated ones. It has been maintained[47] that in order to establish gender equality, women should be allowed to choose as a comparator another woman from a male dominated industry, where earnings are higher. The E.C. Commission was in favour of such a proposal[48] and Article 6 of Directive 75/117 leaves to Member States discretionary powers regarding the appropriate measures for implementing the principle of equal pay.

Equality in social security

In the *Burton* case,[49] the Court held that eligibility for voluntary redundancy/retirement benefit could not be considered, since it concerned the conditions of access to the benefit and therefore Directive 76/207, nor was Article 119 applicable. Then, it accepted that the word dismissal (Article 5(1) of Directive 76/207) should be widely construed so as to include termination of the employment relationship between a worker and his/her employer, even as a part of a voluntary redundancy scheme. The Court used the same formula[50] and recognised that the principle of equal treatment of Directive 76/207 should apply to conditions of access to voluntary benefits schemes. However, as regards to the determination of a minimum pensionable age, the Court held in the *Burton* case that

---

[47] See Szyszczak, "Pay Inequalities and equal value claims" [1985] 48 C.M.L.Rev. 139.
[48] See also *E.C. Commission v. U.K.*: [1982] 7 E.C.R. 2601.
[49] Case 19/81, *Burton v. British Railways Board*: [1982] E.C.R. 555.
[50] *Marshal* case: [1986] E.C.R. 723; Case 151/84, *Roberts v. Tate and Lyle Industries Ltd*: [1986] 1 C.M.L.R. 714; Case 262/84, *Beets-Proper v. Van Lanschot-Bankiers N.V.*: [1986] E.C.R. 773.

pursuant to Article 1(2) of Directive 76/207 and Article 7(1) of Directive 79/7, the determination of a minimum pensionable age and retirement under state schemes and the possible consequences thereof were excluded from the principle of equal treatment. Here, it should be mentioned that the provision of occupational pensions at different ages for men and women is one of the most important causes of discrimination against women in the pension field. Nevertheless, in recent cases the Court departed from the *Burton* reasoning and accepted a stricter and more vigorous approach regarding the social security exception contained in Article 1(2) of Directive 76/207 and Article 7(1)(a) of Directive 79/7. Interestingly, the Court in the *Marshal* case,[51] by drawing a distinction between pensionable age (the age at which a state pension may be claimed) and retirement age (the age at which a person must retire), held that Article 7(1)(a) of Directive 79/7 must be strictly interpreted as being confined to aspects of pensionable age. So, the discretionary power granted by this provision to Member States, is only in determining pensionable age and not retirement age. Therefore, a compulsory retirement for a woman actually amounts to dismissal because she can be eligible for taking a pension earlier, but this does not mean that she would be retiring earlier than a man. It could be inferred from the above mentioned cases that a female employee could no longer be forced by an employer to retire at an earlier age than her male colleague, merely on the grounds that she has reached pensionable age. However, different pensionable ages continue to be permitted with disadvantageous consequences for women.

The legality of the difference in pensionable ages between women and men also exemplifies another form of indirect discrimination. Though women are not forced to retire at a younger age than their male counterparts, the age differences for the age at which pensions may be claimed indicates the paternalistic attitude of policy makers and judicial reviewers which harks back to an era of protectionist legislation for women workers in the guises of shorter work days and no night shifts. Though no case has yet come to light, women hypothetically could be coerced, even forced, by employers to retire upon pensionable age thereby allowing the employers to reduce the total pension payable to women as they are not employed for that many additional years as men. This results in indirect discrimination against women. It also means that occupational pensions payable to women may be less than those paid to men if the pensionable age for women is also taken by them as their retirable age.

Also, the actuarial assumptions regarding life expectancy (longer for women) have a discriminatory result. Moreover, it follows from Article 2(2)(c) of Directive 86/378 that the issuing of a sex distinct mortality table in the calculation of optional forms of benefit will not be prohibited

---

[51] Case 152/84, *Marshal v. Southampton and South West Hampshire Area Health Authority*: [1986] E.C.R. 723.

by this directive. Obviously, there are many issues in the area of social security which remain unresolved.

RELIANCE UPON THE EQUALITY DIRECTIVES AT NATIONAL LEVEL

The question which arises now is whether the directives on equal pay should have direct effect, so that individuals alleging discrimination and inequalities in the field covered by these could rely upon their provisions before national courts. It has been established that directives (it would be better to say provisions of directives) are capable of producing direct effect if they are clear and precise, unconditional and unqualified and do not leave any margin of discretion in the hands of Member States. As the implementing periods of the equality directives have expired, they are capable of producing direct effect, provided the above requirements are met. The controversial matter is whether they produce not only vertical but also horizontal direct effect. The European Court has been asked for a preliminary ruling on this issue on a number of occasions. However, it had never decided on this question until the pronouncement of its judgment in the *Marshal* case, where the Court rejected the horizontal direct effect of these directives. Although it accepted the vertical direct effect of Article 5(1) of the equal treatment directive and the capacity of individuals to rely on provisions of directives against the State irrespective of the latter acting as an employer or as a public authority, it rejected the argument that directives may produce horizontal direct effect on the grounds that their binding nature exists only in relation to the Member States to which they are addressed. The reasoning behind that judgment is open to criticism. Whereas it is admitted that directives are addressed to Member States (which are bound only in respect to the result to be achieved), it does not follow from Article 189 that they should not produce binding effects upon other bodies. According to the *Drefenne* case, the fact that certain provisions of the Treaty are formally addressed to Member States does not prevent rights from being conferred at the same time on any individual who has an interest in the performance of the duties which are laid down. Given the fact that national courts are considered to be organs of the State having the same responsibility for implementing a directive as the legislature and/or the executive of the Member State to which it is addressed, the nature and identity of the party against whom the individual is seeking to invoke a directive are immaterial, since the basis of direct effect is not the duty of the defendant but the duty of the national court to provide for remedies at national level to secure compliance by the defendant with the terms of the directive.[52] Therefore, there would be no objection to horizontal

---

[52] See Wyatt, "New Legal Order or Old" [1982] E.L.Rev. 147.

direct effect on the ground that directives appear to impose obligations upon states and there is no convincing deduction from the wording of Article 189 that they should not also be binding on bodies other than states. Furthermore, the *Marshal* judgment, by denying the horizontal direct effect of equality directives, results in an arbitrary and unfair distinction between state employees and employees in the private sector. The former are able to rely upon the directives against their employer, while the latter—if there is no implementing measure—are not. This runs contrary to the spirit of Article 119 and the equal treatment directives which are complementary parts of a code designed to further economic and social cohesion in the field of employment. On the other hand, action by the E.C. Commission under Article 169 could not compensate for the disadvantageous consequences of the rejection of horizontal direct effect of directives, although it could be maintained that this situation has now, in principle, been mitigated by a possible application of the *Francovich* test at domestic level.

THE CONCEPT OF INDIRECT DISCRIMINATION

As mentioned earlier, equal treatment with regard to access to employment (including promotion and vocational training), working conditions (including conditions governing dismissals) and social security is governed by the equal treatment[53] and the social security directives.[54]

The point of departure for the following analysis is the delimitation of the concept of indirect discrimination contained in the equal treatment and the first social security directive. The European Court of Justice seems to accept[55] that indirect discrimination occurs when a distinction is made upon criteria that do not include the gender of the employee, but through which the same result is intended or reached as in the case of direct discrimination. It should be mentioned that an existing social patterns and conventions render the treatment of men and women equal only in the formal sense; material discrimination still exists, as the traditional gender role partitioning between men and women in modern societies is one of the main causes of job segregation and of indirect sexual inequality in employment. Although the Court follows in principle the above approach, it appears to be reluctant to develop a concrete precedence due to the lack of statutory definition of the concept of indirect discrimination in the laws of the Member States and on grounds that it has not yet pronounced on the direct effectiveness of the equality

---

[53] Council Directive 76/207, [1976] O.J. L39/40.
[54] Council Directives 79/7, [1979] O.J. L6/24, and 86/378, [1986] O.J. L225/40.
[55] See Leenen, "Equal Treatment of male and female employees under European Community law—some recent case law of the Court of Justice" [1986] 1 LIEI 91 at 94.

provisions of E.C. directives. In two cases,[56] the Court decided that an employer who grants maternity leave is not obliged to grant paternity leave. According to its reasoning in the *Hoffmann* judgment, Article 2(3) of Directive 76/207 (measures protecting women in case of maternity or pregnancy as an exception to the main principle of equality) could be interpreted as a recognition of two types of women's needs, biological conditions and the special relationship between a woman and her child. It ruled out, using this approach as reasoning, any obligation by the employer to grant paternity leave. However, the partitioning of the family responsibilities is a very important factor which influences the position of women in the labour market. It is also appropriate here to mention that the Court left to the Member States the margin of discretion in relation to the assessment of the special maternity leave period.

By deciding that it is not a violation of the equal treatment provisions in Article 2(3) Directive 76/207 the Court appears to have perpetuated stereotyped assumptions about the nature of women's work and contributes to the continuance of indirect discrimination against women. It has been argued that women's subordinate place within paid employment (and the actual gender segregated nature of the paid workforce itself) is the result of the division of labour in the home, with women being responsible for most of the childrearing and day-to-day household activities.[57] The responsibility of women for childrearing duties has been translated by the Court in the *Hoffmann* case as the recognition of the uniquely female experience of physically bearing children and the societally sanctioned function of women to rear the children they bear. By deeming maternity leave as an exception to equal treatment provisions, and ruling paternity leave is not legally required to be automatically granted to men who request it, discrimination against both women and men is perpetuated.

The granting of maternity leave only denies women the opportunity to return to previous employment once recovery from delivery and lactation responsibilities are complete, unless children are put into crèche facilities or a childminder is employed as fathers are not legally entitled to parental leave. It also denies men the opportunity to rear their children on a full-time basis without risking loss of employment as paternity or parental leave is not provided for in most Member States. The *Hoffmann* decision unfortunately perpetuates the stereotyped assumption that because women bear children they are therefore, automatically the sex that is responsible for rearing them. There is no "special bond" between mother and child, except for the one that society believes to exist. Once delivery is complete, the tie between mother and child is severed; either parent is capable of performing childrearing activities and responsibilities. However, by not allowing men the opportunity to take

---

[56] Case 163/82, *E.C. Commission v. Italy*: [1983] 9 E.C.R. 3273; Case 184/83, *Hoffmann v. Barmer Ersatzkasse*: [1984] 7 E.C.R. 3047 (reference for a preliminary ruling from the Landessozialgericht Hamburg).

[57] Chodorow, "Mothering, Male Dominance, and Capitalism" in *Capitalist Patriarchy and the Case for Socialist Feminism* (Eisenstein ed., 1979), p. 83.

paternity or parental leave (except under exceptional circumstances such as illness or death of the mother), the relegation of women to the home and childrearing activities ensues. The primary responsibility for child-rearing that is being placed on women has the result of disrupting and hampering female career progression. Women must take time out of their careers (career breaks) to rear children as fathers legally cannot share or take over childrearing responsibilities without leaving their jobs. This results in the indirect discrimination of both women and men because of the utilisation of stereotyped assumptions as to which sex is primarily responsible for childrearing.

In the light of the *Hoffmann* case, the judgment pronounced by the Court on the *Webb*[58] case evaluates the scope of indirect discrimination through pregnancy situations. In the *Webb* case the Court stated that there can be no comparison between a woman who has found herself pregnant shortly after entering into an employment contract with that of a man similarly incapable of performing the work for which he was hired because of a medical or other reason. Pregnancy is not comparable with a pathological condition.[59]

A provision that may be deemed controversial as permitting indirect discrimination is Article 2(2) of Directive 76/207. In particular, under that Article indirect discrimination is not substantiated when the sex of a worker constitutes a "determining factor" for the job. In *E.C. Commission v. United Kingdom*,[60] the European Court of Justice held that this exception does not apply to undertakings or households which employ no more than five people. Moreover, according to the Court's judgment, the principle of respect for private life and personal sensibilities are relevant factors in applying Article 2(2). Also, in *Johnston v. Chief Constable of R.U.C.*,[61] the Court accepted that public safety reasons should require that gender in certain activities could constitute a determining factor. However, in this case, the proportionality principle has to be applied. The tasks of assessing whether the reasons of public safety are well founded and of ensuring that the principle of proportionality is respected, are assigned to the national courts. Because respect for private life, personal sensitivities or public safety are vague concepts, the deter-mining factor exception leaves room for gender bias, even though the Court has introduced the principle of proportionality and strict criteria in its application in deciding that gender can be used as a criterion for employment purposes on grounds of public safety, private life, or per-sonal sensitivities. Arguably, all employment should be gender neutral, if the principle of equality is strictly adhered to; except for employment where biological gender is *the* determining factor for selection, *i.e.* wet

---

[58] *Webb v. EMO Air Cargo Ltd*: [1992] 2 All E.R. 43.
[59] See also Court rulings in C–179/88 *Handels-og-Kontorfunktionærernes Forbund i Danmark* [1990] E.C.R. I–3979 aka *Hertz* judgment and C–421/92 *Habermann-Beltermann* [1993] E.C.R. I–1657 which established that "the dismissal of a female worker on account of pregnancy constitutes direct discrimination on grounds of sex".
[60] Case 165/82: [1983] E.C.R. 3441.
[61] Case 222/84: [1986] E.C.R. 1651.

nurse or surrogate mother. All other occupations can be performed equally as well by both sexes.

Access to justice and the provision of legal remedies at national level

Questions of legal protection and the sanctioning of discrimination were examined by the Court in a number of cases. In *E.C. Commission v. Italy*,[62] it ruled that the existence of any legal remedy seems to be sufficient; whilst in the *Johnston* case,[63] it held that Member States had to ensure that the rights conferred by the directive may be effectively relied upon before national courts by the persons concerned. As regards the question of appropriate sanctions in respect of infringement, the Court held in the *Von Colson* and *Harz* cases[64] that the directive leaves Member States to decide what sanctions should be available to achieve the objectives of the directive. However, an appropriate system of sanctions must be established to ensure real equality of opportunity. So, according to the Court's ruling, the sanctions should fulfil two requirements: (i) they must be such so as to guarantee real and effective judicial protection and (ii) they must also have a deterrent effect on the employer. The Court's decision was very important, since none of the directive's provisions expressly require Member States to lay down any kind of sanctions. However, the Court held that the directive does not require the discrimination to be remedied by a sanction imposing an obligation on the employer to enter into a contract with a victim. Nevertheless, when the penalty is the award of compensation, that compensation must, in any event, be adequate in relation to the damage sustained and must therefore amount to more than purely nominal compensation. Finally, all the above considerations are guidelines for the national courts upon which the victim of sexual discrimination is entirely dependent as regards the award of compensation. It should be noted that the margin of discretion which the Court left to Member States regarding the choice between the right to compensation and the right to the conclusion of a contract could be dangerous for the implementation of the norms of the directive. Nevertheless, this danger is mitigated by placing national courts under a legal duty to review the lawfulness of national law with regard to the equal treatment directive.

---

[62] Case 163/82, [1983] E.C.R. 3273.
[63] See n. 61 above.
[64] Case 14/83, *Von Colson & Kamman v. Land Nordrhein Westfalen*: [1984] E.C.R. 1891; Case 79/83, *Harz v. Deutsche Tradax GmbH*: [1984] E.C.R. 1921.

Concluding remarks

The process of European integration, as conceived by the Treaty of Rome and reinforced by the Maastricht Treaty on European Union, is based upon the concept of a common market, where *inter alia* factors of production enjoy free and unobstructed mobility. The development and provision of homogenous management systems and corporate structures in the European Union is of utmost importance for corporate market participation. Movements of labour and capital and the right of establishment are relevant determinants for the integration of European markets. The right of establishment and the right to provide services within the European Union are fundamental principles of the common market and inherent components for its completion and proper operation. Both principles are crucial for the development of genuine patterns of trade between Member States and are considered necessary conditions for cross-border business development.

One of the most important goals for European institutions is the achievement of growth and enhanced competitiveness of European businesses. This goal has been pursued through the careful application of the competition policy by the Commission of the European Communities and through the provision of a better legal environment for these enterprises. The two main lines along which this goal has been developed are (i) the provision of a uniform legislation on the protection of the various interests touched by the activity of the enterprises, such as shareholders and investors, employees, creditors and, more generally, third parties; (ii) the provision of more suitable forms for the exercise of economic activities in the common market and for industrial concentrations, both at national and international levels, and rationalisation of existing mergers and groups of companies in the European Union.

The European integration process relies on the unobstructed mobility of goods and factors of production (labour and capital) and of persons (natural or legal) seeking establishment and the right to provide services within the common market. The migration of companies follows patterns which are shaped by competitive forces and the need for profit maximisation. By dismantling all internal barriers to trade, the European Community has prepared the legal and socio-economic background for the necessary transfer of resources to the most optimal location within the common market. Corporate migration depicts *inter alia* the market response to the allocation of resources and to performance optimisation *vis-à-vis* European and international competition.

Index

Abuse of dominant position,
See also Market dominance
concentrations compared, 47
Advertisements,
public procurement, 127–130
AGP, 138–142
Agreement on Government
procurement, 138–142
Annual accounts,
banking sector, 149
European Co-operative Society,
36
European Mutual Society, 38
harmonisation of law, 18
Anti-trust,
concentrations, 42
distribution agreements, 91
joint ventures, 53
market dominance, 81
Articles of association,
France, 3
joint ventures, 16–17
Association. *See* European
Association
Auditors,
Belgium, 7
France, 6–7
function, 6
Germany, 7
Greece, 7
harmonisation of law, 18
Italy, 7
Netherlands, 7
powers, 6–7
purpose, 6
United Kingdom, 6
Audits,
European Mutual Society, 38

Banking sector,
annual accounts, 149
consolidated accounts, 149
consumer credit, 149

Banking sector—*cont.*
consumer protection, 148
credit cards, 150
depositers' interests, 148
directives, 146–150
EBSC, 150
European Banking Standards
Committee (EBSC), 150
exposure risks, 148
improvements, 150
integrated payment system,
149–150
integration, 146–150
licence, 148
own funds, 148
payments system, 149–150
solvency ratio, 148
standards, 150
Belgium,
auditors, 7
Board of directors, 4–5
accountability, 5
appointment, 2, 4–5
delegation of powers, 5, 8
France, 8–9
implementation of policy, 8
operation, 5
policy implementation, 8
purpose, 2, 4–5

CAN, 128
Capital,
European Economic Interest
Grouping, 31
harmonisation of law, 18
Cartels,
collusive behaviour, 77
contributions of, 78
control, 77–78
effect, 77
exemptions, 78
incompatible with common
market, 77–78

Cartels—*cont.*
  oligopolistic market, 82–83, 85
Co-operative joint venture, 54, 55
Co-operative Society. *See* European
    Co-operative Society
Co-ordination,
  harmonisation of law, 18
Collective market dominance,
    84–89
Community institutions,
  liability, 118
  non-contractual liability, 118
Company,
  balance of power in, 1–2
  concept of, 1
  decision making, 1
  management systems. *See*
    Management systems
  members, 2
  organs, 2
Competition law,
  cartels. *See* Cartels
  distribution agreements. *See*
    Distribution agreements
  generally, 77
  market dominance. *See* Market
    dominance
  oligopoly. *See* Oligopolistic
    markets
  policy, 21, 77
  purpose, 77
Compliance directives, 116–122
  basis, 120
  damages, 120
  direct effect, 117–119
  discretion of Member State, 120
  entitlement to compensation, 119
  flagrant violations, 120
  infringement, 120
  interested persons, 121
  national courts, approach of,
    117–118
  non-contractual liability, 118,
    119
  obligations of Member States,
    119
  procedural remedies,
    approximation of, 120–121
  public interest, 117
  purpose, 116–117
  remedies, 120
  scope, 121–122

Compliance directives—*cont.*
  scope of remedies, 120
  state liability, 119
  suspension of procedure by
    national courts, 121
  useful effect, doctrine of, 119
  uses, 116
  utilities, 121
Concentrations,
  abuse of dominant position
    compared, 47
  acquisition of control, 51
  actual or potential competition,
    69
  aggregate, 42
  anti-trust authorities, 42
  appraisal criteria, 65–67
  assessment of notification, 63–64
  automatic suspension, 61
  background, 43–50
  basis of regulation, 56–57
  below thresholds, ruling that,
    73–74
  community dimension, 55–56
  compatibility, assessing, 69
  competent authorities of member
    state controlling, 70–72
  competition policy and, 74–76
  concept of control, 50–52
  credit institutions, 51
  "decisive influence on
    composition", 51
  declaration of incompatibility, 67
  definition, 51
  development, 43–50
  dominance, assessing, 69
  duplication avoidance, 57
  Dutch clause, 73–74
  economic perspective, 57–58
  evaluation criteria,
    economic, 57–58
    turnover, 58–60
  examination of notification,
    63–64
  exceptions, 51
  exclusivity of regulation, 69–70
  extra-territorial application, 74
  financial institutions, 51
  forms, 41
  general background, 43–50
  German clause, 70–72
  hearing of parties, 64–65

Concentrations—*cont.*
  hindering of effective
      competition, 66
  history, 43–50
  independence, 51, 66
  insurance companies, 51
  joint ventures, 52–56. *See also*
      Joint ventures
  jurisdiction, 74–75
  legal basis of regulation, 56–57
  meaning, 51
  measuring, 42
  merger control regulation, 47
  newspaper mergers, 72
  notification,
      assessment, 64
      automatic suspension, 61
      disadvantages, 61
      examination of, 63–64
      failure, 62–63
      fines, 62–63
      invalid transactions, 62
      principles, 60–63
      requirement, 60–61
      result, 61
      serious damage to undertaking,
          62
      suspension, 61
      transactions performed during
          suspension, 62
      waiver, 61
  "one stop shop" control, 46, 50
  powers of Commission's decision,
      67–68
  principles of regulation, 50–52
  public interest clause, 72–73
  public security, 73
  relationship between parties, 62
  restrictive agreements compared,
      47
  securities, 52
  suspension, 61
  technical and economic progress,
      67
  third parties, hearing of, 64–65
  threatening viability of common
      market, 42
  turnover calculation, 55, 559–560
  underlying principles, 50
  undertakings, 51
Concentrative joint ventures, 54–55
Concerted practices, 81–82

Concession contracts,
  meaning, 123
  public services, 115
  public utilities, 111
  public works, 104–105, 123
  tendering procedures, 134
Consolidated accounts, 21
  banking sector, 149
  European Co-operative Society,
      36
  European Mutual Society, 38
Construction projects, 125
Consumer credit, 149
Contract Award Notices (CAN),
      128
Corporate structures, 7–10
  approaches, 7
  distribution of power, 7–11
  France, 8–9
  generally, 1
  Germany, 9–10
  importance of, 1
  Netherlands, 10
  two-tier system, 7–8
  United Kingdom, 8
Credit cards, 150
Credit institutions,
  concentrations, 51

Design contests, 113–114, 134–135
Direct effect,
  equal pay, 163
  public procurement, 117
Directives,
  banking sector, 146–150
  compliance. *See* Compliance
      directives
  direct effect, 117, 118, 163
  implementation, 118
  life assurance, 151–154
  motor vehicle insurance, 154–155
  non-implementation, 118
  non-life insurance, 151
  securities market, 155–157
  stock exchange, 155–157
Directors,
  board. *See* Board of directors
  France, 5, 9
  Germany, 5
  Italy, 5
  officer of company, 5
  relationship with company, 5

Directors—*cont.*
  status, 5
Disclosure of financial information,
  18
Distribution agreements, 91–98
  absolute territorial protection, 93
  active sales, 93
  advantages, 91
  anti-trust, 91
  consumer redress, 95
  exclusivity principle, 91–92
  "free riders", protection from, 91
  legal protection, 95
  multiple dealerships, 94–95
  passive sales, 93
  promotion activities, 94
  purpose, 91
  qualified territorial protection, 93
  selectivity, 92–93
  servicing activities, 94
  several dealerships, 94–95
  territorial protection, 93–95
  vertical character, 91
Diversification, 41
Division of public companies,
  harmonisation of law, 18

EBSC, 150
ECSC, 43
EEIG. *See* European Economic
  Interest Grouping
Employee participation,
  European Association, 39
  European Co-operative Society,
    39
  European Mutual Society, 39
  harmonisation of law, 19
Employees,
  information rights, 21
Equal pay,
  Article 119, 160–161
  benefits in kind, 161
  comparitor, 168
  components, 161–163
  definition, 160
  direct effect, 163
  discrimination forms, 163
  effect of, 169–170
  equal work, 160, 168–170
  generally, 159
  ILO Convention, 160
  interpretation of provisions, 161

Equal pay—*cont.*
  introduction of provisions, 164
  job evaluation schemes, 168–170
  meaning, 161
  national level, reliance at,
    163–164
  occupational pension schemes,
    162
  "pay", 161
  pension scheme contributions,
    162
  principle, 161–163
  principle of equality, 160–161
  proportionality, 169
  scope, 161
  travel facilities, 161
  work of equal value, 168–170
Establishment, right of. *See* Right of
  establishment
European Association,
  creation, 38
  employee participation, 39
  establishment, 38
  executive committees, 38, 39
  formation, 38
  function, 38
  general meeting, 38
  genuine cross-border activity, 38
  insolvency, 39
  legal personality, 38
  liquidation, 39
  meaning, 38
  registered office, 38
  registration, 38
  suspension of payments, 39
  voting, 38
European Banking Standards
  Committee (EBSC), 150
European Co-operative Society,
  annual accounts, 36
  consolidated accounts, 36
  employee participation, 39
  function, 35
  general meetings, 35
  generally, 35
  insolvency, 36
  investor shares, 36
  liquidation, 36
  one-tier systems, 36
  powers, 36
  proposals, 35
  purpose, 35

European Co-operative
    Society—*cont.*
requirements, 35–36
structure, 35
suspension of payments, 36
two-tier systems, 36
European Coal and Steel
    Community, 43
European Economic Interest
    Grouping,
activities, 30
address, 31
administrative measures, 34
advantages, 27
aims, 25–26
amalgamation of members, 32
background, 23–26
capital, 31
categories of membership, 30
classification, legal, 28
commencement of regulation, 26
corporate dimension, 29
creation, 25–26, 31
development, 26–28
evasion of national laws, 32–33
exercise of activities, 34
flexibility, 31–32
formation, 30
formalities, 31
function, 24
fusion of members, 32
general background, 23–26
harmonisation, 33–34
holding company, 32
implementation of regulation, 34
intermediary forms, 23–24
legal nature, 28–29
loans, 32
managers, 31
mandatory rules, 33
members, 31
mergers, 24–25
models, 24
multiple membership, 33
natural persons, 30
nature of, 28–29
need for, 24
objectives, 27, 29–33
official address, 31
operation, 31–32, 33–34
organs, 31
profits, 27–28

European Economic Interest
    Grouping—*cont.*
purpose, 24, 25–26, 30
regulation, 24
rules laid down by, 30
scope, 29
small firms, 25
transfers of property, 32
uniformity, 33
workers' participation, 32
European Mutual Society,
administrative board, 37
annual accounts, 38
audits, 38
composition, 37
consolidated accounts, 38
employee participation, 39
general meeting, 37
insolvency, 38
legal personality, 37
liquidation, 38
management, 37
members, 37
one-tier system, 37
registered office, 37
requirements, 37
structure, 37
supervisory board, 37
suspension of payments, 38
winding up, 38
European Union,
corporate structures. *See*
    Corporate structures
establishment, right of. *See* **Right**
    of establishment
generally, 1–2
management systems, 1. *See also*
    Management systems
right of establishment. *See* **Right**
    of establishment
Executive committees,
European Association, 38, 39

Financial services sector, 143–157
background, 143
Banking. *See* Banking sector
capital movement liberalisation,
    145
changes in, 144
completion of internal market,
    144–145
concentrations, 51

Financial services sector—*cont.*
  development, 144
  foundations of market, 145
  generally, 143
  importance, 143–144
  insurance. *See* Insurance sector
  integration in Europe, 144
  investment services, 157
  legislative programme, 145
  motor vehicle insurance, 154–155
  need for common rules, 146
  role, 145
  securities markets, 155–157
  single market, 144
  stock exchange market, 155–157
Formation of companies,
  harmonisation of law, 18
France,
  articles of association, 3
  auditors, 6–7
  board of directors, 8–9
  clause d'agrement, 3
  clause de preemption, 3
  consent clause, 3
  corporate structures, 8–9
  directors, 5, 9
  general meeting, 4
  Groupement d'interet economique,
    24
  pre-emption, 3
  restrictive clauses, 3
  shares, 3
  supervisory boards, 6

GATT Agreement,
  public procurement, 137–142
  public services, 113
  public supplies, 101–102
  public utilities, 109, 113
General meeting,
  European Association, 38
  European Co-operative Society,
    35
  European Mutual Society, 37
  formation, 2, 4
  France, 4
  Germany, 4
  meaning, 2, 4
  multiple voting, 4
  shareholders, 2–3
  voting, 4

Germany,
  auditors, 7
  corporate structures, 9–10
  directors, 5
  general meeting, 4
  preference shares, 4
  shareholders, 3
  shares, 3–4
  supervisory boards, 6
Greece,
  auditors, 7
Green cards, 152
Group accounts,
  harmonisation of law, 18
Groupement d'interet economique, 24

Harmonisation of law,
  annual accounts, 18
  auditors, 18
  capital, 18
  co-ordination, 18
  Directives, 18
  disclosure of financial
    information, 18
  division of public companies, 18
  employee participation, 19
  formation of companies, 18
  group accounts, 18
  mergers, 18
  objective, 17
  one-member private companies,
    18
  process, 17–19
  proposals, 18–19
  purpose, 17
  scissions, 18
  uniform legislation, 17
  Vredeling Directive, 19
Horizontal joint venture, 11

Indirect discrimination, 173–176
Industrial concentration. *See*
  Concentrations
Information, employee rights, 21
Insolvency,
  European Association, 39
  European Co-operative Society,
    36
  European Mutual Society, 38
Insurance sector,
  concentrations, 51
  establishment, freedom of, 152

Insurance sector—*cont.*
  framework, 152
  freedom of establishment, 152
  green cards, 152
  integration, 151–154
  large risks, 153–154
  life assurance directives, 151–154
  mass risks, 153–154
  motor vehicle insurance, 154–155
  non-life insurance directives, 151
  objectives of directives, 153
  reinsurance, 154
  transparency, 154
Intellectual property rights,
  joint ventures, 13
Investment services, 157
Italy,
  auditors, 7
  directors, 5
  shareholders, 4
  shares, 4

Joint ventures,
  anti-trust treatment, 53
  apparent partnership, 13
  articles of association, 16–17
  cartel prohibitions, 53–54
  characteristics, 53
  classes of shares, 16
  classification, 11–12
  co-operative, 54, 55
  committees, 13
  community dimension, 55
  companies, 14–17
  concentrative, 54–55
  conglomerate, 11
  constitution, 15
  contracts, 13
  contributions, 15
  coordinating committees, 13
  de facto partnership, 13
  definition, 11
  development, 11
  duration, 11
  extent of rights and obligations,
    13
  external funding, 15
  funding, 15
  horizontal, 11
  importance, 11
  intellectual property rights, 13
  legal personality, 53

Joint ventures—*cont.*
  liability, 16
  liability of members, 13
  limited liability, 16
  management, 13
  meaning, 11, 53
  members' liability, 13
  merger control regulation, 52–56
  minority shareholders, 17
  operation, 11–17
  ownership, 11
  partnership, 14
  purpose, 53
  registration, 13
  regulation, 16
  scope, 11–12
  several liability, 13
  special advantages, 17
  statement of objectives, 13
  steering committees, 13
  taxation of profits, 13
  third party relationships, 13
  vertical, 11

Liquidation,
  European Association, 39
  European Co-operative Society,
    36
  European Mutual Society, 38
Loans,
  European Economic Interest
    Grouping, 32

Maastricht treaty, 143
Management systems,
  auditors, 6–7
  board of directors. *See* Board of
    directors
  general meeting, 2
  generally, 1
  importance of examining, 1
  organs of the company, 2
  shares. *See* Shares
  supervisory boards, 5–6
Market dominance, 78–81
  anti-trust, 81
  behavioural remedies, 81–83
  collective dominant position,
    83–84
  control, 78–81

Market dominance—*cont.*
  methods of dominance, 78
  oligopoly. *See* Oligopolistic
    markets
  structural remedies, 83–89
  workable competition achieved,
    78
Maternity leave, 174–175
Members of the company,
  meaning, 2
Mergers,
  economic reasons for control,
    49–50
  factors affecting control, 47–49
  harmonisation of law, 18
  mobility regulation, 42
  "newspaper", 72
  "one stop shop" control, 46, 50
  partial, 46
  political reasons for control, 50
Minority shareholders,
  joint ventures, 17
Mobility regulation,
  concentrations. *See*
    Concentrations
  diversification, 41
  generally, 41–42
  importance, 41
  mergers, 42. *See also* Mergers
  multi-product ranges, 42
  multi-range, products, 42
  trends, 41
Monopolies,
  competition against, 78
  duopoly, becoming, 78
  market dominance. *See* Market
    dominance
Motor vehicle insurance, 154–155
Multiple voting,
  general meeting, 4
Mutual society. *See* European
  Mutual Society

NATO, award of contract by, 125
Netherlands,
  auditors, 7
  corporate structures, 10
Non-life insurance directives, 151
Notification,
  concentrations. *See*
    Concentrations

Oligopolistic market,
  absence of competition, 87, 88
  abuses by, 80
  aggregate dominance, 79
  asymmetric, 89
  behavioural remedies, 81–83
  cartels, 82–83, 85
  collective market dominance,
    84–91
  community approach to collective
    dominance, 89–91
  concerted practices, 81–82
  conduct approach, 80
  controlling, 79, 80
  definition, 89
  dependence, 88–89
  disadvantages, 79
  idealistic market, 80–81
  interdependence, 87
  objectives, 79
  parallel behaviour, 81, 82
  perfect competition, 80–81
  performance approach, 80
  policy factors, 80
  prices, 80
  structural remedies, 83–89
  symmetric, 88–89
"One stop shop" control, 46, 50
One-member private companies, 18
Organs of the company, 2

Partnership joint ventures, 14
Periodic Indicative Notices (PIN),
  128
PIN, 128
Pre-emption,
  France, 3
Preference shares,
  Germany, 4
Pregnancy, 173–175
Principle of equality, 160–161
Public procurement,
  advertisements, 127–130
  affiliated undertakings, 124–125
  AGP, 138–142
  Agreement on Government
    procurement, 138–142
  applicability of directives,
    122–123
  automatic exclusion, 129
  award of contract,
    accelerated procedure, 133

Public procurement—*cont.*
  award of contract—*cont.*
    concession contracts, 135–136
    criteria, 135
    design contests, 134–135
    housing schemes, public, 137
    local labour employment, 136
    negotiated procedure, 132, 133
    open procedure, 132, 133
    post-tender negotiations, 134
    restricted procedure, 132–133
    subcontracting, 136
    tendering procedures, 131–134
  CAN, 128
  classification, 98
  compliance. *See* Compliance
    directives
  concession contracts, 123
  construction projects, 125
  Contract Award Notices (CAN),
    128
  contracting authorities, 122
  contracts, 122–123
  definition, 97
  design contests, 113–114,
    134–135
  direct effect, 117
  economic standing, 129–130
  eligibility requirements, 129
  extra-territorial effects, 137–142
  financial standing, 129–130
  framework, 97–98
  framework agreements, 124
  GATT Agreement, 137–142
  generally, 97
  in house contracts, 124–125
  implementation of provisions, 98
  importance, 97
  invitations to tender, 128
  legal requirements, 128–129
  legislative framework, 97–98
  list of recognised contractors, 131
  local labour employment, 136
  mandatory advertisement,
    127–130
  negotiated procedure, 132, 133
  objective of directives, 98
  open procedures, 132, 133
  operation of directives, 122–127
  Periodic Indicative Notices
    (PIN), 128
  PIN, 128

Public procurement—*cont.*
  post-tender negotiations, 134
  principles of directives,
    advertisements, 127–130
    automatic exclusion, 129
    CAN, 128
    Contract Award Notices
      (CAN), 128
    economic standing, 129–130
    eligibility requirements, 129
    financial standing, 129–130
    invitations to tender, 128
    legal requirements, 128–129
    mandatory advertisement,
      127–130
    Periodic Indicative Notices
      (PIN), 128
    PIN, 128
    publication, 127–130
    qualification criteria, 128
    selection criteria, 128
    TED, 128
    transparency, 127
  public contracts, 122–123
  public services. *See* Public
    services
  public supplies. *See* Public
    supplies
  public utilities. *See* Public utilities
  public works. *See* Public works
  publication, 127–130
  qualification criteria, 128
  recognised contractors, 131
  restricted procedure, 132–133
  scope of regulation, 97
  secret public works contracts, 125
  selection criteria, 128
  services. *See* Public services
  size of contracts,
    calculation, 126–127
    estimation of value, 126–127
    lots, contract divided into, 127
    thresholds, 125–126
  subcontracting, 136
  subsidised works contracts, 123
  supplies. *See* Public supplies
  technical capacity, 130–131
    ability, 130
    knowledge, 130
    list of recognised contractors,
      131

Public procurement—*cont.*
  technical capacity—*cont.*
    recognised contractors, 131
    suppiers, 130–131
  TED, 128
  tendering procedures, 131–134
  transparency, 127
  underlying principles, 98
  utilities. *See* Public utilities
  works. *See* Public works
Public procurement knowledge of
    contractor, 130
  ability of contractor, 130
Public services, 113–116
  See also Public procurement
  aims of directive, 114
  background, 113
  classification, 116
  compliance. *See* Compliance
    directives
  concession contracts, 115
  contracts, 114, 123
  design contests,
    introduction of, 113
    meaning, 113–114
  exclusions, 114–115
  GATT Agreement, 113
  non-priority services, 116
  priority services, 116
  purpose of directive, 113–114
  research and development
    contracts, 115
  scope of directive, 113–114
  trade wars, 113
  two-tier approach, 116
Public supplies, 98–103
  See also Public procurement
  aim of directive, 101
  co-ordination of national
    procedures, 99, 100
  compliance. *See* Compliance
    directives
  consolidation of legislation, 103
  contracts, 122–123
  de minimis rule, 101
  effectiveness of provisions, 100
  forms of discrimination, 99
  GATT Agreement, 101–102
  implementation of directive,
    99–100, 102
  improvements to provisions,
    102–103

Public supplies—*cont.*
  negative obligations, 100
  positive obligations, 100, 101
  purpose of provisions, 98–99
  quotas, 99
  reform proposals, 102–103
  scope of directive, 99
  third country products, 99
  transitional period, 98
Public utilities, 107–113
  See also Public procurement
  ambit of directive, 110
  associated contracts, 111–112
  carriers of passengers, 112
  CEPT proceedings, 108
  compliance directives, 121
  concession contracts, 111
  confidentiality, 110
  contracts, 123
  defence, 110
  exceptions, 110–112
  exempted bodies, 111
  explorations, 111
  fuel explorations, 111
  GATT agreement, 109, 113
  legislative background, 109
  passenger carriers, 112
  private enterprises, 110–111
  reciprocity principle, 113
  scope of directive, 109
  security, 110
  supplies contracts, 107
  telecommunications, 107,
    108–109
  third country products, 112–113
  water authorities, 112
  works contracts, 107–108
Public works, 103–107
  See also Public procurement
  aims, 104
  compliance. *See* Compliance
    directives
  concession contracts, 104–105
  consolidation of legislation,
    106–107
  construction projects, 125
  contract, concept of, 104–105
  contractors, 105–106
  contracts, 123
  defence sector, 106
  issues, 103–104
  NATO, 125

Public works—*cont.*
  preference schemes, 106
  requirements of directive,
      103–104
  secret contracts, 125
  special features, 103
  subsidised contracts, 123
  transitional period, 103
  utilities, 106

Quotas,
  public supplies, 99

Registered office,
  European Association, 38
  European Mutual Society, 37
Research and development
      contracts, 115
Restrictive agreements,
  concentrations compared, 47
Right of establishment,
  fundamental principle, 1
  insurance sector, 152
  principle, 1

Scissions,
  harmonisation of law, 18
  meaning, 18
Secret public works contracts, 125
Selective distribution agreements,
      92–93
Sex discrimination, 169
  equal pay. *See* Equal pay
  indirect, 173–176
  maternity leave, 174–175
  pregnancy, 173–175
Shareholders,
  Germany, 3
  Italy, 4
  meaning, 2
  pre-emption. *See* Pre-emption
  rights,
      exercise, 3
      meaning, 3
Shares,
  choses in action, 2
  definition, 2
  France, 3
  Germany, 3–4
  Italy, 4
  nature of, 2–3
  purpose, 2

Shares—*cont.*
  statutory definition, 2–3
  United Kingdom, 2
Social policy, 159–177
  access to justice, 176
  equal pay. *See* Equal pay
  equality directives,
      direct effect, 172–173
      equal pay. *See* Equal pay
      national level, reliance at,
          172–173
      social security, 166–168
      treatment, 165–166
  focus of, 159
  generally, 159–160
  indirect discrimination, 173–176
  legal framework, 159–160
  objectives, 159
  pregnancy, 173–175
  primary legislation, 159
  principle of equality. *See* Equal
      pay
  remedies at national level, 176
  scope of legislation, 159–160
  secondary legislation, 159, 160
  social security, 166–168, 170–172
  treatment, equality in, 165–166
Social security,
  equality, 166–168, 170–172
  social policy, 166–168
Societas Europea, 22–23
  management role, 23
  meaning, 22
  problems, 23
  proposals, 22
  purpose, 22
  taxation, 23
  two-tier system, 22, 23
Stock exchange market, 155–157
Subcontracting,
  public procurement, 136
Supervisory boards, 5–6
  England, 6
  France, 6
  function, 6
  Germany, 6
  meaning, 2
  purpose, 6
Supplies. *See* Public supplies

Taxation,
  Societas Europea, 23

TED, 128
Telecommunications,
  public utilities, 107, 108–109
Tendering procedures,
  concession contracts, 134
  post-tender negotiations, 134
  public procurement, 131–134
Tenders Electronic Daily database,
  128
Transfers of property,
  European Economic Interest
    Grouping, 32
Transparency,
  insurance sector, 154
  public procurement, 127

United Kingdom,
  auditors, 6
  corporate structures, 8
Useful effect, doctrine of, 119
Utilities. *See* Public utilities

Vertical joint venture, 11
Voting,
  European Association, 38
  general meeting, 4
Vredeling Directive, 19

Water authorities, 112
Works councils, 2